PARTNER *to* POWER

PARTNER
to
POWER

THE SECRET WORLD

OF

PRESIDENTS

AND THEIR

MOST TRUSTED ADVISERS

K. WARD CUMMINGS

Prometheus Books

59 John Glenn Drive
Amherst, New York 14228

Published 2018 by Prometheus Books

Cover image © Library of Congress
Cover design by Liz Mills
Cover design © Prometheus Books

Inquiries should be addressed to
Prometheus Books
59 John Glenn Drive
Amherst, New York 14228
VOICE: 716–691–0133 • FAX: 716–691–0137
WWW.PROMETHEUSBOOKS.COM

22 21 20 19 18   5 4 3 2 1

Library of Congress Cataloging-in-Publication Data Pending

Printed in the United States of America

CONTENTS

HOW TO READ THIS BOOK

I n 1956, two Stanford University professors, Alexander and Juliette George, published a groundbreaking personality study[1] of President Woodrow Wilson and his right-hand man, Colonel Edward House, in which they applied psycho-dynamic theory to the biographical examination of the two men and their relationship. The work was influenced by an earlier study by American writer and critic Edmund Wilson (no relation) in which he sought the source of a counterproductive pattern of behavior in President Wilson's professional career stretching back to his days as a professor at Princeton. He colorfully described this pattern as "a curve plotted over and over again . . . always dropping from some flight of achievement to a steep descent into failure."[2] Reflecting on his findings, the Professors George saw Woodrow Wilson's childhood difficulties as motivating factors in his future success, remarking in their own work on how, as president, he was able to "harness and adapt the driving ambition and energy engendered by personal maladjustment into an effective pattern of leadership."[3] In each of these works, the authors sought to understand the biographical experiences that drove the president's behaviors and decision-making. A similar motivation lies at the heart of *Partner to Power*.

This psychologically oriented biography is a non-technical, non-scientific personality study of nine presidents and their closest advisers. The objective is to understand the psychological, biographical and political motivations that drew these individuals into partnership, with the goal of understanding why they needed each other and how they worked together.

Any adequate examination of the lives of these individuals must consider the development of the total personality, up to and including adulthood. Indeed, by the time the nine men profiled here attained the presidency, they were mature

7

enough to have understood their childhood influences and had undoubtedly made personality adjustments that they hoped would be efficacious to their political advancement. In light of this, the goal of *Partner to Power* is to take into account not only the childhood influences on the development of these men and women, but the early adulthood influences as well.

Partner to Power is written for a general reader who is interested in history on the whole and in the lives and accomplishments of American presidents in particular. Additionally, considerable attention has been given to satisfying the interest of readers who are looking for a deeper analysis of the role of American presidents' right-hand men and women. Accordingly, the chapters can be accessed from a number of angles.

Partner to Power can be read as a collection of historical narratives, as a series of personality studies or as a study of the evolution of the role of right hand to the president. Each chapter profiles a key relationship that helped define and drive the development of the role since the first right hand—Alexander Hamilton. The chapters chronicle the development of the role in a cursory way, and the epilogue examines it in more detail. This is to avoid distracting the general reader from what might be best described as "biographical narratives," crafted for entertainment as well as educational value. Those readers more interested in an analysis of the role of right hand will notice that while the chapters touch upon the strengths and weaknesses of each of the models represented here, the epilogue discusses them in depth in order to argue in favor of the vice president as the ideal person for this role.

Although the narratives were crafted with the aid of primary sources, such as diaries and interviews, they rely heavily on secondary sources (described in the bibliographical notes). Also, in an effort to weave seamless narratives or to structure a scene, some liberties have been taken. The reader will recognize these instances by the use of such qualifying words and phrases as "might have" and "may."

INTRODUCTION

Harry Hopkins understood FDR's mind and intentions so intimately that if the president had difficulty explaining himself, even to one of his closest advisers, he would send them to Hopkins for clarification. (*New York World-Telegram* and the *Sun* Newspaper Photograph Collection [Library of Congress])

On January 4, 1941, Harry Hopkins, President Franklin Roosevelt's most trusted adviser, boarded a plane on a top-secret mission to Europe. The five-day trip would take him briefly behind German lines before landing him in southern England, where he would be met by an aide to British prime minister Winston Churchill. Hopkins's health was precarious. The previous year, he had had a large portion of his stomach removed to stave off cancer. Since the operation, he was never without a small black satchel containing the enzymes he needed to inject each day—without which he would literally starve to death. President Roosevelt was fully aware of Hopkins's poor health and his meager foreign policy experience, but the mission was too sensitive to be entrusted to anyone other than his right-hand man. When Hopkins finally arrived, Churchill's aide was shocked by the sight of him. He sent ahead a message to the prime minister describing a shrunken man, as "skinny as a nickname"[1] and too exhausted even to rise from his seat.

Yet Roosevelt had insisted that Hopkins take the trip. As he contemplated a larger role for the US in World War II, Roosevelt needed Hopkins to do what he could not do for himself—go to England to personally size up Churchill. Roosevelt had never met him, so he needed someone to assess whether the prime minister was the sort of man who could be trusted. Only a person like Hopkins, who enjoyed the president's complete confidence, and who knew him as well as any other person in the administration, could make such an assessment.

Hopkins spent a month with Churchill, willing himself to keep pace with the prime minister's punishing schedule of meetings, site visits, speeches, dinners, cocktails, and press conferences. The fact that a man in Hopkins's state of health would undertake such a hazardous mission speaks to the quality of the special partnership he and the president shared.

Special advisers like Hopkins have existed since the earliest days of the American republic. Most Americans are aware of their existence, and although they may chafe at the idea of some unelected presence in the White House pulling strings from behind a curtain like the Wizard of Oz, they also somehow seem to appreciate its value to the president. The fingerprints of right-hand men and women can be found on many of the nation's proudest achievements, from the Emancipation Proclamation and The Great Society to Obamacare. But the country owes many of its saddest moments to their influence as well. The Trail of Tears, for example, might never have occurred but for the terrier-like persistence of President Andrew Jackson's closest adviser, John Eaton.[2]

Partner to Power is a study of the extraordinary relationships between US presidents and their right-hand men and women. It delves into their psychological underpinnings in order to understand how they function and why they are necessary. Although dozens of right-hand men and women throughout history will be discussed, nine are the main focus of this book, each of whom represents one of the five most frequent archetypes[3]: (1) cabinet officer, (2) senior adviser, (3) chief of staff (or chief of staff analogue), (4) family member and (5) vice president. Thinking about the different types of right hand a president can choose from may help us address the following questions: Are such relationships in the best interests of the nation? Are these powerful right-hand men and women sufficiently accountable for their actions? Who are they, and how are they chosen? How do their friendships and working styles impact the decisions presidents make?

Debates continue to swirl about the nature and impact of such advisers and their influence on the president, and *Partner to Power* opens a window on a compelling and contested area of American governance at its highest levels. But, at its heart, this book is about personalities and friendships—some of the most significant in history . . .

George Washington and Alexander Hamilton worked closely together for a decade, creating the office of the presidency as they went along. They shared a partnership so seamless it was as if they knew each other's thoughts. Each man needed the other to achieve his best self, and Hamilton remained at Washington's side long after most of his advisers had gone their separate ways . . .

Abraham Lincoln and William Seward started out as rivals, but they ended up the closest of friends and political allies, fighting to hold the Union together even as men in Lincoln's own cabinet worked against them . . .

The collaboration between President Woodrow Wilson and Edward House would endure a world war and facilitate the founding of the League of Nations, but petty jealousies and misunderstandings would eventually drive them apart . . .

FDR's first right-hand man, the gnome-like and unmistakably working-class Louis Howe, was so strikingly dissimilar from the young, patrician Roosevelt that many people were surprised they even knew each other. And yet their collaboration became one of the most important in American presidential history as the New Deal programs they created helped lift millions of Americans out of poverty during the Great Depression. Their relationship had been established years earlier, before Roosevelt contracted polio; Howe had moved in with the

Roosevelts to help Franklin recuperate from his illness and ended up staying for twenty years . . .

When Clark Clifford started working for President Harry Truman, he was a lowly naval assistant, emptying ashtrays in the War Room. A year later, he was counsel to the president and one of the most powerful men in the world. As he worked behind the scenes to advance the president's Middle East policies over the objections of the secretary of state, Clifford demonstrated how few limits existed on the power of the president's right-hand man . . .

The uncommon power Sherman Adams enjoyed as President Dwight Eisenhower's chief of staff stands unequaled to this day. Like most right-hand men and women before him, Adams preferred to work behind the scenes and rarely spoke to the press. Nevertheless, no one doubted his role. Few were surprised to learn that, during the short period in which the president recovered from his heart attack, Adams secretly ran the government in his place . . .

James Baker, Michael Deaver and Ed Meese were three men who acted as one for the benefit of President Ronald Reagan. Together they oversaw White House operations and policymaking. The skills and qualities each man brought to the task enhanced his individual power, but, more importantly, together they were an unstoppable force. No one would learn this better than Reagan's embattled secretary of state . . .

Although she was not able to get there on her own, for a brief period Hillary Rodham Clinton could say she was "co-president of the United States" as she and her husband translated their unique partnership from the governor's mansion in Little Rock to the White House . . .

And Dick Cheney, the self-professed "Prince of Darkness"[4] and close partner of President George W. Bush, was the most powerful vice president in American history. During the tumult of September 11, 2001, as Bush flew safely above the nation in Air Force One, Cheney was running the government from a bunker buried deep beneath the White House. At one point, a military officer informed the vice president that an unidentified passenger plane had been spotted entering DC airspace and was presumably headed toward the White House. Without skipping a beat or taking a breath, Cheney ordered it shot down.

For the most part, right-hand men and women are chosen because their strengths and temperaments serve the purposes of the president. Though most of them choose to wield their influence out of the spotlight, even from the shadows they impact our lives in deep and lasting ways. These are their stories.

WILLIAM McKINLEY & GEORGE CORTELYOU

DEFINING THE RIGHT-HAND MAN

This photo, taken around the year 1900, captures the nature of the relationship between McKinley and Cortelyou. Here the president shakes hands during a stop in Alliance, Ohio. He is joined by Agriculture Secretary James Wilson and Interior Secretary Ethan Hitchcock. Cortelyou is draped in shadow, observing the scene from the doorway.

On the evening of February 15, 1898, the battleship USS *Maine* suddenly burst into flames in Cuba's Havana Harbor. She sank surprisingly fast, taking three-quarters of her crew down with her. By morning, the charred skeletal remains reached out of the water like the giant claws of a dead crab. The incident might have receded quietly from the nation's memory were it not for newspaper publisher William Randolph Hearst, President William McKinley and his right-hand man, George Cortelyou.

Running headlines that pointed a bloodstained finger at Spain, Hearst whipped the American public into a patriotic frenzy. His paper, the *New York Journal*, led the battle cry, accusing Spain of the "treacherous slaughter" of 260 men. Hearst even offered a $50,000 reward, the equivalent of $1.5 million today, to anyone who brought to justice those responsible. Suddenly, ordinary Americans who had never once given thought to Cuba or to Spain found themselves in the streets, chanting Hearst's ubiquitous mantra, "Remember the *Maine*! To Hell with Spain!" By spring, the country was at war.

The growing influence of the press was changing the way Americans viewed themselves and the world. President McKinley, recognizing its power, looked for ways to tap its potential.

By the time of his death from an assassin's bullet three years later, he had transformed the "American president" into a personality on par with the leading pop-culture figures of the day. People across social strata suddenly were desperate to know what McKinley ate for breakfast and where he purchased his ties. Such intense national interest in the common and everyday affairs of the president was unheard of. Presidents had of course been household names, but, until McKinley, none had ever been a superstar.

Central to this transformation were McKinley's efforts to formalize and deepen the ties between the White House and the media. Working closely with his personal secretary Cortelyou, McKinley created the first White House press office. With Cortelyou's help, he rode the populist wave, sweeping the nation to war and, in the process, introducing a new vision of the presidency: the chief executive as "the people's president."

William McKinley, the seventh of nine children, was born in the small town of Niles, Ohio, in 1843. His strong Methodist upbringing, built on the expectation of self-reliance, produced a disciplined, dutiful and acutely observant child. Friends described him as smart, but more diligent than brilliant. A craving for attention inspired him to pursue a career in politics. After seven successful terms in Congress, in 1892 he was elected governor of Ohio and, in 1896, president of the United States. One of his most important staffing decisions after taking office was to accept outgoing president Grover Cleveland's recommendation to retain Cortelyou as his private secretary. The decision would have long-term consequences for McKinley and for the office.

George Cortelyou was born in New York City during the second year of the Civil War. After graduating from Georgetown Law, he was hired as a clerk at the US Customs Service and the office of the Postmaster General before moving to the White House to work for Cleveland. His extraordinary organizational skills helped make him a central figure in the McKinley White House, but it was his role in shaping the first White House press office that would elevate him to the top of McKinley's advisers.

As the prospect of war increased the need for reporting from the White House, photography and moving pictures were changing how the president was viewed by the public, how he communicated with them and even his policy-making. To this day, presidents still use communication strategies McKinley and Cortelyou developed in the late 1890s to speak directly to the American people through the press. FDR's famous fireside chats in the 1940s and Trump's Twitter spasms in the 2010s can be traced back to McKinley's example.

Before McKinley, there were no White House press releases, the president did not sit down one-on-one with reporters to conduct in-depth interviews, and there were no policy-oriented presidential speaking tours. Cortelyou instituted as a standard practice the creation of daily "press clips" for the president to help give him a sense of public opinion around the country—a first.

Before Cortelyou, the press would show up at the White House only occasionally to gather information on a subject or to seek a quote. Cortelyou raised the importance of this practice by organizing a regular schedule for disseminating information to the press. This crucial change established the White House as a regular stop on newspaper reporters' "beat." Instead of going straight to Capitol Hill for comment on issues, reporters began to regularly and systematically seek the White House's views on subjects. By making the White House a reliable and regular source of information for the press, Cortelyou raised the profile of the presidency in the eyes of newspaper editors and, thereby, the public. Through their partnership, McKinley and Cortelyou ushered the presidency into the modern age.

Before McKinley, the nation's chief executive was seen as co-equal with the other branches of the government. Most Americans felt an emotional bond to their congressman, but their feelings did not extend to the president. As McKinley traveled the nation explaining why the US should go to war with Spain, Cortelyou's skillful use of the media helped create a new way for the president to engage with the public.

Cortelyou was certainly a conscientious and devoted staffer, but he possessed no special gift for media management when McKinley first asked for his assistance. He could not know it at the time, but by helping McKinley create the modern White House press operation, Cortelyou would secure his rank among the most important right-hand men in history.

In the end, the Spanish-American War wasn't much of a war. It was over in five months, and the winner was never really in doubt. But from all the excitement in the press at the time, you would think the entire Spanish Armada had dropped anchor in Boston Harbor. Media empires sprang up practically overnight, struggling to keep pace with the public's insatiable appetite for news. McKinley and Cortelyou quickly recognized that the nation stood at the foot of a cresting wave of irreversible change. How they chose to react influenced how future presidents would govern and how Americans would view them.

Since the founding of the American republic, the right-hand man has filled a role as the closest adviser of the president, and, through time, it has evolved, adapting to the shifting authorities and needs of the office. Though many of the skills and duties of the role have changed since Alexander Hamilton's day, these unique men and women continue to share three key characteristics.

First, right-hand men and women have a limitless portfolio. They may possess a defined and specific job function—White House counsel, for example— but the president is willing to assign them tasks outside of the scope of their official duties—even if those tasks enter into the portfolio of other officials. Hamilton, for example, was officially Washington's treasury secretary, but the president often assigned him duties more befitting a secretary of war.

Second, right-hand men and women possess unequaled access to the president. George W. Bush's right hand Dick Cheney, for example, had three avenues of influence with the president: through his staff, which he took pains to ensure mirrored Bush's personal staff in number and responsibility; through open meetings, in which Cheney arranged to have access to any meeting Bush attended; and through closed meetings. Cheney's schedule included a private weekly lunch with Bush during which no subject was off the table.

Lastly, each right-hand man or woman understands the president's thinking as well as, if not better than, anyone else on staff. Each of President Franklin Roosevelt's right-hand men and women (Howe, LeHand, Hopkins, Moley, Tugwell, Corcoran . . . Roosevelt went through right-hand men like tissue paper) was noted for his or her ability to read his thoughts. One, Harry Hopkins, was so successful that he once personally, and unsolicited by the president, reversed an important presidential directive because he suspected Roosevelt had made a mistake. After being informed of his error and Hopkins's corrective action, Roosevelt thanked his loyal servant.

All the key advisers profiled in *Partner to Power* not only were remarkable individuals, but also filled a role that continues to be unique and contested as a special, necessary and underexplored element of presidential power. Their contributions to history highlight critical moments in the evolution of the president's right hand.

As the partnership between McKinley and Cortelyou illustrates, external forces often influence who becomes the president's right hand. Just as the exploding power of the media drove the subsequent need for advisers with the organizational skills of Cortelyou, shifts in the public's mood may also impact the choice of person in the role.

There was a time when the idea of an African-American woman as the president's chief adviser (as Valerie Jarrett was to Obama) was laughable, and it was only after the passage of the Twelfth Amendment that it became politically possible for the vice president to serve as the president's right hand. These events, and their coming to pass, reflect some of the shifts in the ever-evolving definition—and question—of the "right-hand man."

The profiles in *Partner to Power* trace the path of this unique and controversial role from its amorphous beginnings to the clear, more effective and more accountable contours of the vice presidency. As has often been the case with America's most enduring political institutions, it all began with Alexander Hamilton.

CHAPTER ONE

GEORGE WASHINGTON & ALEXANDER HAMILTON

THE SHAPE OF THINGS TO COME

Washington is often described by historians as the "Hidden Hand President" for how often he used others to execute his agenda. It may have been Washington's hand behind the scenes, but more often than not the fingerprints left behind belonged to Hamilton. (Painting of George Washington by Gilbert Stuart; painting of Alexander Hamilton by John Trumbull)

Very few who are not philosophical Spectators can realize the
difficulty and delicate part which a man in my situation has to
act . . . I walk on untrodden ground. . . . There is scarcely any part
of my conduct which may not hereafter be drawn into precedent.[1]
                                        —President George Washington

*O*n *New Year's Eve, 1793, as Americans lifted their glasses in joyous celebration of the coming year, Alexander Hamilton was imagining himself
in another line of work. He had been at George Washington's side, on and off,
since he was in his early twenties, and now, facing middle age, he was considering a life without him. For a man of Hamilton's mind and abilities, the future
was limitless. He might run for governor of New York or for the US Senate or even
for the presidency. But first, he would need to resign his post as treasury secretary
and reestablish himself as a private citizen. Taking his glass in hand, Hamilton
greeted the new year happily, secure in the thought that this year he might finally
be able to free himself of Washington and move on. To his great disappointment,
he soon discovered his plans to leave were a bit premature.*

*In 1794, the world's two superpowers, Great Britain and France, went to war,
forcing the United States to choose a side. Hoping to avoid inflaming tensions
with the British that had been festering since the end of the Revolution, President
Washington favored neutrality. But the British were not going to make it easy
for him. They had acquired an annoying and dangerous new habit. To cut off
French supply lines in the West Indies, the British forced into the nearest English
port any American merchant vessel engaged in commerce there. The ship was
emptied of its cargo, and its crew members were given the choice of joining the
Royal Navy or finding their own way home.*

*Washington envisioned a treaty with the British that would keep America neutral
while also giving American merchants the freedom to continue trading with the
French. But a huge swath of the American public opposed his efforts. Accusing
the legendary war hero of being unpatriotic for wanting to pursue a peace treaty
with a nation still widely regarded as the enemy, some longtime defenders of the*

president began to wonder aloud whether Mount Vernon was not a more fitting place for the aging president to spend his autumn years.

Further complicating matters, Washington faced this crisis without the help of his secretary of state Edmund Randolph, who was dealing with a crisis of his own-- having recently been accused of treason. Randolph was not his first choice to lead the State Department, but Washington could find no one else willing to replace Thomas Jefferson when he resigned the previous year. A few poorly chosen words by Randolph, to the French ambassador did permanent damage to his relationship with the president. So, when he needed Randolph most, Washington had to look elsewhere for someone to shepherd his treaty with Great Britain. As he so often did in difficult times, he turned to Alexander Hamilton.

Despite years of close and successful collaboration, the partnership between Washington and Hamilton remained on shaky ground. Throughout much of their relationship, there was a tension between them not unlike that between an overly demanding father and a stridently defiant son. But they needed each other. Hamilton desperately needed Washington to support him as he advanced increasingly unpopular programs to strengthen the federal government, and Washington, ever mindful of his legacy, desperately needed Hamilton's programs to succeed. Washington knew that even without Hamilton, he would still be remembered as an important man, but he might never be great.

Deeply self-conscious, sometimes to the point of paralysis, George Washington would become famous for his self-control, though Hamilton knew it was only an act designed to mask his nagging insecurities. Washington was an intelligent man who, surrounded by intellectuals, was keenly aware of his deficiencies. He often worried about being judged out of his depth and went to great lengths to conceal his self-doubts. Alexander Hamilton, a man of incandescent brilliance, was eager to serve Washington without judgment. By helping shape Washington's ideas and then working to bring them to life, Hamilton enabled the president to establish the public image of himself as a man of vision and leadership. Theirs was a truly symbiotic collaboration—with each man needing the other to achieve the best version of himself.

As the crisis with the British unfolded, Hamilton and Washington worked together, in the public eye and in the shadows, to pull the country back from the brink of war. Their successful partnership endures as the most important in American presidential history, for the standards and traditions it set for all subsequent presidential partnerships and for what it did to establish the presidency itself. Had Washington not been in office during this crucial period, when every decision established a precedent, and had Hamilton not been his most trusted adviser, the United States might have developed into a distinctly different nation.

Throughout Washington's presidency, as other men of consequence darted in and out of his life, Hamilton remained a constant. For almost a decade, they held the administration and the nation together through stormy seas, cutting a path for posterity and forever illuminating what it means to be a president and a president's right hand.

I

An Indispensable Partnership

In 1777, Alexander Hamilton was barely twenty years old and not yet the type of man who yielded easily to authority. Most Revolutionary War soldiers would have thought service on the commanding general's personal staff a great honor, but to Hamilton[2]—who had joined the military in search of personal glory—working for General Washington was a source of embarrassment. Instead of leading bayonet charges, Hamilton, a lieutenant colonel, was in charge of writing letters and keeping the general's field journal. His irritation was exacerbated by Washington's temper[3]—which was as fierce as it was unpredictable.

One day, General Washington and his staff were crammed into a small farmhouse in upstate New York after a string of embarrassing defeats by the British. Everyone was on edge—Washington especially, whose head swirled with a list of complaints from Congress about his lack of progress.

After a particularly tense exchange with his senior staff, a still-irritated Washington, passing Hamilton on the stairs, asked for a word. Hamilton begged

Washington's patience as he excused himself to deliver an urgent message, promising he would then meet the general in that same spot. Depending on whom you ask, Hamilton was away for one minute or ten. However long Hamilton's absence, Washington was not pleased about having to wait. When Hamilton returned, the general inquired heatedly what could have kept him for so long and whether he had forgotten that he had been waiting. Hamilton's frustration with his position suddenly became too much to bear. This was the last straw. He had had enough of Washington's little tantrums. If Washington was so offended, Hamilton responded, he would be glad to remove himself permanently from the general's presence. Washington tried to ease the tension, but Hamilton would have none of it.

After giving Hamilton time to regain his composure, Washington sent an aide to convey his apologies, but the damage had been done. Hamilton sent back word that he would stay long enough to train his successor, after which he would be on his way.

The two men did not speak again until after the war. They might not have spoken even then, but, as was often the case in their relationship, Hamilton's ambition would help him swallow his pride. When Hamilton realized Washington's chances of becoming president and that the former general was his best shot at getting a cabinet appointment, he threw himself behind Washington's candidacy. Though Washington's election was never in doubt, the task proved more difficult than Hamilton expected.

First, Hamilton had to convince Washington to take the job. When he wrote the general at Mount Vernon to inform him that people were raising his name as a possible candidate for the office, Washington replied that he enjoyed his calm life in Virginia and was not interested. Hamilton knew Washington well enough to know he was only posturing and that if pressed hard enough he would accept. Hamilton influenced others to reach out to Washington as well, and, after only a little more prodding, Washington agreed to accept the office if it were offered.

Next, Hamilton had to clear the field of rivals. One might expect that with a man of Washington's stature in the race, competition would shrink; however, more than ten people entered. Only two of them—John Adams of Massachusetts and George Clinton of New York—could conceivably muster the votes to defeat Washington. Adams had the greatest chance, but he had openly acknowledged his willingness to accept the office of vice president, which in those days was awarded to the presidential runner-up. Clinton could win only if Adams unexpectedly withdrew his name. Some urged Clinton to consider bowing out, to avoid any chance that Washington might not secure enough votes to win, but Clinton refused.

Hamilton disliked Clinton[4] and was determined to prevent him from spoiling Washington's chance of winning unanimous support. Doing so would require an elaborate series of maneuvers.

He needed to discourage electors from voting for Clinton, and, at the same time, he needed them not to vote for Adams. Electors were required to cast two votes; the person who got the most votes would be named president, while the person with the next most votes would become vice president. The problem for Hamilton was that if he convinced people not to vote for Clinton, and they cast their vote for Adams instead, Adams might get enough votes to win the presidency. So, Hamilton had to convince seven electors to cast their second votes for neither Adams nor Clinton. In the end, Washington won handily, and Adams came in a distant second. Adams was embarrassed by how few votes he actually received, and when he learned about Hamilton's role in his defeat, he never forgave him.

As a reward for his support, Washington nominated Hamilton to be the first secretary of the treasury. It would be one of the most important decisions of his presidency.

II

The Psychology of Symbiosis

On the surface, it might appear as if Hamilton and Washington's partnership was a mere consequence of professional expediency, but it had as much to do with the men's psychology as it did with their ambition. They shared a strikingly similar personal history that must have influenced their understanding of each other. It may also account for why theirs was such a productive partnership.

A series of traumatic events in their childhoods threatened to break them as individuals. Nonetheless, they emerged from these experiences imbued with a fierce personal strength, a keen appreciation for the precariousness of life and an understanding of the uniqueness of the times in which they lived.

Washington and Hamilton were raised by strong mothers who instilled in them the dogged perseverance necessary to create their own luck. When Mary Washington and Rachel Hamilton were abandoned by their husbands, instead of seeking out new spouses to take care of them, they chose to take their fate into their own hands and raise their children alone. They were independent-minded risk-takers, and their sons would be too.

According to legend, Washington is said to have noticed Hamilton for the first time in late August 1776, while American forces were retreating from Brooklyn to Harlem Heights, New York. The Continental Army was on the run. Hamilton was a captain, in charge of an artillery unit that covered the Continentals' rear as they withdrew. As the last of the exhausted and demoralized American troops crossed over into Harlem, Washington noticed how disciplined and energetic Hamilton's men seemed in comparison to those around them. He was so impressed that he invited Hamilton to dine with him that evening. Whether this dinner did actually occur is lost to history, but it is clear that at some point Hamilton was introduced to General Washington, who was so taken with him that he invited him to join his staff. For Hamilton, joining Washington was not at first a compelling proposition.

Hamilton was in pursuit of military glory, and working as Washington's administrative assistant seemed hardly the best path to that goal. But Hamilton was poor and unknown in the Summer of '76, and he knew better than most how limited his prospects were. Washington offered him a battlefield promotion and a central role on his leadership staff. The forty-four-year-old Washington was commander in chief of American forces and at the height of his powers. To the young Hamilton, who was easily impressed by impressive men, the alluringly graceful and immaculately adorned Washington (who stood six foot three, at a time when the average adult stood a full foot shorter) must have been a sight to behold. To win him over, Washington gave Hamilton the "full treatment." Hamilton never had a chance.

Washington was acutely aware of the impression his physical presence made on others. When Washington wanted to impress people, as he did Hamilton at that time, his method was to invade their space.[5] Standing close and facing them directly, he would look straight down into their eyes. The intent was to make them feel as if they held his undivided attention, while also making them aware of his imposing stature. His speech was purposeful, measured and without animation. All this combined to win Hamilton over. Later, as Hamilton got to know him better, he grew to understand that Washington was not always as confident as he seemed. Though he had trained himself to conceal his emotions, he had a "tell" of clenching his jaw during conversation, which must have revealed when his thoughts were straying. The flashy uniform, the graceful, courtly manners and the diplomatic reserve were all designed to conceal a secret that only those closest to him knew.

George Washington was born on the family farm in Westmoreland County, Virginia, on February 11, 1732. He had a tough start in life. He lost his father, Augustine, when he was just reaching adolescence, leaving him to scrabble mostly on his own for success in a world where family and social connections mattered most. Augustine's death left Washington to be raised by his desperate, demanding and disturbingly negative mother, Mary Ball. Due largely to the pressures she placed on him at an early age, Washington emerged from his youth an extraordinarily self-conscious young man, hypersensitive to criticism and plagued by benumbing self-doubt.

Mary Ball Washington was still a young woman when Augustine died. She might have remarried, but instead she chose to single-handedly raise six children and run the plantation on her own.[6] Though only eleven at the time, George was the oldest among Augustine's children with Mary Ball, and was expected to pull the most weight. The family was moderately well-off, but as hard as she worked, Mary Ball was never able to do more than keep the plantation afloat. Devoting so much time to the farm left her little time for her children. To ease the pressure on Mary Ball, George's older half brother Lawrence, from Augustine's previous marriage, offered to take George in. As he spent more time away from his mother, Washington's relationship with her grew strained. Her eventual passing inspired little emotion in him, and in the years following her death he never found the time to place a headstone at her grave.

Washington entered young adulthood spurred by a strong sense of destiny, tempered by loss. Like many others in eighteenth-century America, by the time Washington reached his twenties, he was already intimately acquainted with death. Malaria, diphtheria, tuberculosis, yellow fever and smallpox were common causes of untimely death in colonial America, striking down the old and the young without prejudice. When his brother Lawrence contracted tuberculosis, George traveled with him to Barbados, where it was hoped the climate would improve his health. Lawrence did not recover, however, and George contracted smallpox. Yet his brother's death, and the death of Lawrence's wife and young daughter a few years later, profoundly changed his fortunes in life. By their deaths, Washington inherited Mount Vernon, and his prospects brightened. His good fortune convinced him that he must be destined for great things. When he later joined the military, his belief that he was "protected" was reinforced by his miraculous escapes from injury in battle. Despite having horses shot out from under him, Washington always emerged unscathed.

Washington's physical stature also contributed to his feelings of destiny. In a culture that valued rugged masculinity, even as a young man Washington stood out for his height and powerful build. He was tall, with long, strong arms and big hands. From the front, his narrow shoulders, wide hips, and large, athletic legs made him appear impressively solid, if bottom-heavy. He cut a memorable figure and rarely entered a room without notice.

In his youth, Washington was a bit of a dandy. His letters reveal a man who labored over his appearance with the fussiness of a bride preparing for her wedding day.[7] For the insecure young Washington, who was eager to make a name for himself, wearing a well-made suit or smart waistcoat may have been a way to compensate for the flawed man he believed he was underneath.

The myth about Washington never telling a lie is just that—a myth. The young Washington was not above lying or cheating if it made him look good. When he was a lowly British Army major, years before the Revolution, a skirmish with French troops resulted in the death of a diplomat who was his prisoner at the time. The nervous young major blamed the diplomat's death on the incompetence of his men. And when the poorly constructed stockade he ordered built to house prisoners was easily overrun by a small band of French scouts, Washington could find fault with everyone but himself. As a final and lasting insult to the men he led, after the war he teamed up with a friend to cheat the enlisted men out of the land the colony of Virginia had promised them for their service. He secretly changed the terms of the agreement with the Virginia colonial government to ensure that only officers—not enlisted men—received payment for their sacrifices.[8]

By the time he and Hamilton first met, however, it was decades later, and Washington was more like the honorable figure most schoolchildren would recognize today. The mature Washington was a hero of the French and Indian War, a fabulously wealthy landowner, and a respected member of Virginia's political elite.

Though Hamilton was barely out of his teens when they first met, Washington must have been struck by how much he resembled the young man Washington had only pretended to be. The youthful Hamilton was brimming with promise and the confidence that flowed from a genuine belief that he truly possessed the skills and qualities necessary to achieve his ambitions. Washington saw in him none of the self-consciousness, self-doubt or insecurities that he himself had carried at that age. Even then, Hamilton was a natural leader and a man of undeniable intellectual gifts. And, unlike the young Washington, he believed that honor was more important than riches or fame. Washington could not have known it at the time, but the admirable Hamilton had begun life in conditions just as precarious as he had.

In an age when a person's bloodlines were a large determinant of social success, Alexander Hamilton's family history hung over him like a dark cloud. As he moved in the highest levels of society, he hid the fact that his mother, Rachel, had been briefly imprisoned for adultery and that his father, James, was a depressed, depressing ne'er-do-well and constant disappointment to the most important people in his life. There were rumors, fed by John Adams and others, that Hamilton's mother was a prostitute and an octoroon.[9] The rumors about his mother were unfounded, but the ones about his father James being the black sheep of a noble Scottish family were true. After spending a decade with Rachel and fathering two sons by her out of wedlock, James went out one afternoon to run an errand and never returned. Alexander was ten at the time, and though he would establish an irregular correspondence with his father in later years, they never saw each other again.

After James left, Rachel, brilliant and resourceful, gathered the boys and moved from Nevis to the island of St. Croix, where she opened a shop with money borrowed from family. As an illegitimate child, Hamilton could not attend the local Catholic school, but Rachel was able to afford sporadic tutoring for him and his brother. When Hamilton was eleven, he and his mother contracted tropical fever—he survived, she did not. Hamilton and his brother were shuffled back and forth between relations before finally coming to rest in the company of virtual strangers. His brother became apprenticed to a furniture maker, and Hamilton took a job working for a merchant.

Although his start in life placed him at a disadvantage, it is hard to imagine that someone of Hamilton's ambition and intellectual resources would be down for long. As he entered his teenage years, the shop owners put him in charge of store operations. Though Hamilton hated the work, he applied himself. In his free time, he read every book he could put his hands to. He was poor and lonely, but he was determined to make something of himself. In a letter to a close friend, Hamilton revealed his desperate desire to be something more than a common clerk:

> My youth excludes me from any hopes of immediate preferment, but I mean to prepare the way for futurity. I'm no philosopher, you see, and may be justly said to build castles in the air. My folly makes me ashamed yet we have seen such schemes successful when the projector is constant. . . . [As he continues, he makes clear the extent to which he is willing to go to achieve success in life.] My ambition is so prevalent that I contemn the grov'ling and condition of a clerk or the like to which my fortune &c. condemns me and would willingly risk my life tho' not my character to exalt my station.[10]

While other boys his age were distracting themselves with games and girls, Hamilton applied himself to the mastery of currency exchange rates, to languages and to marketing. Writing would be his ticket to a new life. An article he published in the local newspaper about a hurricane on the island was so well received that friends and acquaintances took up a collection to send him to study in America.

Hamilton was only nineteen when he arrived in New York City, but he was a remarkable figure even then. In the parlance of the time, he was a "pretty fellow." With his waif-like build, thin shoulders and rosy cheeks, he was often mistaken for a child. When he wanted to, he could be charming, but if his intelligence was insulted, his response could be unsettling. In his day, a subtle, insightful witticism was the preferred method of retort, but Hamilton's insults could only be likened to shotgun blasts. His inability to moderate himself in the face of a personal attack was a lifelong weakness.

Hamilton knew his stipend would not sustain him for long, so he sought out ways to stretch his income. He moved in with a friend and considered an expedited course of study—hoping to save on tuition by condensing all four years of schooling into two—at Princeton. Princeton denied his request, but when his same proposal was accepted by King's College—later known as Columbia University—he devoured the curriculum, completing his studies in just two and a half years. And he still found time to get involved in the city's political scene and to organize a campus military drill company. It was his success at training and equipping this small band of followers that led to his commission as an artillery officer. Given his energy, intelligence and resourcefulness, it was only a matter of time before he came to the attention of the commander in chief.

For Washington, conversing face-to-face with the young Hamilton for the first time must have been a memorable experience. His eyes were bluish-purple, his hair was the rusty color of autumn leaves, and the sharp line of his nose and the close set of his eyes gave his face a feline quality. His mannerisms were feminine and masculine at the same time—delicate, but deliberate. Washington would have been struck by Hamilton's intensity and his bristling intellect. It is not hard to imagine Hamilton as a fast-talking youth, moving from topic to topic with the agility of a trapeze artist. Washington would have been impressed by Hamilton's understanding of military strategy, his grasp of economic theory and his deep reading of political philosophy.

Though it was not the custom of the day in polite or professional conversation, had Washington and Hamilton discussed each other's past, they might have shared how they both lost their fathers when they were still boys and how their fortunes had been greatly dependent on the support of older men. They would have discovered how it was their mothers, not their fathers, who were the driving influence in their youth, and they would have seen how they both saw the military as their only real means of ascent in life. They would have seen that they were both huge risk-takers, and they might have recognized how useful they could be to each other. At the time, Washington needed Hamilton more than Hamilton needed him. Washington was leading a war on two fronts—one against the British and the other against Congress over the resources he needed to sustain the army. Washington needed powerful, persuasive writers who could help him win the support of Congress and the backing of the press. Hamilton's decision to join Washington's staff would have monumental consequences for the lives of both men.

As Hamilton and Washington worked together, the huge differences in their temperaments became apparent. Washington learned how impulsive Hamilton could be, and Hamilton saw how paralyzingly cautious Washington was.[11] Hamilton was often reckless. In later life, in a legendary incident involving a sexual liaison with a married woman, Hamilton hastily published a pamphlet admitting his adultery in an attempt to dispel an unrelated rumor that he was speculating with the public's money.[12] Had he been more reserved, Hamilton could have addressed the speculation issue alone without raising the issue of the affair. The unnecessary and unexpected admission effectively ended any chance he might have had of becoming president.

Despite his mercurial nature, Hamilton became invaluable to Washington for the way he inspired him. The fledgling United States was especially dependent upon men like Hamilton who could envision a path through the swirling uncertainty that characterized the nation's earliest days and who possessed the commitment and ability to translate vision into reality. Washington recognized Hamilton's brilliance and potential for greatness early in their relationship, and he had the wisdom—and, perhaps more importantly, the self-possession—to defer to Hamilton's leadership and advice at key times when other officials failed him. The Jay Treaty, in 1794, was one such moment.

By 1794, the Revolution had been over for more than a decade, but residual political and economic issues threatened to push the United States and Great

Britain toward a resumption of hostilities. Many Americans were angry that the British had yet to pay reparations for carrying off American slaves during the war, and trappers, hoping to get rich in the vast forests out West, resented Britain for being deliberately slow to pull out of the territories after the war.

Across the Atlantic, the British were angry that Crown loyalists in America had yet to be compensated by the American government for the seizure of their property during the war and that debts owed to British merchants went unpaid because the American government refused to enforce British collection orders. These issues, although annoying, fell short of inspiring thoughts of a declaration of war in the minds of most Americans—that is, until they learned that the Royal Navy was capturing and imprisoning American sailors in the West Indies.

No one knew better than President Washington and Treasury Secretary Hamilton that the US was not prepared to fight another war with the British. They understood how lucky American forces were to have defeated the British in the first place, and they personally knew how many times the Continental Army had come close to total defeat. The country was still in its infancy, and war at such a vulnerable time in its development could end the American experiment before it had time to fully take root. The conflict was growing into the most serious crisis of Washington's presidency, and it arrived at a time when he was probably least prepared to deal with it.

In 1794, George Washington was getting old. Twenty years in the country's service had left him greatly diminished. The virile, imposing figure most Americans remembered fondly from the Revolution had aged into a slow-moving, slow-talking, dried-up old man. A friend visiting the president could not help but notice how thin he had grown, his face "cadaverous" and his voice "whispy and distant."[13] Washington had wanted to step down the year before, but the fledgling republic would never have survived his departure. So, he soldiered on, surrounded by a team of advisers who themselves wanted nothing more than to beat him to the exit.

At the same time, Hamilton was signaling his own departure from government, but as the crisis with the British grew, he felt increasing pressure to stay on. Though this was an international matter, the treasury secretary felt a need to help Washington since the immensely capable Thomas Jefferson was no longer secretary of state and his replacement, Edmund Randolph, was still learning the job.

Randolph had not been Washington's first choice to replace Jefferson as head of the State Department. Washington trusted Randolph enough to appoint him US attorney general, and would have liked to retain him in that post, but could find no one else willing to succeed Jefferson. Randolph was not a natural in the role, either. On one occasion, Randolph was a little too free while speaking to the French ambassador, Jean Fauchet, and made the mistake of giving the ambassador the impression that he was willing to take a bribe. Unfortunately for Randolph, Fauchet chose to include the secretary of state's poorly chosen words in a diplomatic note home. The message was intercepted by the British navy, which was only too happy to share the information with one of Washington's friends.

During a tense exchange over dinner, Washington took Randolph aside and showed him Fauchet's intercepted letter. Washington had known Randolph for years, and he doubted that he would betray his nation in such a way. But he had to know for sure.

The president closely studied Randolph's face as he read the letter. At first, Randolph showed no reaction, which must have made Washington suspicious, because he pressed him further. Suddenly Randolph exploded. He was insulted that Washington would even accuse him of such a thing. He insisted that he be given a chance to respond in writing once he had had time to gather the necessary materials in his defense—a request that only increased Washington's suspicions. The president agreed, but his mind was already made up.

Even before Randolph had become embroiled in the scandal that would eventually lead to his resignation, Hamilton was deeply involved in the work of the fledgling secretary of state. Washington asked for the help of his full cabinet as he considered how to respond to the crisis with Great Britain, and Hamilton was only too happy to put his hand in.

The first thing Hamilton did was recommend that the president nominate a special envoy to negotiate with the British. The list of qualifications Hamilton recommended for the envoy seemed to suggest himself in the role, but he and Washington both knew he had too many enemies in Congress to hope to win a confirmation vote. So, Hamilton recommended instead their mutual friend Supreme Court Justice John Jay.[14]

Washington and Hamilton's conduct throughout the developmental stages of the treaty illustrates the close, almost intuitive process of collaboration they had developed. Hamilton had learned long ago that there was a right way and a wrong way to approach Washington regarding complicated and serious matters such as this. An intensely cautious man, Washington liked to see a consensus forming around a decision before he felt confident enough to pull the trigger. Hamilton knew he would have to guide Washington carefully.

It was no coincidence that soon an influential member of the Senate visited the president and suggested that he assign Jay the task of negotiating with the British. The senator, a prominent member of the committee that would have to approve the special envoy's appointment, had been recruited to "drop by" the president's residence to effectively second Hamilton's proposal of Jay.

It was Jay's name that would be attached to the treaty, but Hamilton played as great a role as any in its ultimate success.[15] Hamilton was not a man of half measures. When he was in, he was all in. There was hardly a feature of the treaty that Hamilton did not help shape. Not only did he provide Washington with arguments for pursuing the treaty—arguments that Washington would use on numerous occasions throughout the process—he helped get members of Congress on board. After selecting Jay for the post of envoy, Hamilton met with him to lay out the goals and the strategy for the negotiations. To ensure that Jay stayed on message, Hamilton kept up an active correspondence with him throughout the negotiation process.

Washington did not stand in Hamilton's way as he took charge of shaping the treaty. Given what is known about the closeness of their partnership, it is not difficult to imagine that the two men might have, at some point in their relationship—during the Revolution, or perhaps during the early days of the administration—entered into a pact to support each other and to facilitate their mutual success, with Washington the brawn and Hamilton the brains. Washington could personify Hamilton's vision, and Hamilton would attend to the details. As the events surrounding the Jay Treaty unfolded, a portrait of the inner workings of their partnership emerged. As was so often the case during the early years of the American republic, their efforts established a model that similar partnerships would emulate.

III

The Shape of Things to Come

In comparison to what was to follow, negotiating the treaty with the British was easy. The real work began after details of the document were leaked and the American public became convinced, by the friends of James Madison and Thomas Jefferson—the most prominent and persistent political voices in opposition to the treaty—that the agreement should be rejected. Public reaction ranged from resentment that Americans would still not be paid for the property they had lost during the Revolution, to anger that American sailors could still be captured by the British in the West Indies, to confusion about why Washington would seemingly give so much away while securing so little for America in return.

The treaty's boldest critics accused Washington of bending over backwards for the British. They pointed to the fact that England retained the right to levy tariffs against US goods and was granted "most favored nation" trading status. In their minds, the US came out of the negotiations worse off than it had been going in.

After Jay returned to the US and submitted the treaty to Washington, the president asked for Hamilton's help in understanding its details and consequences.[16] He could have relied on Jay's or Randolph's characterization of the agreement, but instead he turned to his right-hand man.

Washington asked Hamilton to prepare a memo arguing the strengths and weaknesses of the treaty—and whether or not he should support it. Hamilton must have wished that Jay had gotten more concessions from the British, but he knew Jay had done his best. It would have been a mistake to expect a treaty tilted in America's favor, given that Great Britain was the most powerful nation on the planet and the US had little with which to bargain. After cataloguing for Washington its strengths and weaknesses, Hamilton urged the president to support the treaty.

Despite Hamilton's recommendation, Washington hesitated, keeping the treaty's full details secret from voters as he decided what to do. Hamilton's analysis had uncovered as many weaknesses as strengths, and Washington instinctively knew the terms of the treaty would not be well received by the public. When he finally released the document, there was indeed an uproar. Jefferson, Madison and their political allies had convinced the press that the treaty was a power grab by the president—that Washington had overstepped his constitutional mandate by negotiating a treaty without the involvement of Congress. They accused him of acting more like a king than the leader of a democratic republic.

In the wake of the negative public response, Hamilton stepped in again to assist the president. This time, his aid came in the form of a carefully calibrated media campaign. Washington and Hamilton shared the opinion that attacking the treaty and the president's authority to negotiate on the nation's behalf was an attack on the foundational principles of the republic and on the presidency itself. It would have been undignified for Washington to answer his critics by arguing the merits of the treaty himself. However, he knew that he would not be faulted for encouraging the effort if someone were to enter the debate on his behalf. There is no record that Washington explicitly requested Hamilton's help, but Hamilton would have known the president well enough to know that such efforts would be welcomed. When the president read the first in a series of essays Hamilton published defending the treaty[17] (written under the name Camillus), he wrote Hamilton to congratulate his right-hand man and to urge him to continue.

Hamilton's handling of the debate was so skillful and persuasive that he was able to reverse public opinion almost single-handedly.[18] He was helped by the fact that Republican criticism sacrificed reason in favor of ridicule in a slow-moving cortege of low blows and cheap shots. Analysis by biographers John Alexander Carroll and Mary Wells Ashworth helps illustrate the reasons Hamilton's work was ultimately judged more persuasive by the public:

> "Camillus," indeed, was distinguished by incisive style, rich citation and a perfectly logical narrative flow. [Hamilton's] evaluation of the first ten "permanent" articles of the treaty were masterful. The central theme was danger: opponents of the treaty were blind to the great interrelated hazards it overcame—a British and Indian war in the Northwest and a Spanish and Indian conspiracy in the Southwest, extinction of overseas trade and decline of prosperity in agriculture as well as in manufactures, increased taxation for defences [*sic*] and, finally, civil war in America.[19]

There were thirty-eight essays in all. Entitled "The Defense," twenty of the essays were written by Hamilton himself. His friend, New York assemblyman

Rufus King, wrote the remaining ten, but even those were heavily edited by Hamilton. The level of scholarship of the essays is remarkable, given the extent of Hamilton's personal and professional obligations at the time. King focused on defending the mercantile elements of the treaty and argued in favor of continued free trade, while Hamilton's essays focused on three themes: defending the treaty and its constituent articles, urging its inherent constitutionality and directly responding to individual criticisms.

Leading a damage-control effort that would put even a modern-day press secretary to shame, Hamilton brilliantly reshaped the debate into a referendum on President Washington's leadership. He argued that an attack on the treaty was an attack on the very man who had led the nation to victory during the Revolution. He urged the public to remember that the US was a new nation with little to leverage and, as such, had little choice but to accept Britain's terms. Putting off a fight with the British today, Hamilton argued on Washington's behalf, would give America time to build up its resources to fight later. Any concessions by the US were worth it if they prevented a conflict. Had Jay pressed harder for better terms, Hamilton argued, he might have pushed the country into the hands of war.

Even Jefferson and Madison had to eventually concede to the strength of Hamilton's arguments. Tellingly, neither man chose to put his pen to the task of responding comprehensively to Hamilton's points—clearly recognizing the futility of doing so. The treaty went on to pass the Senate by a vote of 20 to 10, and, by that time the following year, doubts about the agreement had all but slipped from the minds of most Americans.

Hamilton and Washington had prevented yet another crisis together. This time saw Hamilton a little more behind the scenes than usual, but with the same characteristically successful outcome. Before his death in 1799, Washington would seek Hamilton's special help one last time, in order to write his 1796 address to the people announcing his decision not to seek reelection.

His death would end the first, and perhaps the greatest, political partnership in American presidential history. But it did not end without first helping construct out of whole cloth a republic that would rise to be the envy of the free world. Part of their legacy as a partnership is that they established a template not only for how to be a president, but also for how to serve one.

IV

Hamilton: Partner to Power

What does it take to be a president's right-hand man or woman? Can a person grow to fit the role, or does it require a preexisting set of qualities and skills? Is one adviser possessing a particular political portfolio better suited to the post than another? The answers to these questions lie at the heart of why Washington selected Hamilton, rather than Jefferson or Randolph, to be his closest adviser and provide clues about the selection of subsequent presidents' right hands.

Of the five most frequent models of right hand to the president, Hamilton represents (1) the cabinet officer. Across the arc of American political history, every chief executive has at some time or another employed the services of his own version of Alexander Hamilton. As Washington's experience with his most trusted aide illustrates, the use of a cabinet member in the role comes with challenges, which Washington himself encountered each time Jefferson inferred from an action or comment that the president favored his treasury secretary over his secretary of state.

Had Randolph been free of scandal, Washington would certainly have assigned him total stewardship of the Jay Treaty. The president was hypersensitive to cabinet rivalries after having witnessed the often heated exchanges between Hamilton and Jefferson. After that experience, Washington would not have deliberately instigated a confrontation between Hamilton and Randolph over a matter that fell so squarely into Randolph's portfolio. Managing cabinet rivalries and avoiding displays of favoritism have been a preoccupation of every US president, and this explains why comparatively few right-hand men and women have been members of the cabinet. There have been some notable exceptions, of course . . .

Albert Gallatin, the US treasury secretary from 1801 to 1814, may be the most important of the least-known founding fathers. The longest-serving treasury secretary in history, he was the right hand to both Presidents Jefferson and Madison. Working closely with Jefferson, he devised and executed the financial and congressional plan to fund the Louisiana Purchase and then, interestingly, helped the president plan the Lewis and Clark Expedition. When President Madison wanted to appoint Gallatin secretary of state, Senate leaders objected, so Madison made him treasury secretary instead. But Madison still used him as a secretary of state. Not only did Gallatin arrange for the funding that financed America's role in the War of 1812, he represented the president at the peace negotiations with the British afterward . . .

As secretary of state to President James Monroe, John Quincy Adams is among the few right-hand men who could claim a leading role in establishing the American national identity. Monroe's greatest accomplishment as president may have been what was referred to in his day as the "Principles of 1823" but what we know today as the Monroe Doctrine. Outlining his "Principles" to Congress in his annual message, Monroe declared that the US consisted of all the lands of North America between the Atlantic and Pacific Oceans within the US borders with Canada and Mexico. His assertion put expansionist countries Great Britain, Spain and Russia on notice that North America was closed to settlement. Monroe worked closely with Secretary of State Adams to establish this principle. They were friends and worked closely on a number of foreign-policy issues during Monroe's eight years in office, but the Monroe Doctrine stands as their crowning achievement, partially for the role it played in giving lasting definition to the term "American" . . .

And Attorney General Robert F. Kennedy became his older brother's right hand after the failed Bay of Pigs invasion of Cuba in 1961. International affairs are not expected to be a significant feature of an attorney general's portfolio, but after the secret attempt to overthrow Cuban dictator Fidel Castro went horribly wrong, the president began to reconsider the recommendations he was receiving from his advisers. He started leaning more heavily on his younger brother for advice, eventually coming to rely on him for recommendations on all major domestic and international matters. When in 1962—during what would become known as the Cuban Missile Crisis—the president needed help negotiating with the Soviets, he turned to Robert Kennedy. Working back channels on behalf of the president, the attorney general helped negotiate the removal of Soviet missiles from Cuban soil— neutralizing a threat that might have resulted in nuclear war.

No president since Kennedy has favored one agency head above the rest as he did his brother. This does not mean, however, that it will not happen again—a president can choose whomever he or she wants as a right hand. What is clear is that in the event of such a reoccurrence, there will certainly be unwelcome consequences similar to those experienced by the Washington Administration.

On at least one occasion, Alexander Hamilton bragged that he saw Washington as little more than the aegis for his ambition—the means of his ascent. At some point in the mid-1790s, as Hamilton entered his middle years and as Washington's health began to fail, the two men seemed to switch places in their relationship. Each man still needed the other, and Washington was clearly still in charge, but the power in the relationship, which had tilted so decidedly in Washington's favor for the better part of two decades, seemed to lean more toward Hamilton.

Like Roosevelt and Hopkins or McKinley and Cortelyou, Washington and Hamilton were like two halves of the same person. Washington might very well have become president without Hamilton's help, and Hamilton might have been treasury secretary even if Washington had not become president. But, given each man's strengths and weaknesses, it is difficult to imagine them achieving the same level of greatness without each other.

There are times in American history when the wrong man was in the White House at the wrong time. It is hard to argue, for example, that President Andrew Johnson was the right man to lead the nation through Reconstruction after the Civil War. And, though Herbert Hoover was an extraordinary administrator, he was clearly the wrong man to be president during the Great Depression.

George Washington proved he was the right man at the right time, but he was especially so with Hamilton at his side. Without their partnership, the country might look very different today.

Decades later, when Abraham Lincoln and his right-hand man William Seward inhabited the executive mansion, they could reflect on the example set by Washington and Hamilton as they struggled to hold the country together through arguably the greatest threat the republic had faced up to that point. They could draw strength from the knowledge that, with the right partnership in the White House, even seemingly insurmountable challenges can be overcome.

CHAPTER TWO

ABRAHAM LINCOLN & WILLIAM SEWARD

IAGO AT REST

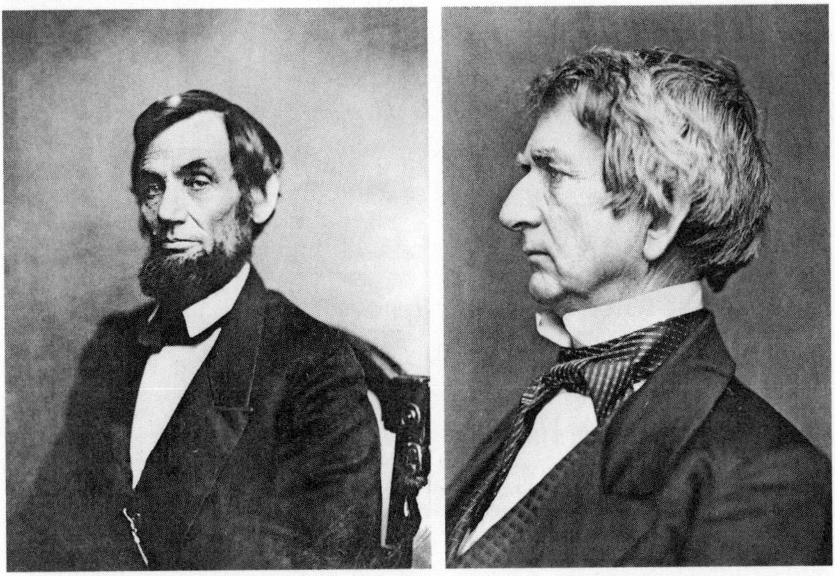

William Seward came to the White House convinced that President Lincoln was out of his depth, but as the pair began to work together, Seward came to admire Lincoln's keen understanding of human nature, his political judgment and his leadership.

> The Presidency, even to the most experienced politicians, is
> no bed of roses.[1]
>
> —President Abraham Lincoln

*O*n an unseasonably warm February morning in 1865, Abraham
Lincoln boarded the presidential yacht, the River Queen, anchored off
*the coast of Hampton Roads, Virginia, for a top-secret conference with Alexander
Stephens, the vice president of the Confederacy. The two men were meeting to
discuss a possible ending of hostilities between the North and South. A gathering
of men of such prominence bode well for a resolution, but after four hours of discussions, the negotiations ended without result. President Lincoln and Secretary
of State William Seward waved goodbye as the boat carrying Stephens and his
party steamed back toward the Virginia shore. As a token of their good parting,
Seward sent a former slave in a rowboat after them with a case of champagne. As
Stephens waved to the president in appreciation, Seward shouted, "You can keep
the wine, but return the negro!"[2]*

*This is the story of how a partnership between two political rivals evolved into
a close professional and personal friendship and the tense secret meeting they
took together with Vice President Stephens that, had it been successful, might
have ended the Civil War. This is also a love story of sorts, about a relationship
that was surprisingly close and that would certainly raise eyebrows today for the
depth of its intimacy.*

*William Seward may very well have been Lincoln's best friend during his White
House years. In his first year in office, the president spent more time with Seward
than he did with his own wife.[3] Both men had difficult marriages[4] and turned
to each other for the companionship they could not find at home. On the day
that Lincoln learned that his secretary of state had been gravely injured in a carriage accident and was lying in bed unconscious at home, he rushed to see him.
Lincoln found Seward resting comfortably. He had recovered well enough to
receive the president, but he was still too weak to sit up to properly greet him.
Quietly entering Seward's room, the president of the United States lay down*

beside him,[5] arranging his long body next to Seward's, and placed his head close on the pillow. Together, they talked softly until Seward fell asleep.

Biographers have described their regard for each other as something akin to unconditional love. To the president, Seward was not just a close friend, but also his closest adviser. Each evening, Lincoln would walk from the White House to Seward's home on Lafayette Park, a block away, and the two friends would sit by the fire—trading stories, talking about history and literature and teasing each other. Lincoln would use the occasions to unpack and analyze the events of the day. Often, after seeking advice from his cabinet, Lincoln would use his evening talks with Seward to settle his mind on the issues. It may have been during one of these visits that Lincoln turned to Seward to help him decide whether to accept Vice President Stephens's request to meet.

The negotiating party aboard the River Queen *consisted of Lincoln, Seward, Stephens, Confederate assistant secretary of war John Campbell, and Confederate senator Robert Hunter. Taking their seats, the men agreed that the discussion would be informal. No papers would be exchanged, there would be no opening statements, and no notes would be taken. Seward had sent ahead a good supply of liquid refreshments, hoping it would aid the discussion among the men, who had all known each other before the war but who had not seen each other in years. Lincoln and Seward, discussing their strategy in advance,[6] decided that they would encourage an open discussion but would accept no terms short of total surrender and that at no point would either of them refer to the Confederacy as a separate country.*

Lincoln was surprisingly forthcoming (maybe even a little reckless), saying things that he perhaps should not have. As they took turns playing "good cop, bad cop," Seward was more consistent in his comments, while Lincoln was all over the map. One minute he was reminding his Confederate guests that they were losing the war and their defeat seemed inevitable; the next he was suggesting that mutually agreeable solutions were available. In one hand, he held out to the South the offer of hope and reconciliation; in the other, only atonement for its sins.

After talking for four hours and coming to no agreement, everyone present real-
ized that there was no point in continuing. As Stephens rose to say goodbye to
his old friend, he took Lincoln's hand and wished him good health. As Stephens
stepped onto the boat that would bear him and his party back to shore, he could
not have known that he would never see Lincoln alive again.

I

"As Men in Rage Strike Those That Wish Them Best"[7]

Some believe Abraham Lincoln first met William Seward in 1848 in Boston, during a political campaign event for future president Zachary Taylor. Seward was one of the most important Whig/Republican leaders in America and was the featured speaker at the forum. The lesser-known Lincoln was the warm-up act. Afterward, the two men are said to have shared a hotel room in nearby Worcester, where they supposedly sat up all night discussing the issue of slavery. Seward biographer Walter Stahr doubts that part of the legend; according to newspaper reports, Seward was in Springfield, Massachusetts, giving another speech at that time, and Lincoln was on a train heading back to Illinois. After the Boston event, the public record does not have them meeting again until just before the 1860 campaign for the Republican nomination, at which they would be competitors.

Following the custom of the day, Seward did not attend the 1860 convention. He kept an eye on the proceedings in the papers and through messages relayed from his friends, convention chair Edwin Morgan, and Thurlow Weed, his campaign manager, who was attending the convention on his behalf. News that Lincoln was among the candidates must have given Seward little cause for concern. He no doubt recalled the disheveled, hayseed giant from their last meeting and perhaps turned his thoughts instead to the three other men on the ballot: Simon Cameron, Salmon Chase and Edward Bates. Each was a man of national reputation and a prominent member of the party from a key state.

Seward was the odds-on favorite—so much so that if a vote had been taken on the first night of the convention, he would have won handily. But the vote would not occur for days, giving Lincoln time to marshal support for himself as a centrist alternative to the "too conservative" Chase and Bates and the "too liberal" Seward. Lincoln ran on the idea that support from all the Northern states would be essential to victory against the Democrats in the autumn and that Seward was too committed to the abolition of slavery to win key conservative states such as Pennsylvania and Indiana.

Seward was so confident that he would be the Republican nominee that, instead of spending the previous year touring the country and giving speeches to shore up his party's support for him, he had taken an eight-month tour of Europe, where he was feted by Queen Victoria and other dignitaries as the presumptive president-elect. On a pleasant early afternoon in spring, as the convention attendees settled in for the first in a series of votes in Chicago, Seward and a small party of friends relaxed in the garden of his upstate home in Auburn, New York, enjoying spirits and cigars as they waited for word of his inevitable victory.

Then, around three o'clock, a courier arrived with a telegram announcing that Seward was well short of the 233 votes that he needed to win the nomination outright, but, with 173 votes, he had a substantial lead over Lincoln, who had 102, and Chase, Cameron and Bates, who had just short of 50 votes each.[8] Seward used the news as an opportunity to educate his guests on the ballot process as they awaited the next courier, who was expected any moment. The courier never came.

Instead, about fifteen minutes later, a friend of Seward's, a visibly shaken Dr. Theodore Dimon, entered the garden shouting something that his distance made difficult to discern. As he drew nearer, he could be heard saying: "Oh God, Oh God, it is all gone, gone, gone! Abraham Lincoln has received the nomination!"[9]

Back in Chicago, in a matter of minutes, the situation in the convention hall had changed dramatically. On the second ballot, Seward's total had increased to 184, but Lincoln was close behind with 181. Convention members, seeing the strong support Lincoln received in the first vote, had decided to change sides. Some of them turned to Seward, but many more chose Lincoln. On the third and final vote, still more supporters joined Lincoln, raising his total to 231—just two votes shy of victory. When the number was announced from the stage, delegates around the hall rose and offered to change their votes so that Lincoln's victory could be unanimous. Lincoln's supporters filled the room with deafening shouts and thunderous applause, while all around them Seward's supporters, some of them men of great dignity and distinction, "wept like boys."

Back in quiet Auburn, Seward's friend John Austin was looking over at Seward when they finally understood what Dr. Dimon was shouting. In his diary, Austin noted Seward's reaction: "A deadly paleness overspread his countenance for an instant, succeeded instantly by a flush, and then all was calm as a summer morning."[10] Composed and contained, Seward turned to resume his conversation with one of his undoubtedly saddened and distracted guests. After a few minutes more, Seward rose and excused himself to go inside the house to share the disappointing news with his family. His daughter, Fanny, recorded in her diary the gentle smile on Seward's face as he uttered the phrase, "Abraham Lincoln nominated," and departed. She wrote that he bore the crushing disappointment with "philosophical and unselfish coolness."[11]

Indeed, he seemed to take the news with grace. Remembering Seward's legendary magnanimity, the editor of the local newspaper approached him to pen a congratulatory opinion piece about Lincoln. Seward agreed. The piece was a strongly worded endorsement of Lincoln's qualifications for office and urged all responsible Republicans to fall into line behind their nominee or risk a Democratic victory in the fall. The result was that even Seward's friends and family thought he had forgiven Lincoln. Yet it must have pained Seward to write that the better man had won when, as his later actions would reveal, he believed in his heart that he had been robbed of his last best chance to become president.[12]

Seward's friends and counselors encouraged him not to withdraw from public life. They suggested that there might be a way for Seward to salvage the situation and perhaps achieve presidential power in deed, if not in name. His campaign manager, Thurlow Weed, and Charles Francis Adams, a close political friend and mentor, suggested that if he worked hard for Lincoln's election—harder than anyone else—Lincoln might reward him with an appointment as secretary of state. They argued that from that vantage point, someone of Seward's experience and abilities could wield significant power from behind the throne, guiding Lincoln much as a prime minister might guide a king.

Seward threw himself into campaigning for Lincoln from Maine to Kansas. Cameron, Chase and Bates also stumped for Lincoln, but none of them did so as vigorously as Seward. In recognition of his hard work and his clear qualifications for the post,[13] President-elect Lincoln offered Seward the position of secretary of state. Seward accepted gladly. Almost from the start, there was friction.

In an effort to smooth over Seward's hurt feelings, after the campaign Lincoln took steps to make friends with him. He shared the draft of his inaugural speech with Seward for comment, hoping it would make him feel like an important member of his soon-to-be cabinet. Seward, perhaps still believing he would have been the better president, edited the speech as if it were his own: He did a line-by-line, deep editorial analysis of the one-hundred-line speech, making significant word and tonal changes along the way. Seward believed Lincoln's language sounded too bellicose toward the South and suggested changes to soften the tone.

When a week passed with no reply from Lincoln, Seward grew agitated. He rushed off an angry letter to the president, threatening to resign unless his changes to the speech were accepted. Instead of confronting Seward, Lincoln simply avoided the discussion. Though he did not acknowledge Seward's contribution, Lincoln did make many of the suggested changes, and he changed the tone of his speech to make it more conciliatory toward the South. But Seward was unaware that Lincoln had accepted his changes until he actually heard the speech.

On the surface, Seward's threat to resign may have looked like a firm stance on principle, but a deeper analysis reveals a characteristic impatience that in this case bordered on arrogance. Such a bold move so early in the administration was a clear indication of Seward's strong reservations about Lincoln's leadership. The observant Lincoln surely recognized this.

If Seward's threat gave Lincoln any concern about his secretary of state, Seward's next act must have convinced him that something must be done about this aggressive and undisciplined adviser.

Less than three months into the administration, Seward decided to pressure Lincoln to turn over the most urgent duties of his presidency to a member of the cabinet to "oversee" on his behalf. In a long memo to the president,[14] Seward argued that, under Lincoln's leadership, the country lacked a coherent domestic and foreign policy and that, perhaps, the president was a bit in over his head. He suggested that the country might benefit from the leadership of one of his senior aides—he did not offer himself, but his meaning was clear.

Seward even went as far as to share his memo with the editor of the *New York Times*, for publication, with the promise that he would also include an approval letter from Lincoln once he received official sign-off from the president. Seward had his son deliver the memo, entitled "Some Thoughts for the

President's Consideration," directly to Lincoln on a Monday morning in April 1861. It is not hard to imagine what Lincoln must have thought of such a letter—what little regard Seward must have had for his abilities to suggest that the president relinquish the duties of his office to the care of an aide! On the following day, Seward received Lincoln's response. The president had written a detailed, strongly worded reply to Seward, but he chose not to deliver it. Instead, he called a personal meeting and expressed himself to his secretary of state in simple but clear terms that essentially amounted to "I'm the president; you are not."

In any other administration, under any other president, a member of staff acting in such a manner as Seward might be asked to resign. Lincoln let the matter pass. In fact, by that time the following year, Seward would be his most trusted adviser. The arrogance and sense of entitlement Seward displayed so strongly in those early days would be supplanted by a deep affection for the president that bordered on love.

II

Janus in Rome

Given how different their personal histories were, some have wondered what it was that drew Lincoln and Seward into such a close friendship. Why did Lincoln get along so much better with Seward than he did with other members of his cabinet? Personality certainly played a role, but more in the way one might expect opposites to attract. Lincoln was pensive and moody, and Seward was lighthearted and jovial. Lincoln could be fun to be around, but, given his history, one imagines it required more than a bit of effort on his part. For Seward, socializing came as naturally as breathing. As is often the case between presidents and their right-hand men and women, their differences were complementary.

They shared at least two similarities that would be immediately apparent to anyone meeting them for the first time—their love for storytelling and their almost juvenile sense of humor. To get a laugh, Seward would draw from a deep catalogue of stories he had collected over his lifetime. For Lincoln, storytelling was more organic and spontaneous—a gift. Friends described how the mere act seemed to transform him. His face, usually morose and sullen, would come alive as the story started to build.

A new acquaintance might also notice that the two men were a bit careless in their dress. While Lincoln rarely gave much thought to what he wore and was often seen wearing the same black suit over and over, there were some who believed Seward's frequent dishevelment was by design. Recalling how the young Seward had loved clothes so much that he and his father had a falling-out over the bills, old friends might have wondered where the dandy they once knew had gone.

Lincoln and Seward could also be crude company. Lincoln sometimes seemed to lack even the slightest refinement, and Seward, despite having been raised among sophisticated ladies and gentleman, swore like an eager young sailor on shore leave. They might have found these qualities endearing in each other. If, during the long hours the two men spent in their talks by Seward's fire, they ever discussed their reasons for entering into politics, they would have discovered that even on that subject they shared similarities.

The motives underlying the decision of the politically ambitious to run for elected office have changed little since Lincoln's day. There are those who profess to being moved to run out of a concern for the struggles of the least fortunate among us. Some believe they are called from on high to correct injustice here on earth. And, of course, some run merely out of a desire to be adored. Among the reasons that Seward and Lincoln decided to enter politics was a mutual and deep need for distraction. Lincoln hoped to outrun his sometimes severe depression, and Seward was drawn to the frenetic atmosphere of politics as a means to escape boredom.

Seward hated standing still so much that he traveled anytime he had an excuse to do so. When he became secretary of state, he would take carriage rides around the city each day just to experience the feeling of motion. A life spent on the move was a quality he shared with Lincoln.

Lincoln's early adult life was spent largely moving from place to place: first, as a twenty-year-old worker aboard a flatboat going south to New Orleans; then, as a surveyor and finally on horseback as a circuit court lawyer. Historians have speculated that Seward's wanderlust began as an effort to escape the orbit of a domineering father. One might say the same of Lincoln, but it could just as well have been that the distraction of motion helped Lincoln cope with what people in his day called melancholy.

Mental illness ran in Lincoln's family.[15] Both his parents were known depressives, but some suspected that in the case of his mother, Nancy, it was more circumstantial than clinical. It was well known by local residents that Nancy had been born illegitimate and abandoned by her mother. She was tall and dark, with an unattractive, coarse complexion, a sunken chest and haunting eyes. Even her friends described her as sullen and gloomy. These were some of the same words used to describe Lincoln's father, Thomas, who had his own reasons for being depressed.

When Thomas was a boy in Kentucky, a Shawnee raiding party came into his family camp and shot his father, Abraham, as he was planting corn. One of the warriors tried to drag off young Thomas, but, as he struggled to free himself, his older brother Mordecai shot and killed the warrior. Despite this painful memory and the occasional dark moments it must have inspired, Thomas still managed to grow up with a reputation for being easygoing and convivial. When the dark clouds lifted and the moodiness receded, he was friendly, boyishly charming and full of humorous stories. It was from his father that Abraham Lincoln inherited his sense of humor and gift for storytelling. Yet Thomas was unlucky in life. Opportunities came, but they always seemed to slip away. As Thomas moved the family from town to town in search of work as a dirt farmer and sometimes carpenter, he left a trail of miscalculations and embarrassing mistakes. The pain of guilt this must have caused him contributed to his depression.

Depression likewise had a strong and lifelong hold on Abraham Lincoln. His struggles with the disease were so severe at times that those close to him feared for his life. His first recorded serious bout with depression occurred in his late twenties, when, after the death of his first love, Ann Rutledge, of typhoid, Lincoln descended into a melancholy so deep it lasted for months.

Lincoln would fall into an even deeper depression years later when his engagement to Mary Todd was called off. For months, he would sit alone in his room as if catatonic. His best friend, Joshua Speed, was so worried he might attempt suicide that he removed the shaving equipment from his room. Once he even locked Lincoln in for his own safety. A friend staying with Lincoln recalled waking in the middle of the night to find him sitting up in the dark talking to himself. Lincoln's depression could be triggered by a memory, the weather or even moments of professional disappointment.

He was close to suicide at least once in his life,[16] but according to historian Doris Kearns Goodwin,[17] Lincoln persevered out of a desire to live long enough to achieve something worthy of recognition. She thought Lincoln's drive was as much fueled by personal ambition as by the memory of the loss of his mother, his sister Sarah, his sons[18] and his first love. It was work that helped shake Lincoln out of many of his deepest funks, and after the deaths of so many of his loved ones, it was work that saved him.

When the burdens of the presidency weighed on Lincoln, especially during the worst of the war years, he would walk across the street from the White House to Seward's home. Sitting by the fire in his friend's parlor, the president would relax and let his mind wander as Seward recounted stories of his world travels.

Seward's wanderlust knew no limits. When he was a young man, with a new wife and young kids, his father invited him on a trip of Europe. The pull of the road was so strong that he accepted without hesitation, even though it meant he would not see his family for weeks. It was as if his restlessness was the sign of an addiction he was powerless to ignore.

William Henry Seward was born in 1801 into a wealthy upstate New York family. His father, Samuel, who had briefly been a member of the New York State legislature, built his fortune from a number of businesses that all revolved in some way around politics. As a reward for backing Thomas Jefferson for president, Samuel was appointed postmaster of his town. Watching his father navigate the world of local and state politics was Seward's introduction to his life's work.

William—or Henry, as he was called as a boy—was a bright, disciplined child. Samuel chose him as the one out of his five children to attend university. At fifteen, Seward enrolled in Union College, near Albany, but before long he grew restless. He abruptly quit college and set off with a friend for Georgia, where he hoped to find a job as a teacher. But after a few months, his father convinced him to return to school. He quickly resumed the rhythm of his studies and ended up graduating first in his class and gaining admission to the prestigious honor society Phi Beta Kappa. After his admittance to the bar, he tried his hand at being a trial attorney, but quickly grew bored and allowed himself to be swept up in the political energy of the day.

For the young Seward, who hated standing still, the frenetic world of 1820s New York State politics was a better fit than practicing law. He found himself spending more and more of his free time attending social events and political gatherings. He slowly built a reputation in local politics based on his political writings and his volunteer work, joining a number of political clubs before becoming a member of the Whig Party—the precursor of the Republican Party.

In 1830, when he was twenty-nine, Seward ran for election to the New York State Senate. In those days, candidates did not openly pursue the seat. So instead, Thurlow Weed, a newspaper friend and political mentor who wielded considerable power in upstate New York politics, campaigned on Seward's behalf. Weed helped orchestrate Seward's political rise in return for helping Weed establish his newspaper, the influential *Albany Evening Journal*. Together they racked up a string of political successes in relatively quick succession.

In 1849, Seward was elected to the US Senate. He was a youthful-looking forty-eight years old, short (even for his day), wiry and bristling with energy. Washington, DC, was soon introduced to his outsized personality, which filled every room he entered. By then, his thick, often unkempt, red hair was turning brown with age. One acquaintance, describing his first meeting with the senator, compared him to a large-beaked macaw with hair that made him appear to be balancing a mulberry bush on his head. The child of a longtime friend thought his suits looked like they had been made of good material by a bad tailor. Most people liked him instantly. Some thought him vain. But, for the most part, people were drawn to his open and unguarded personality. Though he liked to portray himself as a man of the people, Seward was actually a man of refined tastes with a weakness for fine cigars and classical literature.

As mentioned, it was Lincoln, not Seward, who initiated their friendship. Having lost so many elections himself, Lincoln undoubtedly sympathized with Seward's disappointment at having lost the 1860 Republican nomination. Also, understanding human nature as well as he did, Lincoln must have expected that Seward's ego would certainly be too bruised to seek any relationship with him beyond the professional. But the newly elected Lincoln wanted his cabinet to function as a team—a team of which Seward was an important member—so he went out of his way to gain Seward's friendship.

It started with an invitation to meet regularly. He wanted his secretary of state to feel like a valued member of his inner circle and actively sought Seward's counsel. On the occasions when they could not get together, Lincoln would write Seward to ask his advice on a variety of issues. As Lincoln considered whether to suspend habeas corpus and arrest a Maryland state legislator who was hindering the movement of Union troops from Baltimore to Washington, he eagerly reached out to Seward for advice. Similarly, when in 1862 Lincoln received hundreds of letters from citizens requesting that he fire General George McClellan, Lincoln forwarded the letters to Seward at the State Department for comment. Lincoln's efforts to include Seward helped soften his resentment, but it would be a while before Seward could share the president's enthusiasm for the relationship.

In the beginning, Seward thought Lincoln a provincial, unsophisticated hayseed clearly out of his depth and ill-equipped for such a high office. But he soon learned that Lincoln was not only an uncommonly wise judge of character, but also a brilliant manager and a man of great generosity. He was eventually charmed by Lincoln's attempts at friendship, and he tried to reciprocate.

Recognizing how close Lincoln was to his two sons Willie and Tad, Seward reached out to befriend them. He had hoped to do the same with Mrs. Lincoln, but he was never able to get past her icy exterior.[19] Seward began to include the president in his regular carriage rides around the city each evening after work. During these long private moments, Seward came to appreciate their shared sense of humor. Once, while gazing out of the window, Lincoln pointed out a sign that read "T. R. Strong." Lincoln looked at Seward with a twinkle in his eye and remarked, "Tea are strong, but coffee are stronger."[20] They both howled with laughter. Interestingly, the event that transformed their relationship from cordial and collaborative to one of genuine affection would be something that neither man initiated.

Given his legendary ability to read people, Lincoln must have quickly recognized that his treasury secretary, Salmon P. Chase, would be a difficult man to like. Chase was suspicious, openly competitive and petty. He had built a career as a genuine defender of the underclass and had impeccable credentials, but he was also stiff, mean-spirited, and painfully awkward in public. Part of his awkwardness grew out of an extreme nearsightedness that made it difficult for him to read social cues. He was a widower three times over and was devoted to his daughter Kate, who sacrificed her own happiness on the altar of his ambition: she gave up on love to marry an abusive, wealthy older man in order to help her father pursue his lifelong quest for the presidency. On paper, Chase was the worst possible person Lincoln could have added to what he hoped would become a close circle of advisers. Like Seward, Chase accepted the cabinet post with the intention of unseating Lincoln in the next election. Unlike Seward, he proved immune to Lincoln's charms.

Chase was fiercely jealous of Seward's growing friendship with Lincoln, which he felt threatened his own ability to influence the president. In an effort to get Seward ejected from the cabinet, Chase spread harmful rumors about the secretary of state and used his contacts in the Senate to build a movement against Seward. He convinced a number of senators that Seward wielded too much power in the cabinet and was acting more like Lincoln's prime minister than a cabinet secretary. Chase encouraged them to reach out to Lincoln to urge Seward's dismissal. Lincoln knew that the claims against Seward were false, but rather than correct Chase's rivalrous behavior in private, he wisely chose to do so in public.

Lincoln invited Chase, the senators Chase had enlisted and Seward to the White House to hear personally the complaints against Seward. He challenged Chase to say to Seward's face what he had been saying behind his back, but the embarrassed Chase was silent. The meeting ended with the senators leaving discouraged and disappointed. Lincoln knew Chase was the kind of man who would never admit publicly to such small-minded behavior, and he also knew that had he attempted to resolve the matter in private, the affair would not have ended there. By flushing out into the open Chase's base jealousies, Lincoln effectively discouraged him from repeating the offense.

The next day, humiliated and embarrassed, Chase offered to resign. To Lincoln's dismay, Seward also submitted his letter of resignation, on the grounds that he had become a distraction for the administration. Lincoln refused both offers. Later he would say to an aide that Seward and Chase had to both go or both stay. Since Lincoln needed Seward too much to let him go, Chase got a pass.

The incident cast a dark cloud over Lincoln's already strained relationship with Chase, but it deepened his regard for Seward, whom he admired for the grace under which he bore Chase's attack. The incident reinforced Lincoln and Seward's respect for each other and drew them even closer as friends.

After that, Lincoln began to visit Seward more often at his home, where they would sit and talk for hours. They must have realized they had each found a kindred spirit in the other. Over time, as most of the members of Lincoln's cabinet moved on, Seward was one of only two to remain till the end. He became Lincoln's alter ego, his sounding board, his counselor and his conscience. He lifted Lincoln's mood and literally provided him shelter from the rain. Seward would be at Lincoln's side during his darkest days and his greatest triumphs. Together, they shaped the defining achievements of his presidency.

III

Iago at Rest

Chase's plan to drive a wedge between Seward and Lincoln had had the opposite effect. As they became closer, Seward's role as an adviser to Lincoln deepened, and his influence was brought to bear on many of Lincoln's most significant achievements, including the Emancipation Proclamation.

As Lincoln considered how to introduce the Emancipation Proclamation to the public, he raised the issue with Seward to get his thoughts. Seward was rarely at a loss for words, but on this occasion, he could only say that he needed more time to consider the subject. Seward supported the concept of emancipation, but out of the earshot of the president he questioned the value of a proclamation that freed people in areas where the federal government currently had no ability to protect them. He referred to the proclamation as "a puff of wind over an accomplished fact."[21]

When Lincoln presented his idea to the full cabinet, the reception was mixed: War Secretary Edwin Stanton and Attorney General Edward Bates were supportive. Treasury Secretary Chase—perhaps the strongest advocate for emancipation among them—opposed the idea over concerns about the unpredictability of its impact on border states,[22] and he worried about the effect on newly freed slaves, most of whom were, it was judged, unprepared for precipitous emancipation. Seward did not oppose the idea, but he voiced reservations about how England and France might respond, given their dependence on American cotton. The act might push the two countries into the arms of the South, he thought.

Lincoln was prepared to issue the proclamation over the objections of his cabinet and had planned to publish it at his earliest convenience, but Seward said something that changed his mind. The comment was perhaps Seward's most important contribution to the effort.

Lincoln was a careful and deliberate decision-maker. He might spend weeks weighing the pros and cons of a single issue, and he thought he had considered every conceivable implication of the proclamation before Seward surprised him by questioning its timing. Seward thought that to make the proclamation at a time when the Union Army was considered to be performing poorly on the battlefield might be viewed as an act of desperation. He counseled instead that Lincoln sit on the document until the North scored a significant victory. Lincoln later told a friend: "The wisdom of the view of the Secretary of State struck me with very great force. It was an aspect of the case that, in all my thought upon the subject, I had entirely overlooked. The result was that I put the draft of the proclamation aside, waiting for a victory."[23]

Seward's reservations about the document were in no way an indication that his long-held opposition to slavery had changed in any way. He was as fervent an abolitionist as he had ever been, but he believed the proclamation was not the best tool for ending slavery. The energy and determination the secretary of state soon exhibited as he led Lincoln's campaign to pass the Thirteenth Amendment[24] reveals just how far Seward was willing to go when he recognized a viable path to terminating the vile institution.

Passage of the Thirteenth Amendment was a yearlong affair, involving the help of scores of individuals. Other than the bill's sponsors and President Lincoln, no one played a larger role in its success than Seward. The measure passed the Senate almost a year before it passed the House,[25] where opposition was stronger. Seward threw himself into the work, doing everything short of breaking the law to get the amendment cleared.

To win votes, Seward enlisted the help of four Democratic lobbyists of questionable scruples and ordered them to do whatever was necessary. This was of course conduct that Lincoln needed to distance himself from, and many historians believe Seward acted without Lincoln's knowledge. But given how politically careful Lincoln was, and the close relationship he shared with Seward, it is unimaginable that the strategy never came up during one of their private fireside chats. Since one of the cornerstones of the relationship between the president and his right hand is secrecy, the full extent of their collaboration may be lost forever to history. But for an illuminating portrait of how the two men worked together, one might consider their collaboration during the peace conference with Confederate vice president Alexander Stephens. Though there were no notes taken during the conference, and many of the details of the meeting remain murky, what little is known provides valuable insights into the dynamics of the relationship between Lincoln and Seward.

The president did not trust Jefferson Davis. He believed the Confederacy would never accept anything short of independence. So when, on more than one occasion, he received word that Davis wanted to meet, he viewed the request with suspicion. Doubting that the conference would produce anything of substance, he finally agreed to the meeting, but privately he planned to send Seward instead, armed with clear instructions for how to position the discussion for future talks. His plans changed when he received word from General Ulysses Grant that Confederate vice president Stephens had paid him a personal visit and seemed seriously inclined to resolve the conflict if a meeting could be arranged with Lincoln. The president knew that Southern citizens were beginning to turn against Davis in light of a string of battlefield defeats. The pressure Davis was under might be the reason for the urgent request to meet. Perhaps Davis was genuinely open to compromise. At the last minute, Lincoln decided to join Seward.

What would become known as the Hampton Roads Peace Conference was, as mentioned, a failure. Nothing of note was accomplished beyond Lincoln agreeing to free Alexander Stephens's nephew from a prisoner-of-war camp in northern Ohio. But the meeting helps reveal on one hand why Lincoln valued Seward and on the other hand how frustrating many people must have found it at times to work with Lincoln.

The tense meeting exposed some of the good and bad qualities of both men, as well as how well they knew and understood each other.

By today's standards, the room where the conferees met aboard the *River Queen* was tacky to the point of gaudiness. Modern-day travelers entering for the first time might find the decor a bit dizzying. The skylight overhead illuminated a noisy patchwork of ceiling beams, and the beige walls were punctuated at regular intervals by gilded Corinthian columns. A long row of pink- and green-framed windows stood like sentinels on either side of the room. A semicircle of stiff-backed, floral-upholstered armchairs were at war with an ivory, rose and forest-green colored Persian rug, while a lumbering black leather banquette slouched disapprovingly by the door. Vice President Stephens, Senator Hunter and Secretary Campbell stood as they waited for their host. Without warning, a door opened, and in walked Seward, whispering to the president.[26]

Old friends as they were, Stephens and Lincoln's faces came alive as their eyes met. Inquiries were made about the health of mutual acquaintances. Someone asked whether the dome on the Capitol was finished. As the slender Stephens struggled to remove his greatcoat and scarf, Lincoln could not help but poke fun at his friend: "Never has so small a nubbin emerged from such an immense husk." Everyone laughed, but Stephens was the first to show his teeth: "Well, Mr. President, is there no way to put an end to the present troubles and restore the good feelings that existed in the good old days?"

"There is only one way I know of," Lincoln responded. "Those who are resisting the national authority and the laws of the US need to stop."

Stephens immediately steered the conversation to a topic he hoped would be more agreeable—French aggression in Mexico. "Is there no other question that might divert the attention of both parties for a time until passions on both sides cool?"

The Confederates had asked for the meeting in response to a proposal presented to Jefferson Davis during a recent visit from Lincoln's friend Francis Blair. Based on his discussion with Blair, Davis hoped a cease-fire could be arranged so the North and South could unite to stop the advance of French troops in Mexico.

Had Lincoln known that this was the Confederates' main goal for the meeting, he would never have agreed to meet. Stephens's mere mention of the French seemed to annoy him. He had sent word to his Union troops that these Southerners should not be permitted to cross Union lines unless they agreed to discuss only the terms of their surrender. Stephens, however, was unaware that Lincoln had set this precondition.

"Whatever Blair has said was on his own account," Lincoln replied dismissively. "He had no authority to speak for me in any way whatever."

Stephens pressed further. "But suppose that a line of policy should lead to a restoration of the Union without further bloodshed?" The meeting was just beginning, and already Lincoln was out of patience. He did not care about the French; all he cared about was ending the war.

"The existing difficulties [between the North and South] are of supreme importance," Lincoln insisted. Then, something happened that must have immediately revealed to the Southerners the closeness of Lincoln and Seward's relationship.

Recognizing Lincoln's frustration with talk about Mexico, Campbell tried to change the topic by asking Lincoln to explain his strategy for reconstruction, but Seward refused to let Campbell interrupt. Instead, Seward insisted that Stephens be given a chance to fully develop his previous argument. Surprisingly, given his evident impatience with the topic, the president did not object. This was the first in a series of interactions between Lincoln and Seward that showed how they played off of each other. Lincoln listened patiently as Stephens repeated, at some length, what he had already said. The president was clearly uninterested in the subject of a short-term armistice, and Seward knew this, but Seward's insistence that Stephens continue suggests that he saw an opportunity.

Lincoln's acquiescing to a continuation of the discussion suggests that he suspected Seward was up to something. Nothing came of Stephens's further elaboration, but if the Southern conferees wanted an example of how in tune Lincoln and Seward were, this was it. The moment was perhaps valuable to them for what it revealed about Seward and Lincoln—that the president was willing to take a back seat to his secretary of state if it might prove useful to the debate. Stephens, Hunter and Campbell got another chance to witness how Lincoln and his secretary of state related to each other when Stephens asked Lincoln about the Emancipation Proclamation: "Who was freed by the Emancipation and how will property holders be compensated for their loss? Could the document be changed?"

Nothing about the proclamation would be changed "in the slightest particular," Lincoln asserted. He thought the issue of property would have to be settled by the courts. But, Lincoln added, the emancipation was an exercise of his wartime powers. If the war ended, the proclamation would be valid only in the territories that the Union controlled.

Then, Seward interjected in a way that suggests that he and Lincoln must have carefully planned this part of the discussion. Seward reminded their Southern guests that the proclamation, due to its specific language covering certain slave-holding states and not others, freed only two hundred thousand of the three million slaves in the country.[27] If the war was ended by agreement, only those slaves will have been freed, said Seward, but if the war continued, *all* slaves would eventually be freed by force. To add a bit of drama, he then pulled from his pocket a copy of the Thirteenth Amendment.

Hunter, who had been a US senator and Speaker of the US House of Representatives before the war, replied with a provocative comment: "If you could use your war powers to free the slaves, you could use them to end the war and restore states' rights."

Looking at Stephens, Lincoln replied that were he the Confederate vice president, he would go back to Georgia, encourage the governor to rejoin the Union, recall the troops back to the state and convene the legislature to ratify the Thirteenth Amendment as quickly as possible. That way, emancipation could be delayed to some future date, so that all Georgians would have time to adjust. Seward quickly added that otherwise the amendment would be issued by force, and the impact on all parties would be abrupt. By following the president's advice, Seward argued, the South would at least have some control over the process. Then Lincoln added a sweetener.

If the South returned to the Union, he said, Congress might be persuaded to compensate property holders for their losses. As much as $400 million might be appropriated for the purpose. Then, in what was either the first evidence of a dis-agreement between Seward and the president or a bit of theatrics for the benefit of their guests, the secretary of state rose from his chair and, in an apparent display of frustration, walked across the room while mumbling loud enough for all to hear, "The United States has already paid on that account." Lincoln responded to Seward's comments in a way that suggested he might have been sympathetic to the plight of the Southerners: "You may talk so about slavery if you will, but if it was wrong in the South to hold slaves, it was wrong in the North to carry on the slave trade and it would be wrong to hold onto the money that the North procured by selling slaves to the South without compensation if the North took the slaves back again."

Refusing to take the bait, Hunter changed the subject. He asked Lincoln why it was that the South must surrender unconditionally before substantive discus-sions about power-sharing could begin: "Could not the North negotiate terms with the South the way that King Charles did during England's Civil War?"

Lincoln reminded Hunter that at the end of that war, King Charles was beheaded. The Southerners could expect better treatment from Lincoln. "That is less than *I* can expect from the Southern leadership," he joked.

Hunter pressed him: "What you are saying, Mr. President, is that we of the South have committed treason that we have forfeited our rights and that we are proper subjects for the hangman. Is that what your words imply?"

Lincoln's response was short and to the point: "Yes, that's about the size of it."

Sensing that nothing more could—or should be said, Stephens called the meeting to a close. Looking at the vice president, Lincoln asked, "Well, there has been nothing we could do for our country. Is there anything I can do for you personally?"

As the men rose to leave, Stephens asked if his nephew could be freed from the prisoner-of-war camp on Lake Erie. Lincoln agreed. In a last-ditch effort before stepping through the doorway, Stephens asked Lincoln one last time to reconsider an armistice so the North and South could unite against France. The president, not wanting to insult his guests, promised he would consider the issue, but he did not expect to change his mind. The old friends then wished each other well.

Seward and Lincoln waved goodbye as the three Confederate leaders boarded their boat for the return trip home. In a few hours, Lincoln and Seward would be back in Washington, no doubt filled with thoughts about what might have been. Their disappointment did not last long, as the South surrendered to the North three months later.

IV

Seward: Partner to Power

With William Seward, this chapter continues the examination of the cabinet officer as right hand to the president, with a special emphasis on the hazards that can accompany its selection in the role. In chapter one, attention was predominantly focused on how Washington and Hamilton worked together, with comparatively less emphasis on relationships between cabinet members. In this chapter, more attention is paid to what can go wrong when a president appears to favor one adviser over another.

The growing tension between Seward and the rest of the cabinet as he grew closer to Lincoln illustrates why a cabinet official in the role of right hand can be so problematic. Just as Washington's relationship with Hamilton was a cause of friction between Hamilton and Jefferson, Lincoln's relationship with Seward upset the equanimity of his team. A quarter-century before Lincoln took office, when Andrew Jackson was in the White House, his close relationship with one of his cabinet secretaries, John Eaton, threatened his presidency as well.

Eaton was Jackson's one friend in a cabinet of strangers. The two men had known each other for years, and Eaton played a significant role in Jackson's political rise. Jackson was fiercely loyal to his friends, and even after Eaton's conduct put his reelection at risk, Jackson refused to abandon him. Eaton was officially Jackson's secretary of war, but if he is still known today it is for his role in two controversies: first, the tragic mass displacement of Native Americans that will forever be remembered as the Trail of Tears, and, second, the "Petticoat Affair."

The Petticoat Affair centered on Eaton's wife, who was rumored to be a woman of moral ill repute. Eaton first met Margaret in a boarding house frequented by Washington politicians. She was beautiful, intelligent and married. Eaton was so captivated by her that he paid her secret visits and escorted her to social events when her husband was out of town. Following her husband's suspected suicide, Eaton quickly married her. When Eaton introduced his new bride to the wives of his fellow cabinet members, they refused to socialize with her. Jackson rejected recommendations to condemn his friend for bringing scandal into the White House and suffered severe criticism from the public and his opponents for not requesting Eaton's resignation.

Like the conflict in Lincoln's cabinet, the friction in Jackson's was about more than Eaton and his wife. The incident masked a power struggle that pitted Jackson and Eaton against the president's opponents in the cabinet, including Vice President Calhoun. As Jackson's right-hand man, Eaton performed a number of non-war-related functions, including acting as the president's gate-keeper, speechwriter and chief political adviser. Marginalizing the influential Eaton would help shore up the influence of Calhoun and his supporters. To take the pressure off of Jackson, Eaton and Secretary of State Martin Van Buren offered to resign, giving the president the opportunity to request the resignation of the rest of his cabinet. He was therefore able to remake the cabinet more to his liking while taking advantage of a face-saving solution to his Eaton problem.

As mentioned in chapter one, in the modern era relatively few presidents have selected cabinet secretaries to serve as their right hands. Infighting is an important reason why. President Kennedy was the last to pursue this path; subsequent presidents seem to have followed more in the footsteps of President Ford, who famously refused to single out any member of his cabinet as his main adviser.

After suffering as he did over the Eaton affair, Jackson may have learned his lesson about whom to select as right hand. He chose Van Buren for the role after Van Buren replaced Calhoun as vice president on the ticket during the 1832 campaign. Vice President Van Buren was obviously experienced and capable, and he and Jackson liked each other; these were important considerations. But perhaps it was no less important that by selecting the vice president—someone above the rest of his cabinet members—as his chief adviser, Jackson could avoid repeating a painful mistake.

Two months after the Hampton Roads Conference, Seward was badly injured in a carriage accident and was bedridden for weeks. He was at home, resting, when

Lincoln was assassinated at Ford's Theater. Conspirators also targeted Seward that night, and he was attacked with a knife by a crazed Confederate soldier who forced his way into Seward's bedroom. He suffered a deep slash across his face and lost so much blood that he passed out. Days later, when he was well enough to rise from his bed, Seward noticed that the flags in the city were flying at half-mast and understood instantly that Lincoln was dead.

Not since Washington and Hamilton had such a strong and productive partnership existed in the White House. There had been other right-hand men, but, with the exception of Hamilton, none had left such an indelible mark on the presidency. It would be another fifty years before a similarly impactful partnership emerged, in the form of President Woodrow Wilson and Colonel Edward House.

Like Lincoln and Seward, Wilson and House were the closest of friends. Their partnership, however, met a very different end. After forming one of the closest bonds of any presidential partnership and scoring achievements of true historical significance, the two men parted ways forever when it became clear to Wilson that House had ulterior motives.

In the beginning of their partnership, they would sit alone in the president's bedroom, talking intimately, late into the night. They would take long private walks together and even vacation together. Wilson would visit House at home in New York, where they would roam the city streets at night, deep in conversation, ignored by unsuspecting passersby. When, after seven years of close friendship, Wilson suddenly refused to speak to him, House struggled to understand what he had done wrong.

CHAPTER THREE

WOODROW WILSON & EDWARD HOUSE

THE CO-DEPENDENT PRESIDENCY

This photo was taken in 1918, in the days when House, seated here next to Mrs. Wilson, still played the president like a fiddle. In the beginning of their relationship, to fool the president into thinking they were kindred spirits, House would chat with those closest to Wilson to learn the president's thinking on various issues and then repeat what he had heard back to Wilson as if they were his own thoughts.

> Mr. House is my second personality. He is my independent
> self. His thoughts and mine are one.[1]
>
> —President Woodrow Wilson

*W*orld War I propelled the US into the unfamiliar role of world leader for the first time in its history. Other presidents had helped to establish the US as a respected member of the global community of nations, but it was only during Woodrow Wilson's presidency that the US began to be regarded on the world stage as indispensable. This is the story of how Wilson and his closest adviser, Colonel Edward House, helped to bring about that transformation and how they reshaped the American presidency in the process. It is also a story about the damage done to noble causes when petty jealousies and other human failings drive policymaking.

House first met Wilson when the latter was pursuing the Democratic Party nomination for the presidency in 1911. He quickly recognized that Wilson was unlike any other politicians he had known. Wilson needed more affirmation than most, and there seemed to be no limit to the amount of flattery he could absorb. House saw in Wilson the elusive combination of qualities in a candidate that he had been seeking his entire political life. Not only did Wilson possess the gifts and skills to win the nation's highest office, but also his personal insecurities made him particularly amenable to House's preferred brand of influence. House made it his business to become one of Wilson's closest friends. During the president's lowest moments, following the death of his wife, Ellen, House made frequent trips to Washington to console the president. If House stayed overnight, he slept in Ellen's old room next to Wilson's so that they could sit up together when the president was unable to sleep. Their late-night talks, which at times became quite intimate, helped Wilson find the strength he needed to cope with his loss.

History has not been kind to Colonel House. He will always be remembered for his work with Wilson, but historians have not forgotten the acts of selfishness that drove him and Wilson apart. House cared deeply for Wilson, but he never let his personal feelings derail his ambition. He loved being able to help the president in his career and in his personal life, but throughout their relationship he never lost sight of the fact that Wilson was a means of achieving his lifelong pursuit of power without accountability.

The Colonel[2] survived as Wilson's friend and adviser because the president refused to see the truth about him until it was too late. Two events helped open his eyes. The first was his marriage to his second wife, Edith Galt, who was considerably less affected by House's charms than her husband. The second was the Paris Peace Conference, the physical and emotional demands of which drained the patience of both men.

I

Damage

Wilson and House sat down to talk together for the first time on an autumn evening in 1911 at a luxurious Neo-Italian Renaissance hotel in downtown Manhattan. It was a quickly arranged meeting. They had been told by mutual friends that they would like each other and that the meeting could be beneficial politically. They talked for about an hour and parted with great reluctance, both enthusiastically pledging to reunite as soon as possible. They were surprised by how much they shared in common. In Wilson, House finally found a man he could manipulate. In House, Wilson found someone willing to dispense the fawning admiration he so desperately craved. It was as if they had discovered in the other a kindred spirit. Of course, they could not have known it at the time, but the qualities they resonated to in one other had been shaped by troubling childhood experiences. Perhaps it was the scars they recognized.

Edward Mandell House has been the subject of numerous histories, but he is a difficult man to pin down. He was careful about the impression he left behind, taking great care to ensure that only the image he wanted the world to remember endured. He is survived by an uncommonly thorough journal library and a couple of autobiographies, which cover in great detail his life after he entered politics but which say little about his early years.

The latter years are so well documented because House employed a personal secretary whose main responsibility was to record his role in history. He would sit with her each evening and dictate his version of the day's events—adding embellishments here and there, always with an eye toward casting himself in the best possible light. If we were to rely solely on House's account of his life and work with Woodrow Wilson, we should think he was responsible for most of the president's successes and none of his failures.

House's notes are too thorough to be ignored by historians, but gathering a full picture of his life and his work with Woodrow Wilson requires some reading between the lines. This is especially the case regarding his youth.

According to House, he was eleven when his mother died and in his early twenties when his father followed. Judging from the paucity of information he left about them, his relationship with his parents was not a close one. His father gets the lion's share of House's remembrances, but only for how the wealth he provided enabled House to pursue a life in politics. Reflecting on House's account, a reader must surmise that the lack of a driving parental influence in his life increased the importance of his relationships with his brothers—which was intensely competitive, hierarchical, and often violent.

He was born a decade before the start of the Civil War in a boisterous and male-dominated household outside Houston, Texas—the youngest of seven boys—where the only way to get noticed was to be more reckless than the last. His father set the standard. Thomas House was a wealthy entrepreneur who built his fortune outrunning the law. At various times, and sometimes all at once, he was a banker, a cotton and sugar planter and a gun runner for the Confederacy. He raised his boys to be young gentlemen, but he also gave them the unsupervised run of the plantation. Like characters out of *Lord of the Flies*, the boys erected their own personal fiefdom. In the hierarchy they established, where age mattered (though not as much as courage), they carried guns and knives and fought like men.

The boys raced ponies through the countryside and played "gunfight" with real guns and ammunition. House's oldest brother suffered a severe gun wound to the face during one of the games and House himself almost killed two boys.

Living in such a household must have taught House at an early age that if he wanted to get noticed, he would need to fight above his weight. He was the smallest among his brothers, but he was no less violent.

His favorite brother, Jimmie, the one he emulated, was the most reckless of them all. Jimmie died at age sixteen after a careless fall from a homemade trapeze. House almost lost his own life in a similar way when, at age twelve, the rope he was swinging from snapped unexpectedly. He fell and hit his head on a wagon wheel and was bedridden for days. House wrote in his memoirs that the experience changed him forever. Before he fully recovered, he contracted malaria, and the effects of the disease ravaged his health. The reckless, violent little ruffian became a fragile, delicate boy. From then on, he would always be struggling with, or recovering from, some illness. He no longer had the strength, and perhaps even the nerve, to live the boisterous lifestyle he had before. From then on, to get his way, he would need to use his brains, not his fists.

While studying at Cornell, the young House received word of his father's death. Since his mother had already passed, he and his brothers were now on their own. House returned to Texas and was elected by his brothers to manage the considerable estate their father had left behind. After selling off the plantations and rearranging the stock and bond portfolios, each of the House brothers was left with a sizable annuity. With his financial future secure, House turned his thoughts to starting his own family.

By his early thirties, he had a wife, two daughters and one of the largest homes in Austin. House was a man of means, but he was bored. To liven things up, he decided to get involved in politics, but he was unsure where he might fit. He struggled with the idea of running for office,[3] discouraged by the less than striking personal image he cut, but he knew he could at least use his wealth to influence events from behind the scenes. His interest in politics may have had its origins in the lively political discussions the House family had around the dinner table when he was a boy. His father briefly served as mayor of Houston and throughout his life remained politically active, regularly inviting famous political friends over for dinner. Young Edward was old enough to have gotten to know many of them and was undoubtedly impressed by what he saw.

His full political awakening may have occurred during the 1876 presidential race between Rutherford Hayes and Samuel Tilden, a race that would stand as the closest in history until the 2000 campaign between George W. Bush and Al Gore. House was eighteen years old in 1876, and, like so many others at the time, was swept up in all the excitement of the campaign. As a boy, he might have envisioned himself one day running for the presidency, but at forty he was less optimistic about his chances. After careful reflection, he decided he had neither the stamina nor the physical presence to run for office.

He had become a petite, balding man, about five foot six, with a slender build and what might be described as a pencil-thin neck. His large, intelligent, cat-like eyes made him look like he had just stepped out of a Modigliani painting. He had a small head, a severely receding chin and a conspicuous pair of ears that protruded like the handles on a trophy cup. He might have thought his manicured mustache lent his face an air of dignity, but in fact he just looked like a turtle with a mustache. His movements were slow and delicate—some thought them reptilian. His voice had a thin huskiness that one biographer compared to the inside voice one uses in church. And, he wilted in hot weather like a character in a Tennessee Williams play.

Once he decided he preferred managing a campaign to running as the candidate himself, he used his wealth and connections to find the right candidate. His goal was to fashion himself as the powerful presence behind the throne, but he needed to find the right person to back. At first, he thought Texas governor James Hogg would be the right fit. Hogg was running for reelection, and House knew a victory in a statewide governor's race would help establish his reputation as a key political operative. Hogg was victorious, but his relationship with House did not work out as hoped. Hogg was a man of deep political experience and connections and strong views about his own abilities. He was not the kind of candidate who needed much advice, and House quickly understood that the consigliere role he had envisioned for himself might never materialize under Hogg. His next campaign would present him with a more pliable subject.

Charles Culberson was a talented deep thinker who needed a lot of emotional support. He liked the glamour of politics, but he found the groveling and backslapping demoralizing. House devoted himself to helping ease his mind and to raising his spirits during the numerous times that Culberson seriously considered walking away. They would become close friends and have a successful, decades-long partnership. The relationship was a tremendous boost to House's career. House used his role as campaign manager to create the statewide operation on which he would rely for the rest of his life in Texas politics. The Culberson gubernatorial victory put House on the map as an important player among state politicos, and it helped convince House where he belonged.

If the Culberson campaign made House's name, it was the campaign to elect Joseph Sayers governor that transformed him into a Texas legend. Sayers was a mediocre politician who lacked the charm and charisma of Hogg and the intelligence of Culberson. And, he was not much of a campaigner. In fact, he spent much of the governor's race in Washington, DC, where he was serving out his term as a congressman. He was not driven to be governor: he looked at the office merely as an honorable capstone on a long political career. House used his keen understanding of state politics and his good relations with the African-American and Mexican-American communities to outmaneuver all of Sayers's competitors. The victory was one of House's proudest achievements, but Sayers was not open to suggestion the way Culberson was, and House had a difficult time working with the new governor. The relationship helped House make two important discoveries about himself: he had the confidence and resources to get almost anyone elected governor in Texas, and, although he liked being in the company of powerful politicians, he hated the backslapping and the circus atmosphere.

His next campaign, to elect Samuel Lanham governor, would be his last. He literally phoned it in. His statewide operation was so well developed at that point that he could hand off the day-to-day operations to others. House did not feel strongly about Lanham, but he knew he could influence him, so he backed him. He had started to spend more of his time outside of Texas, in hopes of finding a candidate who could help him reach the next phase of his career, when his old friend Governor Hogg offered to introduce him to the famous politician William Jennings Bryan. Hogg thought that Bryan's gifts as an orator and House's skill as an organizer was the perfect combination for winning the White House.

House tried working with Bryan but quickly realized that, for many of the same reasons he and Hogg did not mesh, he and Bryan were also a bad fit. Bryan was far too set in his ways and independent to be open to persuasion. And House was not going to put his resources at the disposal of a man he could not sway in the end—so he looked elsewhere.

The kind of candidate he was seeking would be difficult to find. Such a man would need to be a progressive in order to win working-class voters and a strong Democrat. He would also need to be from the North, yet appealing to Southern and Western populists. More importantly, for House's sake, the man would need to be just emotionally dependent enough to be open to House's personal brand of persuasion—which relied on heaping spoonfuls of flattery and subtle psychological manipulation. House had given up on the idea of finding such a candidate and was considering running his old friend Culberson for the nomination when someone offered to introduce him to the exciting young governor of New Jersey.

Woodrow Wilson and Colonel House could not have been better suited to each other in temperament. House was shameless in his capacity for flattery and skilled at seeming to shrink in the presence of larger personalities. Wilson craved exactly such adoration and deference. Wilson was a man who adored being adored. House must have been elated at having found a candidate who was the complete package: brilliant, handsome, eloquent, a natural campaigner and breathtakingly insecure. As he pondered this new relationship, House might have wondered how Wilson came to possess such a peculiar combination of qualities.

Thomas Woodrow Wilson (or Tommy, as he was called), was born in 1856 in Staunton, Virginia, a small town not much larger today than it was then. He was the youngest child and the only boy in a deeply religious family headed by an ambitious Presbyterian minister whose love seemed to come at a price. Tommy spent much of his youth worried that he would never be able to live up to his father's expectations, because, long after most boys his age had begun schooling, Tommy could not read or write. He was nine before he learned the alphabet and twelve before he could string letters into words.

Historians have speculated wildly about the reasons for Wilson's reading difficulties. Wilson himself suggested[4] he had been a lazy child, perhaps a little too secure in the comfort of being the baby of the family to want to exert himself too much. One pair of historians have suggested that he willfully refused to learn to read, as a way of defying his domineering father—a well-read and eloquent writer and public speaker, but one possessed of a biting and sometimes caustic sense of humor[5]—whom he resented for belittling him in public and insulting his intelligence.[6] Another historian, Edwin Weinstein, has argued that Wilson might have suffered from a developmental form of dyslexia,[7] pointing to Wilson's lifelong difficulty with numbers (arithmetic requires some of the same parts of the brain as reading), his poor spelling and his inability to learn German and French no matter how hard he tried. Dyslexia was not known to science in Wilson's day, but there was clearly something terribly wrong.[8]

It seems likely that Wilson did suffer from dyslexia but, as an adult, overcame the disability by sheer force of will. In order to appreciate the full extent of his achievements in life and his extraordinary work ethic, one has to bear in mind the difficulties he faced. Despite his late start in life and the daily, sometimes excruciating tasks of reading and writing, he excelled as a scholar. He earned a law degree, got a PhD and went on to write important works of political science. Burdened as he was with dyslexia, the sheer effort and rigid self-discipline necessary to accomplish such sustained scholarship over so many years testifies to the almost superhuman will he possessed.

His struggles with dyslexia, and the disappointment he must have felt in himself for those struggles, may not have been the only reasons Wilson came to be so emotionally needy. Doubts he felt about the love of his father and mother may have also played a role.

Professors Alexander and Juliet George have theorized that Wilson was emotionally scarred by the experience of not being able to read.[9] They speculate that his deep need for acceptance in later life was partly the result of his perceived inadequacy in the eyes of his father. They suggest that Wilson emerged from his youth with the belief that his father's love was conditional, a belief that left him with a deep and enduring sense of insecurity.[10] Even after Wilson had attained a measure of professional success, he remained unsure of himself in the presence of his father. In their famous biography, the Georges tell a story in which, during one of Wilson's speeches, he seems visibly unsettled by seeing his father in the audience.

Woodrow's relationship with his mother also had its challenges. To those outside of the Wilson household, Janet (or Jessie, as she was often called), was a conundrum—fiercely loyal to her family and capable of great kindness and sensitivity to strangers, but often standoffish with those whom she regarded as below her social class. She has been described by biographers as a joyless woman, aloof and severe and, perhaps, scarred by a deeply troubling childhood.[11]

As a girl, Janet just barely survived the voyage of immigration with her parents from Europe. Swept overboard into bitterly cold water, she saved her own life by grabbing hold of a rope trailing behind the ship. The experience left her with a lifelong fear of storms, and, according to Wilson, it inspired his own fear of open water. Not long after arriving in the US, Janet's mother died. Her father remarried quickly but paid little attention afterward to Janet. The feelings of abandonment she must have felt as a result of these experiences left her with a negative outlook on life that was sometimes shared by her children. Wilson once said of his mother, "When I feel badly, sour and gloomy and everything seems wrong, then I know that my mother's character is uppermost in me."[12]

By the time he and Colonel House met, however, the sensitive young Tommy—who had faced disappointment, intense struggle and emotional uncertainty—had transformed himself into the brilliant, ambitious, charismatic and desperately needy man that House knew could someday be president. The question in House's mind was whether he would be there when Wilson crossed the finish line.

Just days after their first meeting, House invited Wilson to dinner in his Gotham Hotel apartment. They dined alone. House went to great lengths to make the occasion as comfortable for Wilson as possible and took time before the meeting to research his guest.

House was told that Wilson was a man of deep religious conviction (some even said he believed God had called him to run for the presidency) and a man of remarkable eloquence who was not afraid of engaging critics forcefully and directly with an oratorical style that was part university scholar, part Calvinist preacher. He had moved an aggressive legislative agenda through the New Jersey assembly by verbally bludgeoning his opponents into submission. As House and Wilson talked together over an intimate dinner, House could not help but be impressed.

The Woodrow Wilson sitting before House on that autumn evening in 1911 was already a man of extraordinary accomplishment. In the past decade, he had risen to the presidency of an Ivy League university, where he instituted educational reforms that would one day impact the curricula of every institution of higher learning in the nation—an act that alone secured his place in history. Then, without ever holding a public office, he was elected governor of New Jersey. He ran circles around the legislature, introducing the most progressive agenda of any governor in the history of the state. And now, after only two years in office, Wilson sat before House as a credible candidate for the presidency of the United States.

He even looked like a president. He was fifty-six years old, and, though he was just under six feet tall, his slender frame made him look taller. His smartly tailored suits and high lapels enhanced the effect. His face had Nordic qualities—angular, with high cheekbones, a strong chin, a sharp nose and full lips. His prominent ears drooped severely at the lobe, and all of his energy was compressed into expressive, heavily hooded blue-gray eyes. His movements were compact and purposeful and his smile toothy, uneven, and colored by neglect. A tic in his left eye indicated when he was upset or overtired, and a serious stroke, suffered in 1906, left him with a noticeably flaccid handshake.

If their meeting was like most of Wilson's meetings, he did all the talking. What struck a listener most when conversing with Wilson was the perfection of his speech. He did not pause or struggle for words when he spoke—the river of his thoughts flowed uninterrupted. There were no unnecessary gestures or vocal effects. His grammar was flawless and his diction unimpeachable. He held a listener's attention with familiar metaphors, colorful imagery and lofty, poetic pronouncements. House recognized that Wilson was a far more brilliant communicator than Bryan or Hogg or even Culberson—perhaps the best he had seen.

Unlike their relatively brief first meeting, their dinner lasted for hours. They covered every imaginable topic, and, according to House, they were in agreement on every subject. Afterward, House recorded his thoughts in his diary: "We found ourselves in such complete sympathy in so many ways that we soon learned to know what each was thinking without either having expressed himself. I think he is going to be a man that one can advise with some degree of satisfaction."[13]

Later, House recalled the dinner in a conversation with a friend, saying that he was surprised they had gotten on so well. "From what I had heard . . . I was afraid that he had to have his hats made to order [because of his inflated ego,] but I saw not the slightest evidence of it."[14]

Looking at House, Wilson saw a calm, unintimidating little man with an almost feminine softness. He described House later as "mild, unassuming, unobtrusive, gentle, deferential, confidential and intimate."[15] What Wilson saw in House was partly a persona the colonel had cultivated for the purpose of putting people at ease. While he may have seemed meek, House was rarely passive.

In conversation, House avoided direct clashes or open antagonism, allowing the other person to speak freely while concealing his own thoughts on an issue. People who were his enemies often had no idea. As one former senator said of House, "He can walk on dry leaves and make no more noise than a tiger."[16] When Wilson was president, Secretary of State William Jennings Bryan was deceived into believing he and House were close friends. House went out of his way to nurture this misperception, all the while working behind Bryan's back to undermine him in the eyes of the president and to poach increasing swaths of responsibility from him.

House understood human nature. Having worked with so many political candidates over the years, he understood the dark forces that often inspire their decisions to seek public office. As he tucked into a beautiful dinner of Wilson's favorite foods and listened to the future president expound on where he would like to take the country, he might have let his mind drift just long enough to wonder what dark secrets inspired Wilson's need to be president. Why would Wilson abandon a comfortable life in relatively quiet Trenton for the bloody Roman Colosseum of Washington, DC? He was about to find out.

II

The Art of Manipulation

Part of the myth surrounding Colonel House involves the idea that he somehow manipulated Wilson into pursuing actions that the president might otherwise not have taken. Like most myths, this one contains a kernel of truth. House did indeed know how to pull Wilson's strings, but he rarely convinced the president to do anything to which he was strongly opposed. It was in those areas where the two men shared general agreement that House's powers were most potent. The sly colonel learned that when Wilson trusted a person, he was unusually open to suggestion. It almost did not matter who made the recommendation or what the context was. House took advantage of Wilson's loyal, trusting nature, not just to stay in his good graces, but also to reinforce his own personal influence in the White House. Some around the president could see what House was up to, but Wilson either could not or would not.

The year Wilson and his right-hand man entered the White House, the country was in the midst of a major economic transition and was experiencing explosive economic growth. But not everyone was benefiting. For hundreds of years, the principal drivers of the economy had been agrarian, but a second industrial revolution following the Civil War had changed that. American cities were swelling with a huge influx of workers, many of whom had left family farms or had come from overseas looking for work in the heavy industries of the Northeast and Midwest. Muscled-back cities like Chicago, Pittsburgh and New York strained under the collective weight of reams of forged steel, barrels of refined oil and seemingly endless wagonloads of coal. The change was making some Americans enormously rich, even as the least fortunate among them were introduced to a shocking degree of deprivation.

Andrew Carnegie was one of the lucky ones. He got in on the ground floor of the steel industry and, in time, rose to become one of the wealthiest humans to ever walk the earth. He tried to avoid ostentatious displays of wealth, but he was not above the occasional splurge. He owned a sixty-room mansion on East 91st Street in New York City—a mini Versailles on the edge of Manhattan. Every morning he would wake to the soft, wafting melodies played by his personal organist in his reception room below. Carnegie would rise from his bed and look out the window down into an English garden. To the south, less than an hour away, on Mulberry Street, in what is now Chinatown, the men and women, boys and girls who worked for him slept rough and huddled together in the street for warmth, under squat tarps precariously assembled each night over heating grates.

The rise of progressivism in Wilsonian America was not just about correcting the huge economic disparities between the rich and poor. In the early 1900s, even the middle classes were suffering, as rolling stock market crashes threatened the banks and the financial security of everyday Americans. Protecting the working class from corporate greed became a theme of the 1912 presidential election. Wilson made a number of speeches around the country advocating economic opportunity for all, through genuine bank and tariff reforms. His speeches would become known collectively as the "New Freedom Platform,"[17] and, after his victory, it became the focus of the first two years of his administration. Colonel House was at his side as he contemplated a total reorganization of the US banking system.

House functioned as an unofficial adviser to Wilson. He held no formal office and received no salary but was nonetheless a central figure in the administration. The fact that Wilson would involve House so intimately in his work, given his lack of an official portfolio and how little he understood high finance, speaks to Wilson's trust in his friend.

"What I like about House is that he is the most self-effacing man that ever lived," Wilson said. "All he wants to do is serve the common cause and to help me and others."[18] The colonel worked hard to present himself to Wilson as a selfless and supportive friend, because this was the only real way to get on with someone as self-absorbed as Wilson. The president needed to believe that he was the faultless, unerring center of the universe. House did what he could to perpetuate the charade. In his memoirs, he describes his method of working with Wilson:

> I never argue with the president when we disagree, any more than with any other man, beyond a certain point. When we have talked a matter over and we find that we are opposed upon it, I drop it—unless and until I come across some other piece of evidence to support my views. When the president asks for suggestions in drafts of speeches, I nearly always praise at first in order to strengthen the president's confidence in himself which, strangely enough, is often lacking.[19]

Though he might have disagreed with Wilson, House always couched his comments in terms of approval and praise. His flattery of Wilson knew few limits. House would tell him, for example: "I do not put it too strongly when I say you are the main hope left to this torn and distracted world. Without your leadership, God alone knows how long we will wander in the darkness."[20]

House admitted to his biographer, Charles Seymour, that he fully accepted the fact that in order to work with Wilson he had to constantly stroke his ego. He believed that if he displeased Wilson at any point, their relationship might come to an end.

The compliments House heaped upon Wilson were so extreme that most people would consider them absurd, but Wilson's ego was so fragile that he greedily devoured even the most obsequious compliment. "You are so much more efficient than any public man with whom I have heretofore been in touch, that the others seem mere tyros."[21] There was something almost immoral in the way House would shamelessly feed Wilson's ego. House must have recognized that there was something unhealthy about Wilson's excessive need for affirmation. But whatever the source of this deep need in Wilson, House was only too happy to oblige.

If he was lacking for something sufficiently saccharine to say, House would pass along praise from others. He told Wilson that after his war address to Congress, a British diplomat told him "If Shakespeare had written the address it could not have been more perfect."[22] On another occasion, House passed on a letter from an English friend comparing Wilson to Lincoln. After his wife, Ellen, died, Wilson came to rely on House's extraordinary support even more.

Wilson, in his grief, would roam the halls of the White House at night in tears, talking to himself. His friends and family were genuinely concerned for his mental and physical health. House was abroad when he received the news of Ellen's passing and rushed home to help his friend. He knew Wilson would need him more than ever.

Ellen developed Bright's disease in the summer of 1914 and was overtaken quickly. In her last days, Wilson sat by her bedside for hours on end, watching over her as she slept. The president was by Ellen's side, silently gazing out her bedroom window, when she took her last breath. "God has stricken me almost beyond what I can bear,"[23] he later said to a friend. Wilson's constant need for support made him the type of man who needed to have a companion in his life. Ellen had been his counselor, his cheerleader, and even his research assistant. She was deeply woven into the fabric of his life. As Wilson lay in bed years later, recovering from a stroke and contemplating his own death, he confessed to his daughter that he owed everything he was and had to Ellen.

Her death drove Wilson into a deep depression. He would sit for hours, staring silently into space. His doctor, Cary Grayson, visited his room one morning to find him sitting alone, with tears streaming down his face. Dr. Grayson wrote to a friend, "A sadder picture, no one could imagine. A great man with his heart torn out."[24] Wilson visited Colonel House in New York in seek of comfort from his dear friend. Together they would walk the late-night streets of the city. During one of these walks, Wilson confided to his friend that he had hoped some mad stranger would come along and put him out of his misery. "I don't think straight any longer and have no heart for the things I am doing."[25]

The closest Wilson and House would ever be was in the months following Ellen's death. That summer, Wilson invited the colonel to his vacation home in New Hampshire for three days. House stayed in Ellen's old room next to the president's, and they shared a bathroom. With tears in his eyes, Wilson told House intimate stories about his love for Ellen. He shared photos, letters and poems. From August 1914 to January 1915, House visited Wilson in the White House thirteen times, staying in Ellen's old bedroom. They would sit, talk and read together for hours during these visits. House's warm, easygoing and supportive nature made him the perfect companion for Wilson during his time of grief.

Ellen Wilson died the day after war erupted in Europe. At a time like this, other presidents might use the demands of the office to distract themselves from their grief, but Wilson was the type of man who seemed to need the stability of companionship to find the motivation to work. For a time, House was the source of that companionship, but it eventually became clear that Wilson needed something more. When Dr. Grayson introduced him to his friend Edith Galt, the dark clouds over Wilson began to lift.

He was captivated by Edith. She was independent-minded, smart and a striking beauty. Wilson seized the moment and swept her up into his life. Within months of their meeting, they were engaged.[26] Within a year, they were married. One of the darkest periods of his life had finally come to a close, and he could now turn his thoughts to the many pressing problems facing his administration, not least of which was the war across the Atlantic that some were calling for the US to join.

Wilson's marriage marked the beginning of another highly productive period in his life, but it also set in motion a chain of events that would bring to a painful end his relationship with his closest friend. Edith's memoirs betray her lack of affection for the colonel. If Edith appeared to like House at all, it was only for the president's sake. She seemed to have problems with all the men working for her husband. She thought Wilson's chief of staff, Joseph Tumulty, was crude and lacking in the decorum one should expect of someone working so closely with the president. She thought even less of House, revealing her assessment of the "strange little man" in a note to Wilson: "House looks like a weak vessel and I think he writes like one very often."[27]

Years later, she described him in even less complimentary terms, making it known she considered him indecisive, unproductive, fawning and an intellectually dishonest amateur.[28] Given her distaste for House, it is not difficult to imagine Edith played an active role in the fracturing of relations between the two friends. Indeed, on at least two occasions, Edith attempted to orchestrate House's removal from Wilson's orbit by urging his appointment as ambassador to the UK.

III

The Co-dependent Presidency

As World War I drew to a close, House and Wilson's relationship was beginning to show signs of wear. The colonel was spending most of his time in New York, and with Edith now the dominant force in Wilson's life, the president had fewer reasons to seek out House's companionship. The Versailles peace conference following the war was a chance for the two friends to reconnect.

Though House was not Wilson's secretary of state and, in fact, held no official portfolio of any kind in the administration, Wilson chose House to be his principal adviser during the talks. (Wilson did not have a close relationship with his cabinet members, and he rarely involved himself in their work. The one exception was foreign affairs, in which he shared a keen interest with House. Together they ran circles around Wilson's secretary of state, Robert Lansing.)

Wilson and House began the conference virtually inseparable, meeting sometimes on-the-hour to review strategy and to let off steam. Soon, however, the president noticed House was behaving differently than usual. For years, for the sake of their relationship and to strengthen his own influence in the White House, the colonel had enabled Wilson's worst impulses. But he recognized that the conference was a historic opportunity for them both. House believed he owed it to himself, the nation and Wilson to be more forthcoming and assertive than was his custom with the president, given their mutual goal of securing lasting world peace. So when the treaty seemed to be in trouble almost from the start and House thought Wilson was at fault, for the first time ever he began to openly criticize him. Sensitive to criticism of any kind, Wilson disliked this shift in attitude and began distancing himself from his right-hand man.

The president took a brief break from the conference to attend to pressing business back in Washington. When he returned to the conference, he no longer seemed happy to work with House.

First, as recorded in House's diary, Wilson stopped consulting him on issues. Before, they used to spend hours comparing notes before and after important meetings. Now the time scheduled for their private meetings together was shortened and the number of meetings reduced.

Next, Wilson abandoned the habit of keeping House in the loop on important matters as he had done so carefully in the past. This had an impact not only on their relationship, but also on the conference. As Wilson resettled into the rhythm of meetings of the "Big Four" countries, he refused to even invite House to join him in the most important gatherings between the principals. The other leaders brought their advisers with them, but Wilson chose to go alone. He even insisted that the minutes of any meeting he attended not be circulated to House.

House struggled to understand why the president suddenly refused to speak to him. His critics believe the change in Wilson's behavior when he returned from Washington was not only a result of Edith's influence, but also a response to House's own actions.[29] At the conference, House had been appreciably less deferential than usual toward Wilson at precisely the time when—surrounded by so many world leaders—the president's ego required more stroking than ever. In the relative calm and familiar surroundings of Washington, it had been natural for House to continually kowtow to the president, but in Paris, with the stakes so high and under intense pressure, he may have found it difficult to keep up the facade. During one noteworthy incident, French prime minister Clemenceau walked into a room where House and Wilson were talking. He announced that he had come to discuss an important matter with House (not with the president). The two men excused themselves to go to an adjacent room, where they spoke privately—leaving Wilson waiting in the other room alone. Given Wilson's ego, he undoubtedly was offended. What information could Clemenceau be sharing with House that could not also be shared with the president of the United States?

Wilson also may have been annoyed to find on his return to Paris that House's name was appearing in the European newspapers almost as frequently as his own. The House that Wilson thought he knew preferred to lurk in the shadows, away from the attention of the press. Edith Wilson, who attended the conference with the president, collected copies of European newspaper articles about the proceedings and, one day, confronted House with them, asking why his name came up again and again. In response, House gathered up the articles and left the room, refusing to discuss the matter. Edith later learned from the president's physician, Dr. Grayson, that House and his son had been feeding the newspapers stories that made House look good at the president's expense.

For the first time in their relationship, Wilson saw House as a competitor. The president had never before had to share credit with House for the work they did together. House understood Wilson's personality well enough to know the president did not like to share credit and had built an entire method of approaching Wilson to prevent such a misunderstanding. He made a point of never directly challenging the president; never pushing his ideas on him; and, whenever Wilson made a decision, acceding to the president's judgment regardless of his own views on the matter. But, when it came to the supremely important peace accords, House had at times taken a different tack.

One major area of contention that grew between them was House's recommendation that the US Senate be involved in the peace negotiations. Wilson had fervently opposed this idea, because he did not want to share the credit. Ordinarily House would have stopped there, but he recognized that sign-off from key senators was critical to winning eventual congressional support for the treaty. He pressured Wilson to organize a dinner with important senators during his brief trip back to the US. Wilson reluctantly agreed, but at the dinner the senators realized that Wilson cared little for whether they personally supported the agreement or not. They left the meeting resentful and determined to kill the agreement. Embarrassed at his failure to win their support, Wilson never forgot that it had been House who suggested the meeting. Wilson always bristled at doing things to which he was opposed, and now that the colonel had been a source of that kind of frustration, Wilson's attitude toward him began to change.

House of course knew that Wilson did not like being pushed, but he also recognized that the peace treaty would never win congressional support without the help of key senators. He thought it would be a huge strategic mistake not to include Congress and changed his regular behavior toward Wilson to make this point.

House had reason to be concerned about the health of the treaty. Wilson's many strategic miscalculations during the conference were seriously harming its chances for success. Almost from the start, Wilson carelessly neutralized his most important piece of leverage by making it known that the only thing he really cared about was the creation of a League of Nations. The European powers supported this notion, but knowing Wilson's commitment to it gave them an important advantage over him. They concealed their support for the League and instead used it as leverage to achieve their own objectives.

Another critical negotiation mistake was difficult for Wilson to avoid. One of his greatest strengths had always been his skill as an orator. Most audiences were moved by the biblical imagery and strong moral authority of his ideas. Yet his European counterparts could not relate and were often left unmoved. They would pass notes among themselves during his speeches ridiculing Wilson for his earnestness. He discovered too late that his unyielding moral pronounce-ments were difficult to walk back from. They left no room for compromise and limited his ability to maneuver.

Perhaps Wilson's greatest mistake was his decision, after he returned from Washington, to work alone. By refusing House's help, he cut himself off from an important intelligence resource and a perspective that could have expanded his options and improved his decision-making. Not consulting another set of eyes on the proceedings impaired his ability to see the chessboard in its entirety. And as a result, he could not see all the opportunities that lay within his grasp.

House must have suspected from the start that Wilson was too uncompro-mising to be a good negotiator. And he was not surprised in the end, when Wilson produced a final treaty that might have been much better had he been willing to follow House's advice and include the Senate in the negotiations. Some historians have suggested that Wilson's characteristic unwillingness to compromise was a part of his Calvinist ethos, which required that he be measured not just by his actions, but also by his words: because he invested his positions with moral attributes, to compromise them would be tantamount to compromising his faith. Wilson may have viewed the conference as very much like a battle between the forces of good and evil.[30] He did not realize it, but this was precisely the reason he needed someone like House, who had a more pragmatic perspective.

It is not clear whether there was a single incident that ended the relationship between Wilson and House. Their story is largely one-sided, since House went to great lengths to control the historical narrative about their work together. This is also the reason that details about their rift are so murky. Some historians think the disagreement was largely Edith Wilson's doing:[31] she slowly chipped away at her husband's confidence in House in order to push him out. Another theory is that they simply grew apart as Wilson came to rely more on his wife for advice. He turned to his First Lady for help with all sorts of matters—personal and official. He even regularly shared state secrets with her.

Some historians think the break between Wilson and House was a long and drawn-out process.[32] Others think it was abrupt. In one popular version of the narrative, Wilson returned to Paris from his brief trip to Washington to find that House had negotiated away all the important gains they had made before he left for the US. When Wilson got settled in Paris again, House was invited to the president's rooms to discuss the latest developments. They met alone. After a long and heated conversation, House left abruptly, and the president was visibly angry. If this is in fact how events played out, whatever was said during that private meeting closed the door on their relationship forever.

No matter how they parted ways, one thing is clear: after the Paris Peace Conference, Wilson and House, two men who had been the closest of friends, never spoke again.[33]

IV

House: Partner to Power

It is not unusual for quasi-governmental officials like Colonel House to serve in positions of power in the White House. When Harry Hopkins embarked on his hazardous trip to London in 1941 to make first contact with Churchill on President Roosevelt's behalf (see the introduction), he did so after having resigned from government service for health reasons. However, there have been nagging concerns over such figures, as the recent controversy over President Donald Trump's children working as White House advisers shows. Yet if past is prologue, it appears that men and women like Colonel House and Ivanka Trump are here for the foreseeable future. One of the reasons House has been such a frequent subject of study, especially in recent years, is that his story helps expose the secret lives and activities of these shadow figures. For some historians, House has come to represent what is most troubling about these individuals—lack of accountability.

Many Americans in Wilson's day did not know that, while working on some of the most vital affairs of the administration and speaking on the president's behalf, House was not actually an official government employee. Even at the height of his power, few were aware of his personal beliefs or his qualifications for the duties he regularly performed for Wilson.

Though he was not a member of the cabinet, at various times, and often at the president's direction, House performed special duties that fell within the portfolios of actual cabinet officers—Secretary of State Robert Lansing, for one. Despite his power and the consequential decisions he made on Wilson's behalf, House had not been confirmed by the US Senate, and, as an outsider, he was not subjected to the same scrutiny as actual government employees enjoying the same level of influence. It was as if House functioned under a cloak of secret presidential immunity that granted him all the authorities of an "assistant president for foreign affairs" without any of the customary oversight. As the saying goes, all help is good help until something goes wrong.

A cabinet member acting on the president's behalf with malicious intent could at least be impeached for misconduct. Of course, if House *had* broken the law, he could have been prosecuted, but he could also have easily been pardoned. Impeachment of a cabinet official, by contrast, is reversible only with great difficulty and the involvement of the Congress and the judicial system.

Colonel House and the Trump children will not be the last such figures to walk the corridors of 1600 Pennsylvania Avenue. The criticisms faced by the Trump family underscore the reasons why understanding the role and actions of these figures should be a priority for the president and the American people alike.

The relationship between Wilson and House shows why it takes a special kind of individual to be a right-hand man or woman. Such a person has to be willing to subsume his goals and desires, and even his personality, in ways that most people would find unacceptable. For some advisers, like Alexander Hamilton, displays of devotion on this scale can be a grating experience. For others, like Colonel House, such sacrifices are a bargain that they are only too happy to enter into. But even among those who accept this arrangement willingly, there are some who take their service to the extreme. Louis Howe was one such figure.

Howe sacrificed his financial security, his health, and even a relationship with his family to serve Franklin Roosevelt. When Roosevelt contracted polio, it changed Howe's life forever.

CHAPTER FOUR

FRANKLIN ROOSEVELT & LOUIS HOWE

FIGHTING BACK

Eleanor Roosevelt counted Louis Howe (seated to the right of FDR) among the seven most important people in her life. When Howe died in 1936, President Roosevelt organized a state funeral for him in the East Room of the White House. Before Howe, such honors were reserved only for presidents and members of his family. (Franklin Roosevelt Library, US National Archives and Records Administration)

It was Louis Howe, more than anyone else, who forced father to fight back.[1]

        –James Roosevelt, son of President Franklin Roosevelt

*H*eaven *help you if you were poor or unemployed in 1930s America. Remember those flickering black-and-white celluloid images of desperate, shrunken men weaving sheepishly in and out of the shadows as they waited anxiously for a free bowl of soup? The official unemployment rate in the US at the time was around 25 percent, but the unofficial rate—that which captured those who had simply given up any hope of finding work—was perhaps twice that. If the '20s was the decade of excess and unbounded optimism in America, the '30s was the decade of despair.*

This all began to change when Franklin Roosevelt was elected president. One of his first acts was to establish the Civil Conservation Corps (CCC), a government program designed to put young men to work restoring an American landscape stripped bare and bled white by a decade of self-delusion and mindless consumption. The CCC rekindled the enthusiasm of America's young men and channeled their newfound energy into infrastructure and environmental projects across the nation. They built bridges, put out fires and carved out of the American wilderness scores of national parks and trails. Overnight, men went from sleeping rough and picking through rubbish bins to waking up in warm beds to the smell of freshly baked bread and coffee.

Historians are fond of saying that this or that president might never have obtained the office had it not been for the unique contribution of this or that person. They cite Alexander Hamilton's help in manipulating the vote tallies in George Washington's first election and mention Clark Clifford's drafting of the plan that led to Truman's improbable 1948 victory. For Franklin Roosevelt, Louis Howe was such a person. After Roosevelt was stricken with polio, everyone, including Roosevelt himself, thought he would never again be a viable candidate for the presidency. Howe never gave up hope, and he continued working diligently behind the scenes to ensure Roosevelt's success.

Roosevelt thought, as so many others did, that without the use of his legs, no one would take him seriously as a candidate. Today, FDR is remembered as a supremely optimistic man, but he had never experienced anything as emotionally debilitating as polio. It almost broke him. During the early months of his illness, the man whose pyrotechnic smile would lead a nation through the Great Depression was so consumed by his own hopelessness that he had to move away from his family in order to manage his recovery. Howe, perhaps more than any other person, helped convince Roosevelt that his dreams need not be quashed by polio.

In the pantheon of America's greatest presidents, Washington is credited with founding the nation, Lincoln is praised for preserving it, and FDR is revered for coming to its rescue when destructive forces assailed it from within and without. In some ways, Louis Howe was as responsible for that legacy as FDR himself. Without Howe's contribution, Americans may very well have had a President Franklin Delano Roosevelt, but he would not have been the larger-than-life FDR we remember today. That FDR was largely the creation of Louis Howe.

I

The Feather Duster and the Gnome

For years Louis Howe feared that his wife, Grace, had a lover. He did not know for sure, but there were rumors. Howe's work as a struggling upstate New York newspaper man often kept him on the road. To save money, which was always scarce in the Howe household, Grace insisted on taking their daughter on long visits to the home of her wealthy mother hundreds of miles away in Massachusetts. Howe's inability to provide a stable financial environment for his family was a constant source of embarrassment for him. He always suspected that Grace was deeply disappointed[2] in her choice of a husband.

By the time he reached the age of forty, Louis Howe had convinced himself that his life was a failure. It is not difficult to understand his disappointment. No matter how hard he worked, he could never seem to dig himself out of the financial and professional holes he repeatedly found himself in. He was at a point where even the things that once gave him solace pulled him deeper into despair. As he entered middle age, all the grand expectations he had set for himself had come to naught. Grace found ever more numerous reasons to take their daughter to visit her family in Fall River, and Howe could hardly blame her. The life she lived with Howe was not what she had imagined for herself.

When Grace first met Louis Howe, he was a financially secure and dynamic young man—someone who was going places. He was running the family news-paper, and his father was postmaster general of the city of Saratoga. They lived in a large home on a fashionable street and enjoyed the respect of the commu-nity. Grace was well-off too. Though she was a woman of means, she knew she would need to make a good match in life and thought she had found one in Howe. He had a great foundation on which they could build—he had intelligence, drive, ambition and talent. She thought it was only a matter of time before he came into his own. As they walked down the aisle together, all signs pointed to a happy and secure future. But Grace soon discovered she had married an unlucky man.

Born in Indianapolis in 1871, Louis Howe was a sickly child and the last delivery of an aging mother. Lide, as she was called, was almost forty years old, a widow and the mother of two daughters of marriage age when she met and married Louis's father, Edward, a dashing Civil War veteran. He was young (almost ten years Lide's junior), strong and ambitious. Lide came from a solidly middle-class family, and she hoped her enterprising, energetic new husband would help raise her standing still higher.

Louis was a thin, pale, weak infant. As a boy, he was plagued by asthma and bronchitis, and he developed a heart condition that would persist for the rest of his life. By his teenage years, it was clear he had inherited his father's frenetic and industrious nature. Time would tell whether he had also inherited his bad luck.

Louis's father, Edward, lived a life plagued by professional and financial disappointments. First, he lost the family's money—not just his own and Lide's, but also thousands of dollars he borrowed from the insurance company where he worked and the church he attended—to speculation. Embarrassed and ruined, he picked up the family and moved in with Lide's half-sister in Saratoga.

After five years of small jobs, Edward was finally able to scrape together enough money to buy a local newspaper, which he fashioned into the community mouthpiece of the Democratic Party. As their finances improved, he and Lide could once again hold up their heads in public. The paper struggled at first, but Edward made a success of it. He threw himself into local politics, and when the Democrats won the White House, he was appointed postmaster general of Saratoga. His ample salary enabled the family to move into a larger home on the best side of town. When Louis turned seventeen, his father turned over to him responsibility for the day-to-day operations of the paper while he attended to his postmaster duties. It was during this brief oasis of financial security that Louis met Grace. She was impressed by his optimism and energy and allowed herself to be swept up.

But Howe's luck was about to take a turn, and the descent would be rapid. Within a year of Howe's marriage, his paper failed. He was able to mortgage the small home he and Grace had received as a wedding gift from Grace's mother, but they soon lost the paper to creditors. Edward and Lide also lost their home and had to move in with Louis and Grace. The pressure of so many people living under the same roof put a strain on Louis's marriage. Much of that first year, Grace spent away from Louis in Fall River. After their first child, Mary, was born, whenever Grace needed a break and a taste of the luxury she had left behind, she would retreat to Fall River. Taken all together, Grace would spend years of her life away from Louis while he struggled alone in Saratoga or Albany, trying to cobble together enough work to support the family.

He took writing jobs wherever he could find them—first, at the paper that he and his family had lost to creditors; then, when they fired him, at the paper of a competitor. He wrote for New York City papers, did some freelance writing, tried his hand at writing short stories, even worked as a secretary for an association. Howe did anything and everything he thought might put food on the table. Despite his best efforts, he remained on a downward spiral. He would hold a job for a while and then get fired—find another, and get fired from that one. Grace could not bear to see him grovel for work. "I married you for better, for worse,"[3] she once wrote him, hoping the words would be consoling.

During their long separations, he would sit up nights worrying about his marriage and wondering what Grace was doing with her time. He had heard about someone named "Willie" who had been seen visiting her in Fall River.

When he raised Willie's name to Grace, they fought. He apologized in a letter[4] that reveals at once his deep love for his wife and his blinding insecurities about not being able to provide for her.

Despite the hardship, Howe never gave up. He had a mind for political strategy, and people were willing to pay for his advice. Howe attached himself to a wealthy patron named Tom Osborn, who was a devoted supporter of the Democratic Party and who needed someone to help him come up with ways to outflank Republican efforts in upstate New York. He was a mercurial employer, firing Howe repeatedly only to rehire him days later. In 1911, the year Howe turned forty, he and Grace welcomed into the world their second child, a boy. As he rolled his son around the neighborhood in his stroller, passersby might have mistaken the prematurely aged and shrunken Howe for the boy's grandfather.

Five foot two, rail-thin from chain-smoking and perpetually covered in cigarette ashes, Howe looked like a character from a Tolkien novel. He had long, bony fingers that dangled from his wrinkled hands, a nose that was too big for his face, great bushy eyebrows and dark, sunken pools for eyes. His leathery skin hung from his face in sheets and folds, and a few brave strands of dark hair held on for dear life to his balding, oversized head. The old-style high collars he favored must have helped fortify his short, skinny neck, and he dressed like a mortician. You might have smelled him before you saw him, as he walked around enveloped in a warm plume of body odor and sweet-smelling cigarettes. To his family, Howe was gentle, vulnerable and loving. To others, he was profane, impatient and uncompromising. No one was spared his temper, not even Franklin Roosevelt.

Howe first met the young Roosevelt in 1911, when he was assigned the duty of interviewing the then New York state senator for a newspaper article. Howe never forgot the meeting, but Roosevelt quickly did. The following year, they became reacquainted when Roosevelt took over a leadership role in the state Democratic party and hired Howe as a volunteer to oversee various state campaign functions. They grew to know each other and became friends. Howe was more experienced than Roosevelt, but Roosevelt was the boss. When Howe lost yet another job in the fall of 1912, he wrote Roosevelt a letter begging for work. Roosevelt had recently contracted typhoid fever and needed help with his campaign for reelection to the state senate; he asked Howe whether he would consider running his campaign for him while he recovered from his illness. Howe eagerly accepted. He ran the campaign on his own, with little involvement from the ailing Roosevelt.

1912 was a good year nationally for the Democratic Party, but it was a bloodbath for New York State Democrats, who lost far more seats than they had expected. Roosevelt, however, who had also been expected to lose his seat and who had done very little campaigning because of his illness, won with a higher percentage of the vote than he had during his first campaign. Howe got all the credit for Roosevelt's victory, and, from that point on, he was a valued fixture in Roosevelt's life.

There is a famous photo of the twenty-year-old Roosevelt taken just a couple of years before he married Eleanor that captures him at the height of his physical beauty. He is in motion, facing the camera, his body contorted as if he is about to tumble forward. Though the image is blurred, his expression is one of pure joy— childlike and aglow with hope. He is tall and lithe, like an athlete, and he appears to be darting in and out of the trees in hot pursuit of a fleeing Eleanor.

Almost two decades after that picture was taken, at thirty-nine, Roosevelt awoke from a fitful sleep to find that his left leg was not working properly. The day before, he had been out with the kids, hiking and swimming. After dinner, he said he was feeling under the weather and decided to retire early. Young and vital, Roosevelt went to his bed without a care in the world and woke to find his life on fire.

When the doctors told Roosevelt that he had contracted polio and might never walk again, he refused to believe them. Friends and family were astonished by the force of his denial. He welcomed the crushing pain of daily physical therapy, his muscles fighting him, tightening like a vise as he struggled to stretch them. He refused to accept that his legs would not work. He spent entire days consumed by the task of trying to move a single toe. He had to succeed. If he could not walk, or play with the children, or flirt with pretty young ladies, then who was he?

In college, he had discovered that he was charming and smart. He found outlets for his huge energy – tennis, golf, editing the school newspaper, class president. He was bold and dynamic, and people liked him. He had encountered the same reception at law school and as a young lawyer at the firm of Carter, Ledyard and Milburn, where he boldly confessed, with complete sincerity, his intention to someday become president of the United States. No one laughed— they knew who his uncle was.

Following in the famous footsteps of that uncle, Theodore Roosevelt, he accepted an appointment as assistant secretary of the navy. He loved ships, understood the people and enjoyed the work. Barely thirty years old, Franklin Roosevelt was in charge of the massive naval buildup that preceded World War I. When America entered the fight, he was proud to supervise the navy's role. He hired Howe to be his chief of staff, and together they ran the navy as a partnership—Roosevelt out front and Howe behind the scenes.

As the 1920 presidential campaign season approached, Roosevelt was deeply involved in party politics. He was noticed by the presumptive Democrat nominee, James Cox, and was asked to join his ticket as a candidate for the vice presidency. He threw himself into the work. Sweeping from coast to coast across the country by plane or train or car, he delivered speeches by the quarter-hour. Wherever a speaker was needed, Roosevelt was there. He would attend the opening of an envelope if the crowd was large enough. His energy and movie-star good looks charmed swarms of voters.

A landslide victory for the Republicans swept Warren Harding into the White House, and Roosevelt found himself out on his own. But he was not out of hope or energy. While he considered ways to get his political career back on track, he took two jobs—one as the managing director of the Fidelity & Deposit Company and the other as a partner in a New York law firm. His party was out of power, but he wasn't worried. He was young and popular, and it was only a matter of time before an opportunity opened up. He planned to spend the next four to eight years making a little money while he and Howe worked to lay the foundation for a run at the top job. There was no rush. Though the 1924 presidential campaign season—his next opportunity to run—was years away, he was still in his thirties. He and Howe had plenty of time.

II

Polio

On the morning of August 10, 1921, Howe was finally in a good financial place. After almost a decade of working at Roosevelt's side at the Naval Department and then briefly for Roosevelt's successor, he was well-off enough to send Mary to private school and to own a nice vacation home. The New England Oil Company offered him a lucrative job as an executive, and an important New York newspaper wanted him to be its city editor. His relationship with Grace was still rocky, but with the navy job coming to an end and a chance to move back to New York and make some serious money, he hoped to rebuild their relationship and make her love him again the way she once had.

Howe took the family on vacation to visit the Roosevelts on Campobello Island in Canada's New Brunswick Bay, partially to rest and partially to decide whether to work for the New England Oil Company or the New York newspaper. A minor injury on the tennis court gave him an excuse to sit back and put his feet up. He and Grace sat outside on the lawn enjoying the beautiful summer day, waiting for Roosevelt and the children to return from a short sailing trip they had taken to the surrounding islands. They returned just before dinner, drenched from a swim and exhausted. As everyone gathered around the table, Roosevelt excused himself to go up to bed early. He was not feeling well.

Roosevelt awoke the next morning with a numbness in his left leg. As he rose to prepare for the day, his condition only worsened, and he returned to his room. By that evening, as the numbness spread, he knew he was in trouble.

The first few days of Roosevelt's illness, before he knew he had contracted polio, were the most difficult. He was losing control of his body, and he could not understand why. At first, his only discomfort was a little numbness in his left leg. Then, the leg became immobilized. Gradually the paralysis moved to his right leg and then up his body, into his torso and into his neck. He woke one morning to find he had lost the ability to move one side of his face. It drooped as if he had had a stroke.

The initial diagnoses were wrong. One doctor thought he had the flu. Another doctor suspected a blood clot in his spinal area. It was recommended that Howe and Eleanor take turns massaging his feet and legs daily to help relieve his intense pain. A third doctor finally got the diagnosis right—childhood polio. He ordered Eleanor and Howe to cease massaging Roosevelt's limbs immediately or risk worsening his paralysis.

Eventually he could no longer chew properly or feed himself. Until a nurse could be found, Howe and Eleanor took turns attending to his personal needs, changing his bedding and periodically turning his body to prevent bedsores. When he could no longer control the voluntary muscles in the lower half of his body and needed help with evacuation, Howe and Eleanor helped. Howe slept on a cot outside of Roosevelt's room, prepared to rise at any hour to attend to his friend's needs.

After the initial shock of the news that Roosevelt was suffering from polio and might never walk again, Eleanor and Howe turned their attention to helping him cope with his new reality. Given that his life's pursuit had been to become president, those closest to him wondered how he would adjust to what now might be a life lived on the margins. His mother, Sara, thought she knew what was best for him—permanent rest. She envisioned him living out his days the way his father had, in the comfort and calm of their Hyde Park estate, reading and tending his stamp collection. She clearly did not know her son.

Eleanor knew that such a life would drain all the spirit out of her husband. He needed to be around people. He needed to be active to be happy. Living as an invalid within the walls of a secluded upstate New York mansion would send the thirty-nine-year-old Roosevelt to an early grave. Howe shared Eleanor's belief that Roosevelt must not be permitted to give up on his dreams. Having spent a decade working closely with him, Howe knew that politics was all Roosevelt really cared about.

Since their first campaign together in 1912, Howe had been a close adviser to Roosevelt. And although he had developed great affection for Roosevelt over the years, Howe also had selfish reasons for wanting to see him regain his spirit. If Roosevelt achieved his life's ambition to become president, Howe had every expectation that he would be there by his side when Roosevelt moved into the White House. He saw no reason why Roosevelt could not recover his career after he recovered his health. He needed to convince Roosevelt of this, but first he would need to help him regain his sense of self.

When the news that Roosevelt was seriously ill went public, Howe took over the management of his public relations. For Roosevelt's career to survive, no one could know the true nature of his ailment. When he needed to get back into the city to see doctors, Howe arranged an elaborate method of keeping his travel secret, involving the distraction of the press at the train station. Howe saw to it that a diversion took place at one end of the train, as he and others carried Roosevelt through the cars to the other end.

Managing Roosevelt's illness became Howe's mission. He eventually moved in with the family. From that day forward, until the end of his life nearly twenty years later, Howe would live almost exclusively with the Roosevelts.

Howe knew how fickle the world of politics was, and he knew that if Roosevelt was forgotten, he too might be forgotten. Roosevelt obviously could not attend the sundry Democratic Party events necessary to keep his name in the minds of political leaders, but he understood how important it was to remain relevant. Howe devoted himself to attending political events on Roosevelt's behalf and to keeping his friend's name in the papers. He sent out a flurry of letters over Roosevelt's signature to members of the party; he wrote news articles, op-eds and letters to the editor on Roosevelt's behalf; and, importantly, he convinced Eleanor that for Roosevelt's sake she had to conquer her fear of public speaking and throw herself into New York politics.

"You have to become actively involved in Democratic politics," Howe told her, "in order to keep alive Franklin's interest in the party and the party's interest in him."[5] In her memoirs, Eleanor recorded her thoughts about Howe's recommendation: "I was pushed into the women's division of the Democratic State Committee, not because Louis cared so much about my activities, but because he felt that they would make it possible for me to bring into the house people who would keep Franklin interested in state politics."[6]

It is hard to imagine—given her huge historical stature—but when Eleanor Roosevelt started out, she was a painfully awkward public speaker. She understood how important it was that she help keep her husband's name in front of the public, but speaking to even a handful of people terrified her.

As Howe started to accompany her to speaking events, he noticed she had a habit of allowing her voice to trail off as she spoke. At other times, her pitch would rise sharply and unexpectedly. Her awkward pauses were long enough for listeners to wonder whether something was wrong. He spent hours with her, training her to control her movements and voice, and together they worked on methods to keep her focused on a single theme. He forced her to practice every evening after dinner. Her son James later wrote that she must have made a hundred speeches in the living room of their Manhattan home for an audience of only one—Howe.

When Eleanor spoke at public events, Howe would sit in the back of the room, watching the audience. Using a system of hand gestures, he would guide Eleanor as she spoke until she learned how to capture and hold an audience's attention. With Howe's help, she eventually lost her stage fright and gained a reputation as a skilled public speaker.

Before they were thrown together to help her ailing husband, Eleanor did not really like Howe. She thought he was coarse, crude and cynical. Though they were civil to one another for Roosevelt's sake, they did not actually become friends until years after their first meeting, during Roosevelt's vice-presidential campaign in 1920. By then, Howe was Roosevelt's principal political adviser. He insisted that Eleanor accompany her husband on his whistle-stop tour, to help attract female voters. It was the first opportunity for her and Howe to spend significant time together. In her writings, she described the point at which their relationship changed: "Louis Howe began to break down my antagonism by knocking at my stateroom door and asking if he might discuss a speech with me. I was flattered and before long I found myself discussing a wide range of subjects."[7]

During those times when Roosevelt had to leave the train to attend nearby events, Howe and Eleanor would set off on their own and take walking tours of the town. Indeed, what had been at first a tense relationship became quite close after Roosevelt took ill. Roosevelt's daughter Anna was surprised to find the two alone in Eleanor's room one evening. Eleanor was sitting on the floor next to the bed, at Howe's feet, as he stroked her hair.

Howe's influence on the political lives of Eleanor and Franklin Roosevelt cannot be overstated. Were it not for his guidance and pestering, Eleanor might never have developed into the global figure she became, and Franklin might never have regained the confidence necessary to continue pursuing his dream of becoming president. Howe had more confidence in them than they had in themselves.

While Roosevelt worked to regain his health, Howe and Eleanor worked to keep his career alive. They met with supporters and attended strategy meetings and New York State political conventions. They worked to strengthen or develop relationships that they hoped would be useful to him. But there was only so much Eleanor and Howe could do. Eventually he would need to play an active role in his own political career.

As the 1924 Democratic presidential convention approached, Howe thought Roosevelt might use the occasion to reintroduce himself to the public. Al Smith, the presumptive nominee and governor of New York, was looking for someone to give the nominating speech during the opening ceremonies. It was a necessary, though minor, responsibility. The one benefit was that whoever took on the task would speak to a room packed with thousands of faithful Democrats and have a national audience listening by radio. Howe decided Franklin would be perfect for the job, but Roosevelt was still unsure. Essentially paralyzed from the waist down, he had to rely on leg braces and crutches to get around. What if he slipped as he was walking to the podium? He had fallen before.

III

Fighting Back

By the autumn of 1922, Roosevelt had trained himself to walk again as best he could. Using crutches, he would lean on one stiffly braced leg and swing the other leg forward. Short trips were relatively easy, but a walk of any significant duration required forethought.

Roosevelt is remembered as a man of supreme confidence, but beneath that buoyant exterior, his ego was as fragile as anyone else's—perhaps even more so. (Before his illness, he was occasionally described by those who knew him best as shallow—content to dance along the surface of life like a feather duster, sweeping up adulation along the way.) It was worship Roosevelt craved, not pity. Once he fell victim to polio—a disease that not only sapped his energy, but also made him appear less than impressive—his condition was a frequent source of shame and embarrassment. To avoid having to encounter the look of pity in the eyes of strangers, he put off returning to work for as long as he could.

But after more than a year's absence, Roosevelt decided it was time to return to work at Fidelity & Deposit. After all, he was the vice president in charge of managing the day-to-day operations—it was the least he could do. The plan was for his car to drop him off at the door of the office building. From there he would "walk" the five or so steps necessary to reach the building's entrance. His driver would hold open the door, and he would traverse the long lobby toward the elevators at the far end. They would chat along the way, to make the exercise seem casual. The whole affair, it was estimated, would take no more than a few minutes. He would stay for a bit and then return home. It was a simple enough plan, but he worried about what might go wrong.

On a cool and cloudy day in early October 1922, Roosevelt's car pulled up to the entrance of the Fidelity & Deposit building. Passersby studied the windows as the driver walked around to Roosevelt's side. A crowd gathered as he struggled to raise himself above his crutches. Someone held the door open for him. As he walked through the entrance of the crowded lobby, Roosevelt was suddenly aware of how slippery the floor was.

Concentrating on his footwork, he thrust his right leg forward. As he did so, his left leg swept out from under him and he fell, landing on his back. Lying on the floor, drenched in sweat and embarrassed, all he could do was laugh nervously. He muscled himself up into a seated position and asked for help getting to his feet. Two sturdy men came forward. Someone located his hat, and he was on his way again. The sea of onlookers parted as he slowly moved toward the elevators. With each step, he smiled and nodded to onlookers, in spite of the sweat streaming down his face. As the elevator doors closed behind him, he leaned against the wall and let himself exhale.

Returning to work was only the beginning of Roosevelt's efforts to resume a normal life. He and Howe had agreed that he would eventually restart his political life with the ultimate goal of the presidency, but he struggled to get on board with the idea. Years after FDR had won the White House, his son James recalled a conversation with Howe in which Howe confessed that it had been his plan all along, even during the most difficult times of his convalescence, for Roosevelt to become president. Howe established a timetable for when Roosevelt would seek his next office and even what that office would be. "I'll tell you, Jim, it would make a marvelous primer on politics, on how you can maneuver the right man to the top if you plan properly."[8]

An important part of the plan was for Roosevelt to speak at a prominent political event. As the 1924 Democratic convention approached, Howe decided that giving the speech nominating Smith would be good practice and an ideal place to reestablish Roosevelt on the road to the White House. Howe saw the convention as an opportunity to remind Americans that Roosevelt was still actively engaged in politics and was ready to serve if called. He thought if everyone could see that Roosevelt was strong and capable despite his illness, he would be well situated to run in his own right in eight years.

Howe convinced Eleanor of his plan and urged her to use her contacts in the women's arm of the Democratic Party to persuade Belle Moskowitz, one of Al Smith's chief advisers, to ask Smith if he would permit Roosevelt to introduce him at the convention. At first Smith refused, thinking that he lacked the stamina for the task. He also worried that if convention delegates saw Roosevelt on crutches, the sight would inspire so much pity in the hall that cheering for him (Smith) afterward might seem crass. Roosevelt had similar concerns when Eleanor and his personal secretary, Missy LeHand, raised the idea with him. Howe encouraged Eleanor and Missy to press him, hoping that if he was approached from multiple angles he might relent. When Roosevelt shared his doubts with Howe, Howe enumerated the reasons why the speech made political and strategic sense and assured him that he could do it.

Once Roosevelt agreed to do the speech, the real work began. Ordinarily, Howe would take the first stab at crafting his remarks, but in this case the text was written by Smith's people. All Roosevelt and Howe had to worry about was the walk to the podium. Roosevelt liked people to think he was adjusting well to his physical limitations and that he was confident in his ability to maneuver on his crutches, but even after years of practice, he was still insecure about using them in public. Because he had no control over his legs and hip muscles, the only thing keeping him upright on his crutches was his upper-body strength. He had to balance himself the way a gymnast might balance on the parallel bars. Something as little as an unexpected bump could cause him to tumble. He had not forgotten his fall at Fidelity & Deposit, and he worried about the effect a fall might have on the crowd at the convention.

Howe helped him take charge of the situation. He found out in advance the exact distance from Roosevelt's designated seat at the convention to the speaker's podium and measured off a similar distance in Roosevelt's Manhattan library. Over and over they practiced the steps. Roosevelt's son James was only sixteen at the time, but being tall and strong, he was drafted to escort Roosevelt from his chair to the rostrum. When Franklin leaned on his son's arm, James would have to accept a significant portion of Roosevelt's body weight until he was able to swing his leg around under him and shift his weight back onto the crutch he would be holding in his other hand. At the same time, James would have to show no visible signs that Franklin's progress was in any way difficult for either of them. James's face muscles had to be relaxed and his expression calm at all times. But if Roosevelt lost his balance, James would be the only thing preventing him from collapsing.

The hall would be riddled with obstacles to negotiate. Even if they practiced every day, there was still so much that could go wrong.

On August 18, 1944, President Roosevelt invited his vice president, Harry Truman, to lunch in the Rose Garden of the White House. It was one of the few times Truman had seen FDR in person, and he was shocked by his appearance. Truman described to an aide later how close to death FDR looked. Pale, with dark circles around his eyes, the president was frail and weak. "His hands were shaking . . . physically he's just going to pieces."[9] In the last years of his life, FDR had all sorts of physical ailments—cardiovascular issues, anemia, respiratory problems. There is even speculation that he had advanced-stage melanoma. And yet he still sought a fourth term as president. Historians have wondered why he would place himself under the intense physical strain of a presidential campaign when he must have known that he would not live to complete the term. Given his personality, however, no one should have doubted that he would run. A man like FDR simply could not imagine himself as anything but president.

As a child, he was raised to believe that the world revolved around him. Sara Roosevelt pampered her baby boy like the Prince of Wales—and he fully expected someday to be king. Even when he became an adult, his expectations were largely unchanged. It is true he cared about the public and about public service, but he also liked being in charge. In 1924, even as concerned as he was about failing, he recognized that the chance to give the nominating speech for Al Smith was probably the only way to regain his footing on the path to the presidency from which polio had diverted him.

The old Madison Square Garden was a massive Beaux-art fortress, with what looked like Italian renaissance towers rising from its four corners and a thirty-two-story minaret in the front that reminded some visitors of the ancient lighthouse at Alexandria. It was the second-tallest building in New York City. It was designed by the noted architect Stanford White, who had the unfortunate distinction of having been murdered in the restaurant on the top floor by the husband of his lover.

In the New York summer heat, the building's great hall could be a sweltering place. At capacity, the building comfortably held seventeen thousand souls. When the Democratic convention opened on June 24, the estimated attendance exceeded that figure by several thousand.

The entire convention, stretching over fifteen days, was the longest in US political history. It was dubbed the "Klan-bake" in recognition of the violent protests of Ku Klux Klan delegates who opposed the nomination of Al Smith. In those days, the Klan hated not only racial minorities, but also religious ones. A large Klan rally was organized across the river in New Jersey, where Smith was called dirty names and burned in effigy.

To escape the tumult, Roosevelt arrived at the hall early each morning, soon after the doors opened. The first delegates to arrive would find him already seated and waiting to greet them with his famous grin. At the end of the day, after the last of the delegates had found the exits, Roosevelt might be seen slipping out a side door into a waiting car, which would quickly whisk him away.

He was scheduled to take the stage on the twenty-sixth. James was made a special delegate and was seated next to his father when they received the signal to move to the stage. James rose nervously to his feet. A powerful cheer arose from the crowd as Roosevelt stood up beside him. As he slowly moved up the aisle toward the podium, Roosevelt greeted and thanked his well-wishers. Yet as James later recalled: "I was afraid and I know he was too. As we walked—struggled, really—down the aisle to the rear of the platform, he leaned heavily on my arm, gripping me so hard it hurt."[10]

A few steps from the rostrum, James handed his father his second crutch so that he could take the last few steps on his own. As he neared the podium, Roosevelt nodded at a delegate sitting nearby and motioned toward the speaker's stand. The delegate was confused. "Shake it," Roosevelt instructed. "I must know if it will bear my weight."[11]

For the final step, Franklin leaned his powerful torso forward and let his body fall gently toward the podium. He ignored the sweat bleeding through his jacket and running down his face as he flashed a confident smile to the cheering audience. Al Smith's daughter was nearby. "I shall never forget the thrill I felt as I sat on the edge of my chair and watched him grip the rostrum firmly with both hands and begin to speak," she later wrote.[12]

Roosevelt gave a few opening remarks, thanked the crowd for the standing ovation and then began his speech. When he was done, the ovation lasted for an hour and thirteen minutes. Al Smith, who had been listening to the speech on the radio, said afterward, "Roosevelt was probably the most impressive figure in that convention."[13]

James Roosevelt later wrote, "I never in my life was as proud of father as I was at that moment. And he never again was as popular, as he was in that instant. It has been dramatized, but no re-enactment could capture the intensity of the drama that was played out that day."[14]

In many ways, that speech was the most important of his father's career. Without it, he might never have been asked to run for governor of New York in 1928, where he was once again able to capture the nation's attention.[15] The progressive and bold action he took on behalf of New Yorkers in response to the growing Depression helped build his reputation and would establish him as a leading candidate for the Democratic nomination for president in 1932.

Louis Howe rarely spoke publicly about the 1924 speech, despite its centrality to Roosevelt's return to public life. He thought to do so would only highlight Roosevelt's paralysis.

Al Smith would eventually lose the 1924 nomination to a former congressman from West Virginia, who himself would lose to Calvin Coolidge in the general election. After the loss, Roosevelt and Howe returned to their old lives.

Within a few months, Roosevelt would discover the soothing waters of Warm Springs, Georgia, and for the next several years at least, his activities would revolve around the community there as he built a retreat for young victims of polio. While he was away, Howe fell into a familiar rhythm of attending to Roosevelt's many business and political responsibilities. But he never stopped laying the groundwork for his friend's full-throated return to politics. In the face of President Coolidge's popularity, as victory for the Democrats in 1928 looked less and less likely, Howe threw himself into preparing Roosevelt for a run at the New York governorship.

Years later, someone would ask Al Smith why he would raise up a rival like Roosevelt by giving him a chance to speak at the 1924 convention and then urge him to run for governor. Wasn't he worried that Roosevelt might one day overshadow him? Smith replied that he had not worried because he thought that Roosevelt would never have the stamina for higher office.

IV

Howe: Partner to Power

Louis Howe is featured in this chapter for the way he personifies three important aspects of the particular type of right hand he represents—the chief of staff. First, although he lacked the title, as the person who Roosevelt selected to help manage the day-to-day operations of his administration, he stands as an important precursor of the contemporary White House chief of staff. Second, because Howe's position in the Roosevelt Administration did not require Senate confirmation and his activities were often shrouded in secrecy, he is a critical reminder of the lack of accountability of many of the powerful men and women who have followed in his footsteps. And finally, Howe shows how much of the influence of right-hand men and women is derived from their relationship with the president, rather than from their official title.

Unlike those right hands who must undergo Senate confirmation, such as cabinet officers (like William Seward and Alexander Hamilton), Howe and senior advisers like him do not automatically enjoy the same level of deference throughout the administration. Because he was Roosevelt's chief aide rather than the chief of a federal agency, Howe probably knew as well as most that if he were to suddenly fall out of favor with the president, his influence in the administration would suffer. Of course, a cabinet officer can lose favor as well, but an unpopular cabinet officer can at least still move the gears within his or her own agency. If Roosevelt had turned his back on Howe, busy staffers inside the White House might suddenly have found themselves searching for reasons to take his call.

Howe's official title at the time was "secretary to the president," and, in addition to acting as Roosevelt's chief political adviser, he helped oversee White House personnel (along with Missy LeHand, the president's personal secretary). Though Howe served in the days when much of the White House political staff was borrowed from agencies, given his duties, most Americans would recognize him today as the chief of staff—not by title, but certainly in light of his responsibilities.

The White House chief of staff is a relatively recent invention. In 1953, President Eisenhower was the first to formally confer the title when he appointed his former campaign aide Sherman Adams to the post. In his role as an immediate forerunner of what has now become a widely recognized position within the White House chain of command, Howe enters into an important discussion regarding the accountability of senior White House officials and of the role of the president's right hand himself or herself. Despite his extraordinary influence, Howe was conspicuously exempt from the public scrutiny to which other senior government officials were subjected. Advisers like Howe remind us that some of the most powerful people working in the White House—indeed, in the whole of government—are often unelected, unvetted and little known by the public.

Though Howe lived only long enough to serve the president for a couple of years, in that brief period he helped establish the role of the modern-day chief of staff and, by doing so, significantly influenced the role of the presidential right hand. If today there is an expectation that someone like Howe exists at the side of every president, the assumption is meaningfully attributable to Howe's example.

When Roosevelt was president, he once sent a White House valet with a message to give to Howe, who at the time was living in the Lincoln Bedroom. The message, whatever it was, has long since been forgotten, but Howe's response endures.

Howe looked up from whatever work he was doing and told the valet to tell the president to go to hell.[16] *If anyone outside of the president's family had a right to speak to him in such a way, it was Howe. He had earned it.*

For almost twenty-five years, Howe was a central figure in Roosevelt's political and personal life. Roosevelt consulted Howe after Eleanor asked for a divorce in the wake of his affair with her secretary Lucy Mercer; Howe was vacationing with Roosevelt the day he began to exhibit signs of polio in 1921 and Howe helped Eleanor nurse him back to health afterward. Howe was the one person who never let Roosevelt give up on his dream of becoming president, and he devoted much of his life—at considerable personal and financial cost—to making that dream a reality.

Without his influence and assistance, the achievements that FDR is best remembered for might never have occurred. Howe was responsible for the line "The only thing we have to fear is fear itself," and Howe came up with the idea for the CCC.

After his death, Howe was succeeded by a parade of similarly influential figures in the Roosevelt Administration—Missy LeHand, Raymond Moley, Rexford Tugwell and eventually the most powerful of them all, Harry Hopkins. By the time Clark Clifford arrived in the Truman White House ten years later, people like Howe were widely accepted as a fixture.

Perhaps mindful of Howe's example, Clifford devoted himself to the task of breaking into President Truman's inner circle. He would eventually emerge as the president's most trusted and powerful adviser. He became Truman's eyes, his ears and, more importantly, his voice. During his most difficult moments, it was to Clifford that Truman turned. Such was the case when it became clear that someone needed to remind an insubordinate secretary of state that Truman, not he, was the president of the United States.

CHAPTER FIVE

HARRY TRUMAN & CLARK CLIFFORD

FINDING TRUMAN'S VOICE

Even at their closest, President Truman harbored nagging suspicions about Clifford's motives. Truman appreciated Clifford but thought him at times challenging to work with. He took Clifford's advice and encouraged his efforts on his behalf, but in his private papers Truman confessed that he thought Clifford was a "prima donna." (US Navy/Harry S. Truman Library)

The President is a glorified public relations man who spends his time flattering, kissing and kicking people to get them to do what they are supposed to do anyway.[1]

–President Harry Truman

*C*lark Clifford's official title during the Truman Administration was White House counsel, but he is presented here for his role in helping shape the job of White House chief of staff. He symbolizes a key skill in the arsenal of the type of right-hand men who were particularly relevant during the postwar and post-Depression years and who would become the most effective chiefs of staff: policy synthesizers.[2]

Clifford's keen understanding of President Truman and his ability to translate the president's thinking for others—as well as his ability to assemble, shape and package for the president the ideas of his advisers—would fuel his success in the administration. Even though in later life he would serve as secretary of defense and become one of Washington's most powerful lobbyists, Clifford is often remembered for his service in the Truman White House.

Clifford was an unlikely candidate for the role of right hand. He was unknown to the president when he first joined the administration, he possessed little experience in politics, and he had even less knowledge of policymaking. Yet this outsider desperately wanted to be an insider.

What he did possess was a gift for persuasion and a masterful ability to shape and present the ideas of others, a skill on which Truman grew to depend. From the modest perch Clifford first held as an assistant naval aide, in just two years this modern-day Machiavelli clawed his way up, first into Truman's inner circle and then to the summit of White House power.

A dramatic confrontation between Clifford and Secretary of State George Marshall over official US recognition of the new state of Israel would become one of the events that enabled Truman to wrest control of the nation's foreign affairs *away from the men who believed they knew better than the president what direc-tion to take the country. The incident would also strengthen Clifford's position as Truman's right-hand man. The legendary showdown in the Oval Office has become a critical piece of US-Mideast political history. It all began on a sweltering May afternoon in 1948 . . .*

I

Risk

As each man entered the Oval Office, his eyes instinctively swept the room in search of a place to sit. There was no large sofa welcoming visitors, like there is today—only a few chairs along the wall, which were available to the quick, the clever or the brave. Of course, President Truman was ensured a seat, and surely the two chairs that flanked his desk would be claimed by George Marshall and Clark Clifford, who were, in effect, the guests of honor.

Undersecretary of State Robert Lovett must have been well acquainted with the pre-meeting dance that attended gatherings in the Oval Office and undoubt-edly imagined where he would sit well before entering the room, but the four "backbenchers" who were also asked to attend—Robert McClintock and Fraser Wilkins from the State Department and White House staffers David Niles and Matthew Connelly—might have hung back sheepishly at the door, waiting to see how things played out. When the music stopped, Marshall and Lovett were seated at Truman's left, Clifford sat directly in front of the president and Con-nelly and Niles settled at Clifford's side.

The mood was tense and, for Clifford, fraught with danger. Marshall, the regal US secretary of state, was to be for the next thirty minutes his opponent in a contest in which there might not be a winner, but there would certainly be a loser. Marshall was there to be disciplined for the way he was handling the "Israel issue," but Presi-dent Truman feared offending him too much to deliver the blow himself.

Only days before, Marshall had brought Truman to tears with his touching toast at the president's private birthday celebration. The room sat in a stunned silence as Marshall, a man not given to praise, expressed his genuine respect for

Truman, thanking him for his integrity, courage and leadership in a time of great crisis. Truman rose to respond[3] but could not find the words. Struggling to hold back tears, all he could do was stand with his arms outstretched toward Marshall. It is no wonder that he did not wish to confront Marshall on the Israel issue and passed the hatchet to Clifford.

The fact that Marshall was in the wrong did nothing to calm Clifford's nerves. The stakes are always high at the White House, but it's not every day that a staffer and relative political novice is expected to go toe to toe with someone of Marshall's stature. The secretary of state was no ordinary man. Even among extraordinary men he stood out. If after World War II an award could have been given to the one person most responsible for securing the Allied victory, the name embossed in gold letters on the front would have been Marshall's. He might have been the most admired American on the planet. Marshall knew this, and so did Clifford.

Everyone has a sweat signature. Like a fingerprint—it is unique. Though the physiology of perspiration is the same for us all when we are nervous—the heart beats a little faster, the capillaries swell and the blood flows more liberally, elevating the body's temperature and raising pearls of moisture to the skin's surface—where and how much we perspire varies from person to person. For some people, sweat pools on their upper lip. For others, it collects on their chin or in the small of their back. Rolling Clark Clifford in tissue paper as he waited anxiously to face off against Marshall would have revealed a Rorschach image that he alone would recognize.

This was a meeting President Truman had hoped to avoid, but the unacceptable and possibly insubordinate actions of his secretary of state had made it necessary. Truman had decided to officially recognize the new state of Israel, but Marshall and other State Department officials disagreed publicly with the decision, making the administration appear embarrassingly out of sync.

Marshall was visibly agitated by Clifford's presence at the meeting. He had counseled the president strongly against recognizing Israel too early, and the presence of Truman's counsel[4] only confirmed to Marshall that the president was pursuing recognition not for geostrategic reasons but simply to score political points with Jewish voters in the upcoming elections. Marshall arrived at the meeting with his Mideast experts in tow, hoping to convince the president that recognition would be a grave foreign-policy mistake, but Truman was not there to be persuaded.

When the room settled, the president made a few opening remarks and then gave Marshall the floor. The secretary of state began with a brief description of battle conditions on the ground in Palestine, including which territories were held by Arab forces and which were held by Israelis. He then deferred to Under-secretary Lovett, who presented the consensus of the Defense Department, the State Department and the CIA that the US should not recognize Israel.

Lovett argued that there was no need to rush toward recognition. A truce between the Israelis and Palestinians, he thought, was still possible. He described the dangers of prematurely supporting Israel. He explained that the Arabs, and especially the Saudis, would not receive the news of American recognition well and that US access to oil in the region and its own strategic ambitions in the Middle East might be permanently damaged if the US did not tread carefully. He summarized the latest intelligence reports that showed that the Arabs were better armed than the Israeli soldiers and held better-established and reinforced positions on the battlefield. The Arab troops, having been trained by the British, he said, were better equipped and prepared than the Israeli forces, which were composed mostly of unseasoned volunteers.

Marshall reinforced Lovett's points by emphasizing the strategic challenges the Israelis would face if the conflict expanded and added that premature recognition could pull the US into a quagmire that had no real end in sight. Satisfied that he and Lovett had presented a compelling and persuasive case, Marshall ceded the floor. The president invited Clifford to respond.

Prior to leaving government service, Clifford would build an almost legendary reputation as a man of extraordinary gifts for presentation. Those who personally witnessed his performances often described their effect as mesmerizing.[5] "After sitting through one of his presentations, one often paused to reflect because his delivery was so authoritative," a colleague once said. All the elements of his delivery were painstakingly crafted to persuade the audience completely.

Before speaking, Clifford would sit silently gathering his thoughts as the room settled. When all was calm, he would begin slowly, letting the words gather momentum dramatically as he went. Sometimes for effect, he would sit erect, with his palms pressed together and his thumbs stacked as if in prayer. Words used to describe Clifford's manner have included "deliberate," "sonorous,"

"eloquent" and "uninterruptable." His voice was clear and deep, with the resonance of a news anchor. The experience of arguing dozens of cases in front of
juries had taught him to use the acoustics of the room and fertile silences to add
gravity to his delivery. He would let the carefully chosen words reverberate in his
chest before freeing them to rise up and hang in the air irresistibly like the call of
a bell or an echo in a cave. As he faced Secretary Marshall directly, Clifford's first
words were a quote from Deuteronomy: "Behold, I have set the land before you:
go in and possess the land which the Lord sware unto your fathers, Abraham,
Isaac and Jacob, to give unto them and to their seed after them."[6]

Clifford argued that the land rightfully belonged to Israel. It had been given
to them by God himself and paid for with the lives of more than six million Jews.
Surely every human being must feel that they deserved a home of their own. He
argued that Israel would not stop fighting until the land was theirs, and, so, a
Jewish state was inevitable. The Russians had been looking for an excuse to stick
their claws into that part of the world for some time; not supporting Israel now,
Clifford added, would give them the justification they needed.

As Clifford spoke, he could see Marshall glaring back at him angrily. He
later described Marshall's expression as "reddening with suppressed anger."[7]

Clifford rejected out of hand two key assumptions held by the State Department: First, the truce between the Arabs and Jews that Marshall and Lovett
believed was possible was not going to happen, because both sides had already
rejected that option. Second, Clifford took issue with Marshall's belief that Palestine could be turned over to the United Nations and governed under a trusteeship. He felt that this was a flawed assumption because it presupposed the
existence of a single state to govern. Given that the Arabs and Jews had already
begun dividing up the territory, a trusteeship obviously could not work.

Clifford concluded by insisting that recognizing Israel was consistent with
long-established White House policy and that it would be an act of humanity in
keeping with American values. In total, Clifford spoke uninterrupted for almost
fifteen minutes.

In what Clifford later described as "barely contained rage and more than a
hint of self-righteousness,"[8] Marshall released the anger that had been welling
up inside him: "Mr. President, I thought this meeting was called to consider an
important and complicated problem in foreign policy. I don't even know why

Clifford is here. He is a domestic adviser, and this is a foreign policy matter. I fear that the only reason Clifford is here is that he is pressing a political consideration with regard to this issue."[9]

Hoping to ease the rising tension, Lovett jumped in to say that even a delayed recognition of Israel might not be necessarily in US interests. He cited intelligence reports that many of the Jewish immigrants arriving to the new state would be communist and Soviet sympathizers, to suggest that the US would ultimately be doing itself a disservice by supporting what might end up being a pro-Soviet state.

Despite what Marshall viewed to be an unimpeachable argument against recognition, he saw that Lovett's remarks were not convincing the president. Thinking that only a political argument would work, Marshall added one final point to punctuate Lovett's comments—and it sucked all the air out of the room: "Mr. President, Mr. Clifford's recommendations are wrong. If you follow his advice and I was to vote in the next election, I would vote against you."[10]

This was no common threat. Coming from perhaps the most trusted American in the world, these words carried immense weight. If Marshall were to make his threat known publicly, it could sink Truman's chances of holding on to the presidency. Truman abruptly called the meeting to a close, rushing Marshall and his staff toward the door without resolving the matter. As Marshall and Lovett left the room, it was clear to Truman and Clifford that they would have to take matters into their own hands. If Marshall thought the issue was closed, he did not know Truman.

When Harry Truman was a child, he dreamed of becoming a concert pianist. For a boy growing up in rough-and-tumble Independence, Missouri, in the late 1890s, such an aspiration was highly unusual. When asked years later what he had been like as a child, Truman replied, "To tell the truth, I was kind of a sissy."[11]

He was a small, delicate boy in a town where people rode horses and carried guns and where barroom brawls were not uncommon. While other boys his age played and wrestled in the streets, Harry Truman diligently practiced his piano at home and socialized with his little sister and her friends. His mother, Martha, was raised in a pioneer farming family, but she had the extraordinary distinction of having attended college, where she studied art, literature and music. She hoped Harry would follow in her footsteps and encouraged his interest in the piano.

His father, John, a tough mule trader, came from a long line of pioneers and, unlike his son Harry, was not afraid of a fight. He was only five foot four, but he was scrappy. Once, during a court trial, a lawyer accused him of being a liar. John chased the man out into the street, threatening to beat him up.[12] Stubborn and uncompromising, he was long remembered by his neighbors for his work ethic, his integrity and his temper. The dogged persistence for which his son Harry would become known was no doubt inspired by John's "never give up" attitude.

Harry also inherited his father's appetite for risk. John believed in hard work, but he also believed every man needed luck to be successful. The trouble with John was that so few of the risks he took paid off.

Once, he lost the family's savings in a bet on grain-market futures. Afterward, Harry had to abandon his dream of attending college in order to help pay off the debts: he worked as a mailroom attendant, a bank teller and then a railroad timekeeper. After another risky venture, his father lost the family home and the Trumans were reduced to running the farm of a family relation. Harry left his job in the city and moved back home to help with the labor. He was not the outdoorsy type, but he did his best for eight years at his father's side. His hard work revealed a rugged determination that his father had not known existed. He might have lived out the rest of his days as a farm laborer had his father not been injured and died after straining himself lifting a boulder. On his deathbed, John catalogued his regrets, telling his son that he believed his life had been a failure.

Remembering his father's last words, Truman set off on a string of risky ventures of his own. First, he borrowed money to invest in a zinc mine—it failed. Then he borrowed even more money to invest in an oil business—that too failed. Hoping to change his luck, he enlisted in the Missouri National Guard after the US entered World War I in 1917. As a thirty-three-year-old farmer, Truman was not required to serve. He had never been in a fight in his life, but he was put in command of an artillery company.

The rigors of war reinforced Truman's confidence in himself. During one harrowing battle, under heavy fire, his men panicked—scrambling in every direction—but Truman kept his head. As shells exploded around him, he shouted orders to his men, rallying them into ranks, and marched them out of danger.

Not a single one of Truman's soldiers lost his life that day. Truman's grace in battle won him the enduring respect of his men and would one day be the source of his professional resurrection.

When the war ended, Truman returned home to Missouri and tried his luck at business again, this time selling menswear. Sadly, after just two years, he and his partner decided to close the shop for good. He was thirty-eight and up to that point had known mostly failure in life, but his luck was about to change.

In 1922, an old reserve buddy remembered Truman when his uncle, the legendary Missouri political boss Tom Pendergast, was looking for someone to run for Jackson County commissioner. Truman agreed to throw his hat in the ring. He was no public speaker, but his military record helped him stand out as a candidate. He discovered that he enjoyed campaigning and was able to win a narrow victory. For the next decade, he built a reputation as an honest and hardworking public administrator.

In 1934, after deciding to take another risk and run for the US Senate, Truman surprised everyone, including himself, by winning. As the junior senator from Missouri, he put his head down and applied himself to the task of slowly building a reputation for energetically fighting waste, fraud and abuse in government contracting. In the process, he saved the nation billions of dollars and established himself as a well-regarded national public figure.

Truman's fortunes took another positive turn in July 1944, when Democrats arrived in Chicago to nominate Franklin Roosevelt for a fourth term as president. A group of powerful back-room operators considered the choices for Roosevelt's running mate: former Supreme Court justice Jimmy Burns was a staunch segregationist and unacceptable to the liberals; Henry Wallace, the current vice president, was a champion of civil rights and too liberal for the conservatives. Hoping to strike a compromise, Democratic leaders chose Truman. The president did not know Truman, but he was too preoccupied with the war and with his own failing health to care who his running mate was. When Truman's name was raised, he accepted with little objection. That decision turned out to be one of the most important of FDR's presidency. He died in office eighty-two days later.

In April 1945, as he prepared to assume the presidency, Truman understood Washington and politics, but he must have wondered whether that would be enough to guide the nation. After all, he was following in the footsteps of a man who, after three full terms in office, was the only president an entire generation had ever known. And Roosevelt had only ever met with Vice President Truman twice and had never accepted him into his inner circle, so not only was now-President Truman ill-prepared for the immense public commitments of the office, he was unaware of even the most urgent matters President Roosevelt had been dealing with before his death. Making matters worse, the new president stepped into the shoes of the great FDR surrounded by people who shared his doubts about his abilities.

The new president was a short, stocky man, who never left the house without his suit pressed and his shoes shined. His daughter, Mary Margaret, described his appearance as that of someone who had just walked off of the band stage. His hands were powerful and rough from his years spent behind a plow. He had a nasally but resonant voice that had a gravelly quality and that easily betrayed his discomfort with public speaking. When nervous, he would stumble over his words, pause and then repeat himself. He wore thick spectacles that magnified his eyes into great orbs. Though he did his best to look confident, he confessed to his family that in the beginning of his presidency he was genuinely scared. He was a small-town guy suddenly elevated to the head of the most prosperous country and most powerful army the world had ever known. He made no secret of the fact that he felt entirely out of his depth.

The press picked up on Truman's discomfort and reported on his blunders so often that even ordinary Americans began to wonder whether Harry had it in him to be president. In two important ways, Clark Clifford helped change perceptions about the new president. First, where Truman was awkward in public, Clifford was graceful. In his effort to surround himself with his own people, Truman had chosen men who, unfortunately, were not as polished as one might expect. Clifford's smooth elegance helped change the negative reputation of the men around the president. Second, Clifford was a highly capable and disciplined adviser, able to delve with confidence into any policy area. He was the ideal right-hand man—articulate, competent and completely committed to the president's objectives. Like a figure out of central casting, he emerged on the scene precisely when Truman needed him most.

In the immediate aftermath of the showdown in the Oval Office, Clifford had one chief aim: to help Truman officially recognize Israel before the clock ran out. He would do this with or without the help of the secretary of state. He did not have a background in foreign affairs, he knew little of the history of the region and he lacked many of the key foreign-policy contacts that would be crucial to his effort. Armed only with his keen persuasive gifts, his intelligence and the imprimatur of the president, he set to work doing what the rest of Truman's foreign-policy team would not.

Clifford arrived early at the White House on the morning of May 14, 1948, with the equivalent of a month's work to do in just ten hours. He needed to do an end-run around the secretary of state and identify a powerful ally in the State Department to help him keep the UN delegation out of his way as he single-handedly executed a major foreign-policy shift. Without alerting the Russians or the Arabs to what he was doing, Clifford needed to convince the Israeli leadership to officially request recognition from the US. Finally, Clifford would need the US delegation in the UN to get on board at the precise moment and help him convince other countries not to oppose US efforts—and he would need to accomplish this by 6:00 p.m., to coincide with Israel's planned announcement of statehood.

Clifford first reached out to Eliahu Epstein, who he knew would probably be the first Israeli ambassador to the US, and asked him to approach the Israeli provisional government to request an official letter of recognition from the president. Clifford would need such a letter to protect Truman in case Marshall decided to object in public.

After receiving the request for recognition from Israel, and with only fifteen minutes left on the clock, Clifford called Dean Rusk, the deputy secretary of state, to inform him that the US would be issuing a press release recognizing Israel in a matter of minutes. He instructed Rusk to inform the UN delegation immediately. Rusk objected, saying that it would be a great embarrassment to them, given that they had been working for weeks to delay the recognition of Israel. He warned Clifford that the entire US delegation might resign in protest. Clifford didn't care. This was going to happen over the objections of Marshall or Rusk or anyone else who stood in his way.

When the head of the UN delegation, Warren Austin, got the call that US recognition of Israel was imminent, rather than face the embarrassment, he hung up the phone, called for his government limousine and went home without informing anyone, including the rest of the US delegates, of what he had learned.

Then, around 6:15 p.m.,[13] as the UN was about to debate an issue regarding the Middle East, a seemingly bizarre rumor began to circulate that the US had just officially recognized the state of Israel. The rumor drew laughter from everyone who heard it, including the US delegates, who immediately discounted it as ridiculous. Then someone produced a press release stating that recognition had in fact occurred only moments ago. When Marshall was informed of what Clifford had done, he called Rusk from California, ordering him immediately to New York to keep the US delegates from resigning en bloc.

Marshall would never speak to Clifford again. For Clifford, it didn't really matter—he didn't need Marshall. His performance proved that as Truman's right-hand man, he could be just as powerful as the secretary of state when he needed to be. Only three short years before, Clifford had been a newcomer in the White House, an unknown quantity, an outsider. Now, he was arguably the most powerful staffer in the government—and his greatest accomplishments still lay before him.

II

A Gambler's Heart

Clark McAdams Clifford grew up in St. Louis at a time when people still rode in horse-drawn carriages and when a man went around each evening at dusk lighting the gas-powered street lamps by hand. The young Clark was not an indifferent student, but he preferred to focus his attention on baseball and tennis. In college he followed his mother's advice and joined the theater club, where he developed a flair for the dramatic that would be the foundation of his gifts for persuasion and presentation in later life.

In his memoirs, Clifford told a story that captures who he was at his core. He recalled a childhood memory of something no son should ever have to see—the breaking of his father's spirit. An unassuming, mid-level railroad executive with few ambitions beyond serving his family, Frank Clifford had learned early not to expect too much from life. Then, one day the railroad company assigned a new boss to his division, and it was as if the clouds had parted. The new boss had big dreams, and he offered to take Frank along for the ride. Clifford described the transformational effect this new opportunity had on his father and how his characteristic pessimism was supplanted by an energy and optimism that Clifford had never seen before. Then suddenly Frank's boss suffered a heart attack, and, like a smoke ring, the promising career path vanished into thin air. Crestfallen, Frank reverted back to the passive, quiet man his son knew all too well. Frank's reaction to his sudden misfortune etched forever in Clifford's mind the image of the type of man he never wanted to be. For decades, Clifford told this story to explain the driving need for independence that inspired his decision to become a lawyer, but listeners must have wondered whether he knew how much more it said about him.

That painful childhood experience might have taught Clifford persistence, but it must have also taught him the importance of making his own luck. Clifford would spend his whole career making and capitalizing on opportunities he generated on his own. The first of such opportunities came not long after he graduated from law school.

Coming of age during the Great Depression, when jobs were hard to come by, Clifford struggled to find a firm that would hire him. He finally decided he would settle for gaining legal experience any way he could. He walked into the biggest firm in St. Louis and convinced one of the partners, Jacob Lashly, to permit him to sit in the firm's library and work for free over the summer. He offered to keep the library tidy and run whatever errands the attorneys needed. Lashly agreed, and at the end of the summer, Clifford met with him to express his gratitude for the opportunity.

Lashly had been watching Clifford closely and had come to appreciate his ambition and dedication. He offered Clifford a job doing pretty much what he was already doing. Clifford would work ten years for the firm, with ever-increasing responsibility, eventually making partner.

Not long after the US entered World War II, Clifford took a leave of absence from the firm to join the naval reserve. He sent his wife and three young daughters to live with a family member in Boston and divided the days of his military service between Washington, DC, and San Francisco, where it was his job to assess and catalog inventory for the Pacific Fleet.

Clifford intended his stint in uniform to be a short one, and as the war began winding down he started to look forward to resuming his comfortable life in Missouri. One day while on duty in San Francisco, he received an unexpected call from an old friend that would change his life forever.

Jake Vardaman, a Missouri business associate who was also in the naval reserve and who was working in the White House, needed an assistant. He offered Clifford a chance to serve at his side. For Clifford, taking the job meant trading the stable, predictable life he hoped to resume in Missouri for the frenetic atmosphere of Washington. Life as a White House official would be a risky pursuit,[14] especially given that he had a young family to support, but Clifford must have seen the possibilities as well. After some hesitation, he accepted the offer, and the Cliffords moved to DC.

On his first day on the job, Clifford recognized that he was in an environment of great and rare opportunity. From the sidelines, as he emptied ashtrays and straightened chairs in the Map Room, he closely watched each of the men in Truman's inner circle—Samuel "Judge" Rosenman (White House counsel), James "Jake" Vardaman (naval aide), John Steelman (special assistant) and Harry Vaughn (military aide)—in order to assess their strengths and weaknesses and compare them to his own. Clifford saw a Truman White House that was riddled with problems of inefficiency and amateurism. He shared with his wife, Marny, his conclusion that Truman was in desperate need of talented, professional advisers. The right man, with the right qualities, could go a long way in such an environment if he could only gain the trust of the president.

By his own admission, Rosenman's days as Truman's counsel were numbered. Since he was a lawyer like Rosenman, Clifford must have thought about succeeding him when the time came. As a man given to careful and strategic planning, Clifford undoubtedly recognized that there were at least four things he must do to succeed Rosenman: First, he would need to prove that he was a team player. Second, he would need to show why his talents qualified him for membership in the president's inner circle; from there, he could carve out an area of influence and begin to make himself indispensable to Truman. Finally, he would have to bring all these elements together in a way that established him, and him alone, as the best replacement for

Rosenman as counsel. It would be an uphill battle. To rise through the ranks, he would need to make Truman and those closest to the president view him as something more than a glorified room attendant.

As he had done with Lashly at the law firm, Clifford made it known to the key figures around the president that he was willing and able to take on any task, for the opportunity to put his gifts on display.

Rosenman would supply an important opportunity when he began assigning Clifford occasional speechwriting assignments—one of the most important jobs in the White House. The task required involvement in all aspects of Truman's policy affairs, and the person who held the post possessed the greatest opportunity to influence Truman's thinking as they worked together to shape a speech. Rosenman was that person for Truman in the first year of his presidency. His duties as counsel effectively made Rosenman Truman's right-hand man. But it was a title he wore loosely.

As Rosenman's de facto deputy, Clifford soon began to see Truman more and more often. But though Truman was beginning to recognize Clifford's potential for doing more than emptying dustbins, he still viewed Clifford as an outsider. An opportunity for Clifford to begin to change that perception arrived on the day both Rosenman and Vardaman decided they had grown tired of government service. Rosenman wished to leave for the greener pastures of the New York legal scene, and Vardaman, hoping to capitalize on his background in banking, wanted to join the Federal Reserve Board. Since the only members of Truman's inner circle were Vardaman, Steelman, Rosenman and Vaughn, the departure of Rosenman and Vardaman would present a huge opportunity. When Truman asked Clifford to help secure Vardaman's confirmation on the Federal Reserve Board, the significance of the request was not lost on him.

Rosenman had by then recommended that Clifford succeed him as counsel, but Truman was not so sure. Clifford knew guiding Vardaman through the Senate confirmation process would permit Truman to judge up close his political instincts and persuasive skills. Clifford would be required to meet privately with Truman, and he would need to lobby and possibly testify before members of Congress. Given that Vardaman's abrasive style had made him many enemies in Washington, drawing accusations that he used government workers to perform personal tasks, his confirmation was hardly expected to be a slam dunk. Thus the experience would test Clifford's political skills. But he was not discouraged. He met with senators of both parties and convinced enough of them that the claims against Vardaman were simply his political enemies' attempts to settle old scores. Clifford's professionalism and tactical sense helped secure Vardaman's confirmation.

This was a big win for Clifford. But although he had shown he was capable of being effective with Congress—a key element of the job of White House counsel—Truman still wasn't sure how Clifford would perform when the stakes were highest: when the president's own credibility was in question. Clifford's chance to show Truman he had what it took came only a few weeks later, when the administration was confronted with its first real challenge—the labor strikes of 1946.

Millions of Americans had spent the war years standing by without complaint as their wages stagnated, even as they watched their corporate bosses grow fat on profits from government contracts. When the war ended, so did their willingness to sacrifice. After years of barely getting by, they felt they had earned the right to be paid a fair market wage. When their repeated requests went unanswered, the strikes began.

On a single day in May 1946, more than a million Americans—eight hundred thousand steelworkers; two hundred thousand meatpackers; and tens of thousands of glass workers, telephone operators and electric company employees—walked off the job. One electric plant shut down when its thirty-five hundred employees walked out, impacting a hundred thousand workers in other areas. And then came a thunderbolt—rail workers, the custodians of the nation's transportation and commercial arteries, threatened to cut off the country's blood supply unless they received a substantial pay increase. Unlike the other strikes, the rail strike was deadly serious. It meant no mail delivery, no food on the store shelves, and no coal to heat people's homes in the winter. Truman had to act.

After a few false starts, Truman, with the help of his chief labor adviser, John Steelman, finally got a handle on things. Steelman managed much of the negotiation for the dispute, while Clifford was tasked with drafting a speech for Truman criticizing the rail workers' union for putting the country's financial health at risk. By now, Rosenman and Vardaman were no longer with the administration. Of the president's original inner circle, only Steelman and Vaughn remained.

Clifford had assumed Rosenman's role in all but name, and Steelman, who had risen to prominence due to his deep involvement in White House operations, appeared to be filling the advisory and personal role of Vardaman. A new team was forming, and Truman was watching to see how everyone jelled.

On the day of Truman's big speech to a joint session of Congress, Clifford spent most the day working on the draft while Steelman continued to seek a resolution with the union. Clifford finished only just in time and placed the draft in the president's hands on the limousine ride to the Capitol. As Truman spoke to a packed congressional chamber, Steelman was still working feverishly against the clock with the railroad unions. Clifford was watching the president's speech from the antechamber when Steelman called to announce a last-minute concession by the unions. The strike was over! Clifford quickly scribbled a note to Truman, which someone handed to the president during a pause in his speech. Truman looked up from the note with a smile and announced that the rail strike had just been resolved—and that it had been resolved on his terms. The room erupted in celebration, with mighty cheers and applause.

The ending of the rail strike was a great success for Truman, and it improved his public image as a decisive and strong leader. It was also a great success for Clifford, who was from that day forward embraced by Truman as a full member of his team. Clifford's conduct under the pressure of the whole affair must have put to rest Truman's doubts about Clifford's readiness for the bright lights of White House politics. Without ceremony, on June 27, 1946, Truman notified Clifford after a meeting in the Oval Office that he was to immediately leave the naval reserve and assume the full duties of White House counsel.

Clifford now held the office that had enabled Rosenman to become Truman's right hand, but Clifford was under no illusions. He still had much to do if he wanted to enjoy the same respect Truman held for Rosenman. Vardaman and Rosenman were gone, but Vaughn and Steelman remained as credible threats to his ambition to become the president's chief adviser. Vaughn and Clifford had never really gotten along well, and the rail strike had exposed a bitter rivalry between Steelman and Clifford that would fester for as long as Clifford worked in the White House. Truman's new inner circle would be an uneasy alliance.

By any measure, John Steelman was a success story. The former hobo, who had ridden the rails during the Great Depression, was smart and competitive and had the ego of two men. Before entering government service, he clawed his way to a PhD in economics at the University of North Carolina. He joined the Roosevelt Administration to work on labor issues and accepted Truman's offer to assume the same duties in his administration. He became one of the most important members of Truman's staff, and some regarded him as the first White House chief of staff.

Clifford and Steelman had a strained relationship for much of the time they served together. Even years later, in an interview, Steelman betrayed a strong note of bitterness toward his former colleague.[15] As rivals for the post of Truman's chief adviser, Clifford and Steelman were on a collision course, and they came crashing together during the next major labor crisis of the administration.

The coal miners' strike was unexpected. The matter was thought to have been resolved after a contract between the miners and the administration some months earlier. Then, out of the blue, the charismatic leader of the coal miners' union, John L. Lewis, decided to use the upcoming congressional elections as leverage to squeeze more concessions out of Truman.

Lewis's threat was potent. Coal fueled nearly all the locomotive activity in the country, at a time when trains were the only real way to move large quantities of goods. It also powered most of the nation's electricity. Truman interpreted Lewis's reneging on the signed agreement with the coal miners as a personal affront and a threat to national security. He called his team together to discuss a solution.

Steelman advised appeasement. The coal miners were a large and formidable force in American politics, and Steelman felt the only way to deal with such a force was to roll over and give them what they wanted. Clifford disagreed.

Clifford believed giving in to the miners would make Truman look weak and could hurt the Democrats' chances in the upcoming elections. He advocated for an uncompromising insistence that Lewis fulfill the terms of the signed agreement. During a particularly heated exchange after a few drinks in the second-floor residence of the White House, Steelman and Clifford debated their points directly to the president. In the end, Truman decided in Clifford's favor.

The president had the US attorney general file a lawsuit against Lewis accusing him of contempt of court for not adhering to the terms of the agreement, and the union was slapped with a fine of $3.5 million. In addition, Lewis was personally fined, to the tune of $10,000—the equivalent of $100,000 today—with the threat of jail time if he failed to pay up. Lewis made repeated attempts to reach the president, hoping to negotiate, but on Clifford's advice, Truman refused his calls. Accepting his loss, Lewis called a press conference and announced that the miners would honor their commitments under the contract. Clifford had gone toe to toe with Steelman and won.

Prevailing in his struggle with Lewis and Steelman elevated Clifford to the pinnacle of Truman's advisers. His promotion was unwelcome news to Steelman as well as to Vaughn, who had watched Clifford's swift rise from assistant naval aide to naval aide to White House counsel with growing unease, worrying that Clifford might replace Rosenman as Truman's number-one adviser.

If there was any lingering confusion about who was Truman's right-hand man, it was laid to rest on the day Truman asked Vaughn to surrender Rosenman's large West Wing office to Clifford and to move into Clifford's modest office on the other end of the White House. When Rosenman left, Vaughn had been quick to seize his office, recognizing the importance of proximity to the president, whose office was next door. By giving Clifford Rosenman's old office and his old job, Truman was communicating to his inner circle that Clifford was now his most important adviser—a remarkable achievement, given where he started.

III

Finding Truman's Voice

As Clifford settled into his role as Truman's counsel, he came to be involved, to some degree, in every major decision Truman made. Clifford was at Truman's side, for example, when the president decided to undertake a major government reorganization. Leading a consolidation effort throughout the executive branch, with Clifford's help Truman recast the federal government—in particular, the national security structure[16]—into a more efficient and responsive tool, one that would give the president better control of domestic and international affairs.

Truman's reorganization comprised three main goals: a downsizing of the federal government to match diminishing postwar burdens; a reshaping of the military to address the emerging threat of Soviet expansion; and the development of his own national security advisory apparatus within the White House. Of these three goals, downsizing the government would happen with the least effort on Truman's part.

When FDR entered the White House in 1933, approximately five hundred thousand people worked for the federal government. By the time Truman took over twelve years later, the number had risen to more than three million. Much of that growth was associated with the war and with efforts to stand up New Deal programs. Now that the war and the Depression were over, hundreds of thousands of men and women were leaving the government for opportunities elsewhere—relieving Truman of the burden of having to find a way to dismiss them. Dealing with the problems associated with the national security system would be far more challenging.

Truman knew that any reorganization of the country's national security structure must begin with the military, which had long suffered from the effects of disunity and inter-service rivalry. In fact, during the war, there had been so much infighting in the military that Truman thought the US was lucky to have won at all. "We must never fight another war the way we fought the last two," he once said. "I have the feeling that if the Army and Navy had fought our enemies as hard as they fought each other, [World War II] would have ended much earlier."[17]

At various times, Secretary Marshall, Defense Secretary James Forrestal and President Truman himself were each credited with espousing the virtues of greater cooperation among the military agencies, but nothing ever seemed to get done to address the problems. Truman resolved to be the first president to change this.

Some trace Truman's idea of military reform to the famous Elsey Report of 1946, a comprehensive national security analysis based on the famous "Long Telegram" written by renowned American foreign-policy expert George Kennan. The report was largely the work of its namesake, Truman adviser George Elsey, although Clifford enhanced it by soliciting and incorporating ideas from others and edited it to appeal to Truman's sensibilities.[18] The report argued that the Soviet Union was emerging as a major threat to the US and that the president needed to change direction in his foreign policy in order to meet the challenges of the situation.

The foreign-policy successes for which Truman would later become known—the Truman Doctrine, the Marshall Plan, the creation of NATO and the policy of "containment" with regard to communism—were all reactions to international events, but they were influenced heavily by what he learned from the Elsey Report. The legislative platform Truman created to help him institute these policies was the National Security Act of 1947, and Clifford was essential to its passage.

Behind the scenes, as Truman's point person for guiding the bill through Congress, Clifford contributed substantially to the creation of the CIA, the National Security Council, the Joint Chiefs of Staff and even the Defense Department—an agency that he would lead himself some years later. Clifford wrote for Truman the letters to Congress explaining the rationale for the reorganization. He acted as Truman's liaison between the army and the navy to iron out differences between the two departments. He helped draft various versions of the legislation. It was his idea to house the National Security Council in the White House rather than in the Pentagon under the control of the secretary of defense. And it was he who drafted the executive orders to implement the reorganization when the legislation passed Congress.

Clifford played another, less obvious role in the process, without which the reorganization might have happened quite differently. He was Truman's eyes, ears and voice. Other presidents' attempts at reorganization had failed largely because the navy and the army actively opposed them. On Truman's behalf, Clifford fought all the petty turf battles that would have been undignified for a president to fight. Clifford gathered intelligence and brought it to Truman; together they would analyze it to determine how to implement their agenda. Clifford sat in all the meetings that were beneath the office of the president and steered them in Truman's favor.

Though the reforms Truman established in 1947 would not take full effect for months, and what we recognize today as the National Security Council would not emerge until much later, they ultimately made the White House the unqualified leader in the shaping and articulation of the nation's foreign policy. As a result of Clifford's actions on Truman's behalf, no president would ever have to suffer the same frustration as Truman did in May 1948 when he brought his secretary of state to heel in the Oval Office.

IV

Clifford: Partner to Power

Like Louis Howe, Clifford represents the chief-of-staff model of presidential right hand. In Clifford's case, in his capacity as White House counsel, he functioned like a chief of staff, though the title did not yet exist. Today the White House counsel functions as one might expect a counsel to, with defined legal responsibilities, but in Clifford's day the duties of the position were significantly broader.

In the Truman Administration, the responsibilities of today's chief of staff were divided between two positions—the White House counsel (Clifford) and the assistant to the president (Steelman). The former was responsible for helping the president with policy planning and synthesis. The latter oversaw White House operations. A visitor to the executive mansion in 1948 might easily recognize that Clifford was the most powerful member of Truman's staff, but on paper he and Steelman were regarded as equals.

The next president, Eisenhower, combined the duties held by Clifford and Steelman into a new position. Doing so helped prevent the overlapping of responsibilities—which had been a frequent source of friction between those two men. Eisenhower placed this new position, his chief of staff, at the top of the White House chain of command—on a par, in many ways, with his cabinet members.

As White House counsel, Clifford was followed by notables including Ted Sorensen, who worked for President Kennedy; Lloyd Cutler, who worked for Presidents Carter and Clinton; and Fred Fielding, who worked for Ronald Reagan and George W. Bush. None of the thirty-six men and women who succeeded Clifford, however, enjoyed the same level of sweeping influence as he did—with the possible exception of John Ehrlichman, who was a key player in the Nixon White House. Because Nixon's circle of advisers shrank as the Watergate scandal grew, Ehrlichman quickly became one of the most powerful people in the administration.

Clifford would serve as Truman's chief adviser for three years, helping the president win a surprising reelection campaign in 1948 before leaving to establish a lucrative Washington legal practice. He would return to the highest levels of government only once more, twenty years later, to become secretary of defense to President Lyndon Johnson.

Even with the changes to the federal bureaucracy instituted with Clifford's help, the US government was still a writhing, unwieldy behemoth. In order to gain better control of an executive branch that was too massive to maneuver, Truman's successor, President Eisenhower, with the help of his closest aide, Sherman Adams, would introduce an organizational framework that would permanently change how subsequent presidents oversaw White House operations.

Eisenhower is credited with the creation of what we recognize today as the White House chief of staff. Afterward, every US president would have one, and this person often would be the president's principal adviser. Yet Eisenhower's chief, Sherman Adams, remains the most powerful one to date. The scope of his influence would become clearly apparent to all involved in the autumn of 1955, when together, he and the president guided the country through what in less capable hands might have developed into a major constitutional crisis.

CHAPTER SIX

DWIGHT EISENHOWER & SHERMAN ADAMS

POWER BY PROXY

Three months to the day after this photo was taken, President Eisenhower suffered a debilitating heart attack. Afterward, his chief of staff, Sherman Adams—pictured here during their golf outing in New Hampshire—kept such a tight grip on power in the White House that advisers started referring to him as "the abominable 'no' man."

A man like Adams is valuable because of the unnecessary
detail he keeps away from the President.[1]

—President Dwight D. Eisenhower

*S*ince the founding of the American republic, the vast majority of presidents
have acted as their own chiefs of staff.[2] The need for a change only arose
in the twentieth century as the size of the White House staff mushroomed to match
the explosive growth of the federal government. After taking office in 1953,
President Eisenhower granted his chief of staff, Sherman Adams, viceroy-like
authority over the scope and direction of White House operations and domestic
policymaking. For Adams, the immensity of his responsibilities would come into
full relief during the weeks following Eisenhower's heart attack in late 1955. The
president's illness would test the limits and loyalties of his cabinet, and, by the
time the crisis fully subsided, the presidency would be forever changed.

Eisenhower's heart attack introduced uncertainty into a White House culture that
he had worked hard to make appear serene and predictable. As he lay unconscious
in a hospital in Denver, not only was the public unsure of how the government
would operate without him, his own agency heads wondered as well. Eisenhower
had assembled in his cabinet a team of extraordinary men, many of whom could
have been president in their own right. This first great crisis of his administration
might have driven a wedge into the cabinet had it not been for the efforts of four
men who would literally hold in their hands the life and legacy of the president . . .

Howard Snyder, Eisenhower's doctor, confirmed the suspicions of many critics
that he was in over his head as White House physician when his initial misdiagnosis almost cut the president's life short. Snyder would spend the rest of his
days telling and retelling a carefully embroidered and misleading account of the
critical first hours following Eisenhower's heart attack in order to conceal his
embarrassing error . . .

John Foster Dulles, Eisenhower's secretary of state, an evangelical Calvinist who
once considered disowning his own son for choosing to become a Catholic, was one

half of a powerful foreign-policy team with his brother Allen, the director of the CIA. Together they personally oversaw the overt and covert foreign affairs of the nation. Eisenhower's sudden illness, a huge jolt to the status quo, threatened every-thing Dulles and his brother had built together. If he wanted to retain his almost complete control of foreign-policy matters, he would need to cleverly sidestep a power struggle with not one, but two of the most influential cabinet members . . .

Richard Nixon, the young and inexperienced vice president, was struggling to stay relevant in an administration that frequently regarded him as a liability. Eisenhower's incapacitation gave him the opportunity of his dreams: to lead the nation through a crisis and thereby secure his claim to the unofficial title of "president-in-waiting." But it would be ripped from his grasp even before he knew what had happened . . .

And Sherman Adams, the president's chief of staff—and the widely recognized power behind the throne—would be caught "on the back foot" as forces within the cabinet mobilized to challenge his power.

Each of these men would play a major role in how the administration navigated the crisis. Outside of the White House, the public saw an administration striding confidently with the nation's affairs well in hand. But inside, the mood was less certain as the gathering of alpha males, each used to the sound of his own voice, circled Eisenhower's empty chair like hungry vultures.

I

Liars' Club

Adams was just ending a month-long tour of military installations in Europe when he learned of Eisenhower's heart attack. It had been an exhausting trip, and Adams was looking forward to resuming his routine back in Washington. While waiting in line for his flight home from Scotland, he was recognized, pulled aside and given the news.

Drizzle blew sideways across the tarmac as he approached the plane. The image of the legendarily vigorous Eisenhower lying helpless in a hospital bed must have dominated his thoughts as he mounted the stairs. Like most of the public, Adams knew only sketchy details about Eisenhower's condition. He would not get the full picture until the next day, when he called the president's press secretary, James Hagerty.

At 2:30 a.m. on September 24, 1955, President Eisenhower was awakened from a restless sleep by a sharp pain in his abdomen. He and his wife, Mamie, slept in separate rooms, so, with difficulty, he raised himself out of bed and walked across the hall. Mamie awoke to find the president standing above her in the dark, breathing hard and clutching his chest. She walked him back to his room and helped him into bed. Thinking that he might be experiencing another one of his regular bouts of indigestion, she convinced him to take milk of magnesia. Then she lay down beside him, rubbing his back in the way that always calmed him, until he fell asleep. What happened next depends on who was asked and when.

For years, much of what was known about the president's heart attack came from his personal physician, Dr. Howard Snyder,[3] whom Mamie phoned soon after the president fell asleep. Over the years, as he retold the story, Snyder's description of the events of that morning grew more elaborate and boastful of his skills as a physician. In his favored version, he arrived at the Eisenhower family home to find the president in pain, which he immediately recognized as a heart attack. He administered a series of drugs to relieve Eisenhower's discomfort and to prevent further damage to his heart. Once the president was out of danger, Snyder administered a second dose of morphine to enable him to rest comfortably. He allowed the president to sleep late into the morning; then, after calling in a leading Denver cardiologist to confirm his diagnosis, Snyder had the president moved to nearby Fitzsimons Army Hospital.

If this was indeed what happened, Snyder should be commended for his quick thinking, his discretion and his discipline. But this is not how events actually unfolded.

In his 1996 book, *Eisenhower's Heart Attack*,[4] University of Texas professor Clarence Lasby argued that Snyder initially misdiagnosed the president's condition and the delay of appropriate care exacerbated his ailment. Even more damningly, Lasby's research reveals that Snyder's actions suggest that he deliberately tried to cover up his mistake. Even a cursory review of Snyder's efforts on that morning show that Snyder was clearly operating under the assumption that the president was suffering from indigestion, not a heart attack.

According to Lasby's research, at six in the morning, Snyder telephoned the president's driver to inform him that a car would not be needed until later in the day because the president was not feeling well. Afterward, he called the president's private secretary to convey the same message. Mindful of the press conference held each morning at eight, Snyder then called Murray Snyder (no relation), the president's deputy press secretary, to inform him that Eisenhower had an upset stomach and would have a delayed workday. Based on Dr. Snyder's information, Murray reported at the eight o'clock press conference that the president was suffering a stomach ailment, and he made a similar announcement at his eleven o'clock press conference. That would be the last time Eisenhower's illness would be described as indigestion.

When the president awoke around eleven that same morning with no change in his condition, Snyder realized that something more serious than indigestion must be affecting him—yet he took no extraordinary measures to determine the source of the symptoms. Instead he permitted Eisenhower to rest two hours more. Only when it finally dawned on him that Eisenhower must have had a heart attack did he seek outside assistance. He called Dr. Byron Pollock, the chief of cardiology at Fitzsimons Army Hospital outside Denver, and asked him to come at once and to bring an electrocardiograph machine.

When the ECG showed that Eisenhower had suffered a major heart attack, Snyder must have been deeply embarrassed. The president's driver was quickly summoned, and Eisenhower was rushed off to Fitzsimons, where he was injected with blood thinners and placed in an oxygen tent to relieve the pressure on his heart. Press Secretary Hagerty finally reached the hospital from Washington later that evening.

For years, Snyder labored to conceal the fact that he had badly misdiagnosed the heart attack and that his error might have ended Eisenhower's life. Of course, few cover-ups succeed without help, and there was no lack of senior officials willing to help keep Snyder's secret—even Sherman Adams did his part. In his memoirs, Adams recounts almost word for word Snyder's version of events. Given his centrality to the administration, it is difficult to imagine that Adams did not know the truth. As press secretary, Hagerty was probably the person most responsible for keeping the lie alive. He wanted to control the narrative, so instead of entertaining media inquiries about the inconsistencies in the timeline of Eisenhower's illness, he focused attention on Eisenhower's progress in recovery. Eventually questions about Snyder simply died away, only to reemerge decades later in Lasby's book.[5]

As the administration went into crisis mode to manage public perceptions surrounding the president's illness, the central question became what to do if Eisenhower remained too ill to perform the functions of his office. There was a plan in place for what to do if Eisenhower died, but there was no playbook for how the government should function if the chief executive was only severely debilitated.

All this still lay in the future as Adams struggled to sleep on the long flight home from Scotland. As the plane prepared to land in the drizzle and fog of Washington, DC, Adams looked out the window at the city below, contemplating what awaited him. Eisenhower had assembled an extraordinary cabinet, and, for the most part, its members functioned as a well-oiled team. But they had never faced a challenge like this.

II

Covert Actions

As Eisenhower lay unconscious nearly two thousand miles away in Denver, concerns about how the government would function without him were on the minds of everyone in his cabinet. Vice President Nixon was now in the spotlight in a way that he had never been before. All the eyes upon him must have seemed to ask: "Are you in charge? Are you ready?" Ducking into the president's shadow was no longer an option. Adams, no doubt, felt a similar pressure looking into the eyes of men who regarded him as Eisenhower's de facto deputy.

Secretary of State Dulles had much to lose from Eisenhower's absence. A healthy president meant access, influence and recognition as arguably the third most powerful person in the administration. Now, with Eisenhower gone, Dulles was just another member of the cabinet. Worse still, Eisenhower's absence might mean foreign policy would be made by consensus, which Dulles, who was intent on maintaining control over foreign affairs, could not countenance.

In the fog swirling around the presidency in those critical first days, Dulles would need to move aggressively if he wanted to protect his power. Because of their authority, he perceived Nixon and Adams as real threats. By virtue of their positions in the administration, Nixon and Adams both had arguable claims to leadership of the cabinet. Like a character in a Shakespearean drama, Dulles would need to act swiftly and carefully if he wanted to marginalize Nixon and Adams and preserve his grip on foreign affairs.

Of the two, Dulles was less threatened by Nixon, whom he knew would be too worried about appearing power-hungry to overtly snatch control of foreign affairs from him. Since Nixon's only real involvement in foreign policy was his participation in meetings of the National Security Council, ordinarily he posed no major threat to Dulles. But as vice president, no one would question him if he decided to take command of the cabinet on behalf of the ailing president. What if he started poking around in Dulles's secret affairs?

Adams posed a much larger danger. He was seen as the power behind the throne in the White House, and no one would blink if he decided to assume control, on Eisenhower's behalf, of the one small area of policymaking that he did not already dominate. If necessary, Dulles could tolerate Nixon's leadership, knowing that his own vast experience would give authority to his complaints if he decided to push back. But it would not be as easy for Dulles to assert himself under Adams—Adams could be prickly. Twenty years in politics had made him an experienced and particularly vicious knife-fighter whose greatest strength may have been his lack of shame. Unlike most people in Washington, Adams was not burdened by ego. He did not care what people thought of him. If he was perceived as rude or callous or even deliberately mean-spirited in the pursuit of presidential business, so be it.

At fifty-nine, Adams was at the pinnacle of staff power in the White House. Though small in stature, he cast a colossal shadow. He had the cool, detached bearing of a man used to being in charge—and he looked the part, with his shock of white hair, compact athletic build, clenched jaw and steely blue eyes. He was a man of immense authority, with a temper to match. Those unfortunate enough to make him angry would face an assault of finger-snapping vitriol intended to cut deep. No one who worked for him in the White House left the job unscarred.

Adams was born in 1899 in a small farming community in eastern New Hampshire to a journeyman father who moved aimlessly from job to job. His summers were spent on his grandfather's Vermont farm, where he was introduced to the true meaning of hard work. After graduating from Dartmouth, he took a job in a logging camp. It was there, biographers think, that he acquired a talent for offending and alienating people. As a small man among brutish lumberjacks, he needed to be direct and imposing. His words had to inflict the blows that his modest frame could not deliver.

He was a man of contradictions. The Ivy League graduate and aspiring musician, who regularly attended the symphony and read poetry in his free time, often recalled with good humor being kicked in the face by a horse and losing his front teeth while logging. He wore flamboyant neckties, sheer silk socks and ill-fitting suits that hung from his sharp angles like cheap drapes in a storefront window. His speech had a calm, languid quality similar to a Southern drawl, but clipped with the economy characteristic of those accustomed to New England winters. His manner was sophisticated and yet pedestrian. It was as easy to imagine him in a tux at the opera as it was to envision him out on a brisk November morning, wrapped in flannels, pulling up lobster traps. His voice was deeper than you would expect given his size, and he sometimes spoke with his tongue pressed tight up against his bottom teeth as if trying to conceal a secret.

He pursued a career in government as a way to provide for his growing family. Although he eschewed the backslapping kabuki of politics, his rise was swift. Soon after being elected to the New Hampshire House of Representatives, he was elected speaker. He left briefly, to serve a single term in the US Congress, before returning to run for governor. During his second term as governor, he was persuaded to join General Eisenhower's campaign for president. Eisenhower was so impressed with Adams's abilities that he convinced him to resign from the governorship to work full-time on his campaign. When Eisenhower won the election, he made Adams his chief of staff and vested him with powers that rivaled those of past presidents.

Eisenhower assigned his chief of staff three principal responsibilities: (1) to oversee White House operations, (2) to control the paper flow in and out of the building and (3) to prevent all disagreements, big and small, from reaching the president's desk. The structure and procedures Adams instituted to perform these tasks would make him the most powerful man to ever work for an American president.

As Eisenhower's secretary of state, Dulles was the highest-ranking cabinet official besides the vice president, but he had good reason to tread carefully around Adams. As chief of staff to a man like Eisenhower, who delegated freely and who trusted him completely, Adams was the only man in the administration with the authority to reach into the portfolio of other staff members at his own discretion. If done by anyone else, such "poaching" of another's duties would be abhorrent, but Adams had been granted access to any matter worthy of Eisenhower's attention. In essence, this is what Dulles feared. He had created a bubble around himself and Eisenhower that he wanted no one—apart from his brother Allen—to penetrate.

To fully grasp the extent of Adams's power, and therefore the delicacy of the task before Dulles, one must understand the potency of a position like chief of staff when combined with the role of right hand to the president. The president's chief of staff is not always his or her right hand. But, in Adams's case, he was. His portfolio covered almost all aspects of the president's policy and political work. Eisenhower did not want to be bothered with detail, so he gave Adams the responsibility of determining what to deal with on his own and what, on the other hand, rose to the level of the president's attention. This responsibility comprised everything from whom Eisenhower met with, to what policy recommendations reached his desk, to what Eisenhower read. Their arrangement went both ways. Adams kept unnecessary detail away from Eisenhower, and the president would not even read a policy brief unless Adams had read it first and visibly indicated his recommendation on the page. Since Eisenhower disliked reading long documents, Adams would distill them into single-page reports. This process practically ensured that Adams had the final say on most issues before they reached the president.

This was not the only source of Adams's power. Eisenhower abhorred politics and counted few politicians among his close friends. Since Adams was the only member of the staff who had actually held a senior political position before joining the administration, he was put in charge of maintaining relationships with important elected officials. Nowhere was this duty more important than in the patronage system presidents use to reward friends of the administration—which itself can be an enormous source of power. Not only did Adams do the hiring and firing for Eisenhower, he vetted and personally approved political appointees at all levels. Eisenhower, for the most part, simply signed off on Adams's recommendations.

To manage the paper flow in and out of the White House, Adams devised an intricate process to oversee the advancement of recommendations from agencies. All policy initiatives that were to fall under the eye of the president would systematically traverse every relevant agency for input before a final recommendation document was generated for Adams to give to the president. For Eisenhower, the underlying assumption was that Adams had a very good reason for the recommendation he was making. Thus he often signed off without question.

As Eisenhower's gatekeeper, Adams personally approved most meetings with the president—even the ones with senior cabinet officials. Adams determined who got in, how long they stayed and what was discussed. The only person exempted from this process was Secretary Dulles. He alone was permitted to make unsolicited calls to Eisenhower and schedule private meetings with him. Eisenhower viewed Dulles as a mentor and afforded him a level of autonomy over foreign affairs similar to that which he granted Adams over domestic affairs. An important difference, however, was that Dulles was required to provide hour-by-hour updates on developments. Adams was not subjected to the same reporting requirement. Furthermore, Adams had the authority to reach into Dulles and Eisenhower's special partnership if the matter they were dealing with could be interpreted as political. A frequent problem for Dulles was that Adams was given to a broad definition of the word "political."

In the first years of Eisenhower's administration, Dulles could count on getting his way on foreign-policy matters. After Eisenhower's heart attack, he feared that foreign affairs could become subject to decision-making by consensus among cabinet members or, worse still, that he could lose control over foreign affairs completely. Before Eisenhower's illness, urgent national security matters were often discussed in a group setting, but Dulles and Eisenhower would decide together in private how to resolve the issues. In those first critical days after the president's hospitalization, when everyone was scrambling, Dulles's number-one priority was securing his grasp on the area of influence he had carved out for himself.

John Foster Dulles and his brother Allen could easily be described as the very definition of the "ugly American." Their arrogance and refusal to even countenance the idea that non-Western cultures were worthy of an equal political footing with Western ones produced in them a prejudiced and myopic view of the world, which informed a dangerous foreign policy.

In many ways, the two brothers were opposites—Allen was charming and a notorious womanizer, and John was reserved and moralistic—but on the issue of which country should dominate global affairs, they were in full agreement. Modern observers are only now beginning to understand the great harm they did together.

John Foster was a devout Calvinist, and his faith determined his approach to life. In his youth, he was handsome, tall and lanky, with high cheekbones that gave his face a movie-star quality. He had an aloof, serious manner and a severe social awkwardness. In college, he had a crush on a male schoolmate, an attraction that he was ill-equipped to understand and that he only fully recognized when the other boy tried to raise their relationship to the physical.[6]

He developed a facial tic that would surface whenever he felt pressured, and he was given to over-blinking in an attempt to conceal it. He had a tendency to speak with his lower lip protruding—which, later in life, when combined with his hunched shoulders and large ears, gave him the appearance of an aging chimpanzee. At parties, he would often stir his drinks with his index finger and was once noticed squeezing candle wax into little balls and chewing on them.[7] He was a man of unquestioned intellectual gifts, but his discomfort in social situations made him prone to gaffes. Winston Churchill once described him as the only bull who carried a china shop around with him.[8]

In youth, Dulles was imbued with the belief that he bore a special duty in life: to go out into the world and eradicate the forces that threatened Western civilization. Decades of work at the international law firm of Sullivan and Cromwell, where it was his job to bully foreign countries into accepting the will of American corporations, only deepened his commitment to this mission. Once he was appointed secretary of state, this activist sentiment was the driving force behind an aggressive covert foreign policy that included the use of assassination and other cloak-and-dagger tactics, details of which were closely guarded at the highest levels of the administration.

Eisenhower's presidency is often described as an oasis of calm between periods of global political tumult, but recently declassified documents are beginning to reveal that Eisenhower led a tremendously active secret foreign policy that the Dulles brothers helped implement. His administration would be dubbed the "Hidden Hand" presidency for the ways in which Eisenhower was involved behind the scenes in global affairs. He used the CIA as a covert army to overthrow governments[9] and to install regimes friendly to the US. For Dulles, preserving his power in the cabinet after Eisenhower's heart attack was about not only preserving his standing as secretary of state, but also about protecting the secrets that only he, his brother Allen and Eisenhower knew.

With Eisenhower incapacitated, Dulles imagined that rolling Nixon would be easy. The vice president's relationship with Eisenhower was already on shaky ground.[10] But Dulles worried about Adams. The president was permissive of his chief of staff's "political" activities. Adams could be trouble if he chose to view Eisenhower's heart attack in purely political terms. Dulles had tangled with him before.

One time, Dulles had tried to appoint a Democrat, Benjamin Cohen, to an important post at the UN. When Republican leaders complained to Adams, he reached out to Cohen—without consulting Dulles, who was abroad at the time—and encouraged him not to take the position. By the time Dulles returned, the matter was settled, and there was nothing he could do about it. With the president in the hospital and the next presidential election not far down the road, what was to stop Adams from similarly declaring everything "political"?

Dulles also feared that Adams's dominance over cabinet affairs might affect his work. The chain of command put Adams in firm control of all cabinet matters; the staffers who handled the schedule and paperwork all reported to Adams. It was Adams's job to set the agenda for meetings and to ensure follow-up. Dulles feared that with the president out of the way, Adams's role might become even more invasive.

Dulles did not want to destroy Adams or even to usurp his power. All he really needed was to get Adams out of the way so that he and his brother Allen could go about their business without anyone asking difficult questions.

The instrument Dulles would use to marginalize Adams and the vice president was a simple one—a common press release.

Dulles had a law degree, but he was not really a lawyer in the traditional sense. At Sullivan and Cromwell, he had functioned more like a diplomat than an attorney. But anyone trained as a lawyer is trained in the writing of contracts, and Dulles must have recognized that getting the cabinet to approve a press release that codified cabinet operations in Eisenhower's absence would serve as a contract of sorts. On the surface, it would appear intended to put to rest any public fears about the smooth functioning of the administration during the president's illness. But in reality, Dulles was orchestrating what could be interpreted as a soft coup on paper. If Dulles could convince the entire cabinet, including Adams, to approve the press release, he would effectively marginalize Adams and Nixon. The contract ensured that no one, especially Nixon or Adams, would be able to disrupt any of Dulles's covert actions.[11]

Dulles drafted the release and presented it to Attorney General Herbert Brownell for comment along with the suggestion that Brownell get the views of the cabinet on the draft at the upcoming cabinet meeting. Having the attorney general read the release during the meeting would lend it authority, but, more importantly for Dulles's purposes, would make it seem less like a power grab. Neither Adams nor Nixon knew about the draft until the day Brownell presented it to the cabinet.

The weekly meetings of the cabinet were always well attended, but on September 30, 1955—the first meeting after Ike's heart attack—the room was swollen with officials of all ranks. Any White House staffer who could justify his attendance squeezed into any available space. The mood of the room was somewhere between opening night and a funeral. An apprehensive Dulles claimed his regular seat and waited for Nixon to call the room to order.

Nixon began the meeting at 9:30 a.m. by inviting everyone to observe a moment of silence. As he lowered his gaze to say a prayer for Eisenhower, Dulles's thoughts might have strayed from thoughts of the Divine just long enough to alight upon his own situation. Had he done a good enough job drafting the release to throw off any suspicions about his motives? What would he do if Adams or Nixon challenged the release?

Nixon broke the silence with a reading of the latest medical report of Eisenhower's condition. The president was recovering well and was out of danger. He had been removed from the oxygen tent and was sleeping comfortably through the night. The vice president then invited Dulles to report on any foreign-affairs matters deserving of the cabinet's attention. This was a routine practice to which Dulles was accustomed, and usually he would go around the globe highlighting all the issues worthy of note, but on this occasion his comments were understandably brief. He mentioned the turmoil brewing in Cyprus and then raised the possibility that the Russians were sending weapons to Egypt for use against Israel. He concluded his report with a short description of the recent foreign ministers' meeting in Geneva, after which he looked over at Nixon. The vice president then introduced the topic that everyone had been waiting for—how the government would operate going forward.

Dulles and Adams listened closely as Nixon suggested that work go on as normal and with dispatch, with an eye to avoiding logjams. He advised that all urgent matters be channeled through the NSC or the cabinet and that any other new business be placed on the back burner until the president's return. Attorney General Brownell saw this as the opening he needed to raise the issue about the draft press release.

The only part of the release that sparked discussion involved the recommendation that the chief of staff, Adams, leave immediately for Denver. Adams did not react, but Nixon did. He interrupted to question why Adams needed to leave at all. Nixon said he assumed that Adams would be in charge of the White House while the president was away. Dulles jumped in to argue that it was essential that Adams be in Denver because Adams was recognized nationally as the official most closely identified with Eisenhower and he needed to be near the president in the event that some influential outside person tried to take advantage of Eisenhower's reticence. Here, Dulles mentioned no names, but in his memoirs, Adams wrote that he believed Dulles was referring to the president's brother Milton, who was widely thought to be positioning himself for a run for the presidency.

Not wanting to appear discordant, Nixon quickly agreed and recommended that Adams's deputy, Jerry Persons, oversee White House operations in Adams's absence. Dulles scanned the room, prepared to pounce on anyone else who might want to challenge the press release. Adams said nothing. The document was summarily approved, and the cabinet turned its attention to other business.

As the meeting adjourned and he rose to leave, Dulles must have felt a tremendous sense of relief. He had just marginalized the vice president and chief of staff, and no one seemed to have noticed. We know now, according to Adams's memoirs,[12] that he did in fact notice, but no one objected strongly, because to have done so would have appeared uncooperative and, more importantly, no one had really lost anything. Dulles left the meeting confident that Nixon and Adams would not be sticking their noses into his affairs. In a few days, he would be on a plane to Paris to attend a meeting of European foreign ministers, while Adams would be harmlessly tucked away on the second floor of an anonymous building on the outskirts of Denver, waiting for the old lion to recover his strength.

Dulles may have succeeded in getting Adams out of the way, but Adams was hardly out of the picture. If anything, his proximity to Eisenhower only enhanced his power. A popular joke during the Eisenhower Administration captured the scope and scale of Adams's influence during the president's long convalescence: "What if Eisenhower should die and Nixon should become president? Worse still, what if Adams dies and Eisenhower becomes president?"

In the days ahead, Adams would tighten his grip on the White House and experience a level of influence the likes of which had never been seen. And there was nothing Dulles or his brother Allen could do about it.

III

Power by Proxy

When Adams arrived in Denver and saw Eisenhower for the first time, he found him cheerful but weak. Victims of acute anterolateral myocardial infarction—Eisenhower's eventual diagnosis—often experience severe fatigue. Without timely emergency medical care, they may suffer cardiac arrest and die. Eisenhower's heart attack was caught in time, but the episode left him unable to maintain focus for extended periods.

Adams left their meeting knowing that three main tasks lay before him: keeping issues away from Eisenhower until he was lucid enough to deal with them; matching the president's work schedule to his energy level; and controlling staffers' access to him. As a fan of the symphony, in his childhood Adams must have fantasized about what it was like to conduct an orchestra. Wielding Eisenhower's power by proxy like a baton, for weeks Adams would be the White House equivalent of a conductor—guiding the ebb and flow of events around the president.

Adams was Eisenhower's gatekeeper: he worked with the physicians to choreograph the flow of the president's visitors, by determining which cabinet members could visit and in what order. As was his custom in Washington, Adams attended many of these meetings to ensure that they stayed on point and that the necessary actions were taken as a result.

Adams controlled the president's reading: He had always managed the paper flow to and from the president, but during Eisenhower's illness, he was more selective than usual. In the interest of stabilizing his mood, Eisenhower was not presented with any information that might upset him. For much of his illness, Adams kept even newspapers away from the president.

Adams controlled the pace and intensity of Eisenhower's work schedule, slowly increasing the load as the president's health improved. Within a week of his attack, before Eisenhower could even walk, Adams brought in his first item of business—the approval of a list of "pre-approved" government appointees.

Determining what rose to the level of the president's attention and the packaging of policy presentations had always been an immense source of power for Adams, along with the benefit of being in the room when Eisenhower talked himself through important problems—at such times, Eisenhower did not need someone to guide his thoughts as much as he needed the feeling of urgency that came from having someone with him in the room; normally, Adams would sit quietly and listen as Eisenhower spoke. During Eisenhower's illness, it is not hard to imagine Adams guiding the president's thoughts and decision-making in a way he had not done in the past. Eisenhower had confidence in his right-hand man. Years spent leading large military operations had taught him the importance of people like Adams.

During his many visits to the White House as a senior army officer, Eisenhower had been surprised by the level of chaos and mediocrity surrounding Presidents Franklin Roosevelt and Harry Truman. When he became president, he brought Adams—whom he had worked with during his election campaign, and whose masterful administration of floor operations during the 1952 Republican convention had shown how disciplined and effective an organizer he was—with him to establish a formalized decision-making structure in the White House. The management process they developed together helped relieve much of the pressure on Eisenhower while he recuperated.

During this critical period in the nation's history, there was no staffer working more closely with the president and none more vital to the proper functioning of the government than Adams. He had always played an outsized role on the staff, and there were times when he was criticized for it. When Eisenhower was still healthy, Adams could always defend himself by saying that he was simply executing the president's wishes. As Eisenhower lay in bed in Denver, unable to sit up on his own, Adams's go-to defense must have lost some of its resonance.

The president spent seven weeks recovering in Fitzsimons Army Hospital and another six weeks at his 500-acre farm in Gettysburg, Pennsylvania. Historian Stephen Ambrose wrote in his biography of the president that he was lucky to have suffered his attack when he did—with Congress out of session and no events of urgent importance occurring domestically or abroad.[13] But of course, there were crises occurring in the US and around the world—the Soviets were selling arms to the Egyptians to be used against the Israelis, the French were at war in Algeria, the US had officially entered the conflict in Vietnam—and, at home, the Montgomery Bus Boycotts had begun.

These were undoubtedly events that would have been meaningful to Eisenhower and worthy of his full attention, but Adams kept them from him until he felt the president was strong enough. He handled what issues he could himself and left the rest for future days.

IV

Adams: Partner to Power

The White House chief of staff is a relatively recent invention, but its many precursors have existed since the Washington Administration. President George Washington had what was referred to as a "private secretary." In those days, the executive mansion was small (the White House had not yet been built), and there were few staff employees to oversee, so the president's private secretary, Tobias Lear, functioned as one would expect a modern-day secretary might—managing correspondence and appointments.

President Thomas Jefferson appointed the famed explorer Meriwether Lewis as his secretary. Presidents John Quincy Adams, Martin Van Buren and Millard Fillmore employed their sons in the role. Later, as the White House staff grew, the title changed to match the evolving responsibilities. President James Polk's wife, Sarah Childress Polk, was the first woman to serve as a president's private secretary. Given her extensive influence in the White House, one might stretch the definition and pronounce her the first female chief of staff, though some have reserved that distinction for Missy LeHand, FDR's personal secretary.

At the dawn of the twentieth century, the role expanded to somewhat resemble the modern chief of staff. George Cortelyou was President William McKinley's secretary, but, as mentioned in the prologue, his duties were wideranging and included overseeing the president's press operations. Later, when the White House staff mushroomed during the Great Depression and World War II, Louis Howe was appointed "secretary to the president," with responsibility for overseeing the growing staff and managing the policies and politics of the president.

Under Harry Truman, the title was changed to "assistant to the president," to settle a staff dispute (between Clark Clifford and John Steelman). Sherman Adams was the second person to hold the title of assistant to the president, but, in private, Eisenhower referred to him as his chief of staff. He rarely used the title in public, to avoid making the White House sound like a military operation.

The more memorable chiefs of staff have been the ones who oversaw major changes in how the position functioned or who added to its responsibilities in a significant way. Of the postwar presidents, John F. Kennedy had the fewest number of chiefs of staff—only one. And Obama had the most—five, including Peter Rouse, an interim chief of staff who happened to be the first Asian American to serve in the post.

The most powerful chief in history is Sherman Adams; the least powerful is either Ken O'Donnell, who functioned more as Kennedy's appointments secretary than as a chief, and Mack McLarty, who served in the Clinton White House during the brief period when First Lady Hillary Clinton's power was at its peak—more about this later. McLarty had a notoriously light touch when it came to management, and Hillary encouraged his appointment as a way to ensure her own influence in the West Wing.

James A. Baker has the distinction of having served as chief of staff to two presidents—Ronald Reagan and George H. W. Bush. He joined Bush to lay the groundwork for the president's reelection campaign. It would be the last in a long string of political campaigns of which Baker would serve at the helm and which his candidate would lose.

For the most part, all the men and women who have served in the evolving role of chief of staff, since Tobias Lear worked for President Washington, have done so with distinction and honor. The few possible exceptions include H. R. Haldeman, Sherman Adams (yes, Sherman Adams) and John Sununu.

H. R. Haldeman was convicted in 1975 of conspiracy and obstruction of justice for helping conceal President Richard Nixon's role in the Watergate affair. Haldeman might have gotten away with his crimes had President Nixon pardoned him as he requested, but Nixon refused. (In the end, Nixon was too worried about saving his own skin to worry about anyone else.) Sherman Adams was asked to resign in Eisenhower's second term after a congressional committee revealed that he had accepted expensive personal gifts. John Sununu was asked to resign under President George H. W. Bush for racking up thousands of dollars in personal travel expenses on government aircraft. (The White House counsel was able to convince Sununu to repay the tens of thousands in fees he owed only after persuading the Republican Party to tighten the screws.)

Sherman Adams will long be remembered as perhaps the most powerful chief of staff this country will ever know. Though a scandal ended his political career, in his role as the first fully formed White House chief of staff, he helped establish a tradition and practice that endures to this day.

Eisenhower respected Adams immensely and bestowed upon him a level of trust that is unimaginable in present times. If a less trusted person had been Eisenhower's chief of staff before, during and after his heart attack, his administration might not have survived. The next time a president would place so much authority in the hands of staff would not occur until almost three decades later, when President Reagan invited James Baker, Michael Deaver and Edwin Meese to help him run the government.

Eisenhower and Reagan are two presidents known for their willingness to delegate authority, though they had different reasons for doing so. Reagan was an extraordinary leader but a poor manager. As a consequence, he needed three men to do what Sherman Adams could do alone.

The team of Baker, Deaver and Meese—or the "Troika," as they would become known—was unique in American history. At no other time had staffers functioned in the way these three did for President Reagan. Separately, each man had immense influence, but together they were an awesome force. The president's number-one cabinet officer and secretary of state, Alexander Haig, would learn the hard way that it was a mistake to underestimate their power.

CHAPTER SEVEN

RONALD REAGAN & "THE TROIKA"

TO PLAY THE KING

President Reagan's secretary of state once confessed that Reagan was so dependent upon his staff that he was rarely seen in public without Baker (second from right), Deaver (right) or Meese (left) nearby in case someone were to ask him a question. Despite the fact that Baker and Meese frequently disagreed, the "Troika" was successful because Deaver used his influence with Nancy Reagan to act as the deciding vote. (Ronald Reagan Presidential Library)

It's true hard work never killed anybody, but I figure why take a chance?[1]

—President Ronald Reagan

*H*istorians *who rank Ronald Reagan among the greatest American presidents often point to his gift for communication, the clarity of his vision and his unwavering self-confidence as a source of strength and inspiration for generations of leaders. Reagan was surely an inspiring leader and perhaps even a visionary, but was he a great president? The success of his efforts to quell the Soviet Union is undeniable and well worthy of praise, but when President Reagan is measured against all the great men who have inhabited the White House, there is one area where he comes up severely lacking—people skills.*

Unlike the truly extraordinary presidents Franklin Roosevelt and Abraham Lincoln, Reagan lacked the talent, or perhaps even the will, to effectively manage the men and women who served him. Reagan was no FDR, who had a gift for identifying and exploiting people's strengths. And Reagan was no Lincoln, whose staggering skills as a manager enabled him to rein in legendary egos such as William Seward and Salmon Chase, who, had they worked for Reagan, might have torn the cabinet apart. Reagan hated conflict and avoided any personal interaction that required more than a superficial engagement. These are hardly the hallmark characteristics of an effective manager.

As far back as his days as California governor, Reagan had to lean heavily on his advisers for assistance. In the White House, he depended on the tightly knit trio of James Baker, Michael Deaver and Edwin Meese, who each addressed one or more of Reagan's biggest deficiencies in leadership: Baker compensated for Reagan's weakness as a strategist, Meese stood in for him as a policymaker and Deaver managed the interpersonal details that Reagan found so painful. At the dawn of the twenty-four-hour news cycle, when staged images were often mistaken for reality, this trio, or "Troika," as they would become known, fooled the public into believing that Reagan was more involved as president than he actually was.

In 1981, an unprecedented tax cut capped a highly successful first year in office for Reagan, and that success helped lift him—in the eyes of conservatives, at least—into the upper ranks of postwar presidents. But the Ronald Reagan most Americans remember today would not have been possible without the Troika.

The legend of Ronald Reagan was almost extinguished even before it had a chance to fully ignite when, on March 30, 1981, the Troika's greatest test and finest hour converged in the face of a major crisis. Less than three months into his first term, Reagan was shot coming out of a side entrance of the Washington Hilton Hotel by a deranged twenty-something who thought the act would somehow charm actress Jodie Foster into acknowledging his love letters. The incident would throw the White House into chaos and test the bond of Reagan's new team of advisers . . .

James Baker, Reagan's chief of staff, was the oldest member of the team. Largely distrusted by the "Reaganauts" for having spent much of his political career trying to defeat Reagan, Baker was a master political strategist whose personal power grew with each passing day in the White House . . .

Ed Meese, counselor to the president, whose broad and sweeping authorities made him—on paper at least—the Troika's most powerful member, was essential to the team in the early days, but as time progressed, it became clear that he was out of his depth . . .

And Deputy Chief of Staff Michael Deaver, "body man to the president," who served as liaison and interpreter for the Reagans, was so close to the president that he was treated like a member of the family. Deaver became what all presidents must have—a hatchet man, someone to thin the herd by cutting out staffers who proved ineffective or were no longer useful.

Together, these three men of no great distinction or accomplishment carved up the planet and divided the pieces among themselves in the name of Ronald Reagan. Nothing like the Troika had ever existed before and perhaps never will again.

I

Child Monarch

When former Speaker of the House Tip O'Neill once accused Reagan of being lazy, he was not referring to his administration. The large tax cut and Pentagon budget increase the Reagan Administration achieved in its first year in office is considered extraordinary even by today's standards. Another success, the administration's election victories, helped reshape the national political landscape for more than a generation. And this is to say nothing of Reagan's historic foreign-policy endeavors. What is important to note, however, is that most of these accomplishments occurred without Reagan's direction and often with only his minimal knowledge.

Reagan's widely acknowledged passive management style was due largely to the fact that he lacked the interest, and perhaps the energy, to be more engaged. It was not simply a matter of being unprepared. After all, the presidency is not a job for which one can ever really be sufficiently prepared. Nothing in President Woodrow Wilson's experience, for example, suggested that he possessed the knowledge or skills to lead the Paris peace accords. And yet, there he was, sitting at the big table, making deals and literally writing history. The same might be said of President Lyndon Johnson, the small-town Texas politician who found himself calling in airstrikes from the White House as the Vietnam War raged half a world away. Most presidents have simply thrown themselves into the work whether or not they felt they were ready. As President Harry Truman famously observed, the buck stops with them. Reagan had a different approach.

On the morning of August 19, 1981, in the skies above the Gulf of Sidra in the southern Mediterranean, two American F-14 fighter jets were fired upon by two Libyan warplanes. The American pilots immediately returned fire. In the span of a minute, the battle was over. As the F-14s returned to their aircraft carrier, USS *Nimitz*, two Libyan parachutes could be seen floating downward into the gulf— one of them aflame. Soon after, the US secretary of defense called the Century Plaza Hotel in Los Angeles, where Reagan was staying, to inform the president of the incident. It was 11:00 p.m. in Los Angeles, and Reagan was asleep. Ed Meese took the call. He saw no reason to wake the president.

As the commander in chief lay slumbering in the next room, Meese dealt with the immediate aftermath of what would become the first violent act committed by the US armed forces during Reagan's presidency. He determined when and how the American people should be informed of the incident, and he determined when to brief Reagan—around four in the morning, after which the president promptly returned to the warmth of his bed.

The media had a field day when it discovered how disconnected Reagan was from the affair. Reagan just laughed it off, yet it was a prophetic indicator of just how disengaged he would be in the years ahead.

Why did Meese wait so long to inform the president? Former *Washington Post* reporter and Reagan biographer Lou Cannon's assessment of Meese and the rest of the Troika was that "no one in the presidential entourage had confidence in the judgment or capacities of the president. Pragmatists and conservatives alike treated Reagan as if he were a child monarch in need of constant protection. They paid homage to him, but gave him no respect."[2] President Reagan was not informed about this international incident because, in the eyes of his closest advisers, he did not *need* to be informed. For Reagan, the presidency was a nine-to-five job.

In 1964, two decades before the Libyan incident, Reagan was staring down sixty and living a comfortable, though unsatisfying, life in suburban Los Angeles. He had enjoyed some success as an actor, but his career had sputtered, and he now found himself struggling to break the chains of the middle ranks of Hollywood stardom. A couple years before, he had been fired from his longtime job as a pitchman for General Electric for sharing his controversial views about the growth of the federal government. He had once been a strong supporter of the Democratic Party, but, if the legend is true, it was while traveling the country on behalf of GE that he experienced an ideological conversion, transforming him from a stalwart stump-man for the Democrats into the conservative "true believer" that we know today. By the end of the decade, he would ride that new-found conservatism into the California governor's mansion.

Whatever Reagan's motivation for leaving the movie business, he must have soon realized he was not quite cut out for a life in politics. His communication skills were outstanding, but government was possibly the least appropriate career choice for a man of his temperament.

Reagan was interested into politics only in the general sense, and he was not "political." A friend once described him as not the kind of person who sat around at the end of the day discussing politics over cocktails like FDR. Even at the apex of his political power, he was oddly indifferent to the process of governing. During the 1980 presidential transition, outgoing president Jimmy Carter arranged a detailed presentation for Reagan describing and explaining at length the particular issues and obligations a president has to deal with. Carter noted in his memoirs how utterly disinterested Reagan seemed in even the most urgent matters of the office. Reagan sat quietly and listened as Carter spoke, asking no questions and taking no notes. When Carter offered him a pen, Reagan declined. "I will remember," he said.[3]

He was even less motivated by policymaking. Reagan preferred to be the "pitchman," leaving the management of the pesky policy details to others. In his memoirs, General Colin Powell, Reagan's national security adviser during his second term, expressed the frustration that was commonplace among Reagan's closest advisers: "The President's passive management style placed a tremendous burden on us. Until we got used to it, we felt uneasy implementing *our* recommendations without a clear decision (from Reagan)."[4]

For a politician, Reagan was also unsettlingly aloof. Not just with strangers, but with everyone. Reagan's own children spoke of an impenetrable wall around him.[5] He could be charming and engaging in social settings, and he had the interpersonal skills suited to short, casual encounters, but he seemed to have little interest in anything deeper. His wife, Nancy, once said of him, "Although he loves people, he often seems remote, and he doesn't let anybody too close."[6] His longtime friend Charles Wick observed, "No matter how close anybody was to him, maybe with the exception of Nancy, his openness is such that there still is a very slight wall that you don't get past."[7] Reagan's distance made it impossible for him to attend to the delicate interpersonal matters that are an unavoidable part of effective management.

Some have suggested that his emotional distance was the consequence of a long career in the public eye. Others, including Nancy Reagan, have pointed to his childhood.

Ronald Reagan was raised by a deeply religious mother and a frustrated, alcoholic father whose difficulty holding down a job required the family to move more times than any child should. Ron attended four different schools in as many years. Even after the family finally settled in Dixon, Illinois, they lived in five different homes, making it difficult for Ron to build lasting friendships. He spent hours reading by himself, playing with toys, or alone in the woods nearby. Biographers believe he emerged from this period of his life completely self-contained and independent, seemingly without a need for close companionship. He liked people and enjoyed their company, but he was not dependent on them.

In 1964, as Reagan contemplated a career in politics, he must have known enough about the profession even then to realize that, on paper, he was not suited to it. He must have known that his detachment and his indifference to the process of policymaking might pose problems for him down the road. But his experience as president of the Screen Actors Guild and working for GE must have convinced him that, with help, he might succeed. So, he began to assemble a team of men and women whose qualities and skills helped him overcome his deficiencies as a policymaker and as a leader. Three men in particular would become vital to his success. Each of them had challenges of his own, but, together with Reagan, they would scale great heights.

II

The Privy Council

On a brisk autumn morning in 1981, Ed Meese sat alone on the small stage in the Old Executive Office Building, waiting for each of the thirty high school students to take their seats. They knew they had been granted a special privilege in getting to spend an hour with the counselor to the president of the United States, but the impressionable young men and women must have been disappointed when they realized that the man smiling back at them from the stage was the featured speaker.

Those expecting to see an impressive figure were greeted instead by an ordinary-looking man of middle age, with slumped shoulders and a slightly disheveled aspect. His blotchy and bloated face, ample midsection and meaty hands gave him the appearance of a neighborhood butcher. He might have reminded them of a favorite uncle or even their grandfather. Then, he started to speak, and they understood immediately why he was there.

As counselor to the president, Meese was responsible for helping shape Reagan's policymaking in all areas—domestic and international. Reagan's chief of staff, James Baker, and Meese had decided early on to share the responsibilities of running the White House, with Baker overseeing relations with Congress and the media and with Meese managing the Domestic Policy and National Security Councils. The sweep of Meese's responsibilities was immense, requiring more than a working knowledge of every imaginable subject that the president might encounter: interest-rate fluctuations, Supreme Court deliberations, crop prices, Soviet leadership turnover. As Meese spoke and responded authoritatively to questions on a myriad of subjects, the students recognized there was more to Meese than met the eye.

Raised in Oakland, California, in the last years of the Great Depression, Edwin Meese grew up the eldest of four boys in a strict Lutheran middle-class household. He attended Yale on scholarship before studying law at Berkeley. His first job after law school was in the office of the Alameda County District Attorney. It was while lobbying for the State Association of District Attorneys in the early 1960s that Meese first came to Reagan's attention. In 1966, after winning the California governorship, Reagan needed someone to handle judicial issues for him, and Meese came highly recommended. On the spot, Reagan offered him a job running the extraditions department, where he quickly gained a reputation for steady and reliable leadership.

Reagan was drawn to Meese's upbeat, easygoing personality and appreciated the patience he displayed when explaining complicated matters. Reagan grew to trust his judgment and his leadership, and Meese quickly rose through the ranks to become the governor's chief of staff.

When Reagan won the White House, he shocked and disappointed Meese with his decision to appoint James Baker chief of staff. For more than a decade, Meese had been Reagan's right-hand man, and Meese could claim a healthy portion of the credit for his election as president. As post-election DC watched the White House leadership chips fall into place, most observers shared Meese's expectation that he would be tapped for chief of staff. But, unbeknown to all but a handful of insiders, there was a secret effort underway, led by Michael Deaver, to prevent Reagan from giving Meese the job.

Deaver respected Meese's command of policy but thought he lacked the experience and organization skills to manage the White House.[8] He discussed the issue with Reagan's campaign chairman, Stuart Spencer, and together they decided that James Baker was the better candidate for the post. After Deaver convinced Nancy Reagan, together with Spencer, he and Nancy went to work on Reagan. Well acquainted with Meese's flaws, and understanding the need for an experienced Washington hand to manage his team, Reagan agreed to give Baker the post, but he insisted that Baker find a way to share the job with Meese.

As in Sacramento, Meese played a vital role for Reagan in the White House by stepping in to compensate for Reagan's flaws as a manager of the policy process. The problem with Reagan was that he delegated easily, but he never followed up with staff on issues he assigned them. He expected staffers to manage themselves. Additionally, his trust in staff, and his disinterest in the details, made him vulnerable to exploitation. It was dangerous to leave Reagan alone with a staffer. The viewpoint of the last person to speak to him on any given issue often prevailed. Meese understood this about Reagan and took over the supervision of the staff for him. To an eye untrained in the ways of Washington, Meese's broad portfolio may have appeared to make him the center of power in the White House—even Meese thought so for a while, but the real power center in the West Wing was James Baker.

Ronald Reagan might very well owe the success of his presidency, his reelection and perhaps even his lasting legacy to Baker's legislative accomplishments in the president's first two years in office. Reagan may have provided the vision, but he lacked the skills and the interest to translate that vision into actual policy accomplishments. Baker is widely considered one of the greatest White House chiefs of staff in history for his control over its internal affairs and his nuanced and agile handling of the policymaking process. As a member of the Troika, he was first among equals. He played Deaver and Meese like the master manipulator that he was. It has been said about Baker that you sometimes do not know he has played you until the game is over.

Despite Reagan's insistence, Baker had no intention of sharing power equally with Meese. He invited Meese to lunch on the first day to discuss staff organization and presented him with a rough contract he had drawn up that divided the leading White House duties between the two of them:[9] Baker would manage relations with the world outside of the White House, and Meese would manage relations within. Baker would retain the title of chief of staff, and Meese would be named counselor to the president. Meese would oversee policy, while Baker would be in charge of politics. As a cherry on top, Baker suggested that Meese have cabinet rank, which pleased Meese because he thought it meant he had parity with Baker. It would not take long for him to realize that cabinet rank was not all it was cracked up to be.

Baker gave up nothing of great value in his bargain with Meese. Meese had cabinet rank and control over White House policymaking, but Baker controlled all the real levers of power. As chief of staff, Baker had final say in who was hired and fired; Baker retained the traditional chief of staff office next to Reagan's, giving him immediate access to the president; Baker retained control of the flow of paper to and from the Oval Office, thereby controlling what Reagan saw and what was said to him; Baker could sit in any of Reagan's meetings, ensuring that he had a say in any decision; and Baker would be the White House liaison to Congress. This last responsibility was perhaps the most important. While Meese controlled the policymaking organs within the White House, Baker controlled the congressional ones—where Meese's policies went to grow up. The agreement between the two guaranteed Meese access and influence, but the real power lay with Baker.

Born into a wealthy family of Houston lawyers in 1930, James Baker came from a long line of master negotiators. He was named after his famous grandfather and family patriarch, James Addison Baker, who established a law practice that endures to this day and was a successful banker and a founding father of Rice University. Baker was taught early that he had a major legacy to live up to, but his mother and father gave him a good head start.

He attended the exclusive Hill School in Pennsylvania and received an undergraduate degree from Princeton before returning home to attend law school at the University of Texas–Austin. He served briefly in the Marine Corps in the early 1950s before accepting a job at a competing Houston law firm. Hoping to make it on his own, he chose not to work at the family firm. He married, started a family and began building a successful career helping make rich Houston oilmen richer. Then, tragedy struck.

His wife developed an aggressive form of breast cancer that quickly took her life, leaving Baker alone with four young boys to raise. By his own admission, during this difficult period he drank heavily.[10] He described returning home at the end of each day to a sad house where he had to maintain the semblance of hope as he tried to raise his boys without their mother. Each night, after putting them to bed, he would go to his room with a bottle of scotch tucked under his arm. This was his life until he got a call from his good friend George H. W. Bush asking him to run his campaign for the US Senate.

Bush lost the race. Nonetheless, Baker was given a chance to run President Gerald Ford's reelection campaign—which he also lost. He tried his hand at running his own campaign for Texas attorney general. Again, he lost. Bush gave his old friend another chance, this time leading his campaign against Ronald Reagan for the Republican nomination for president. Bush lost. Though Baker failed to ever run a winning campaign, he built up a reputation as a shrewd strategist and a talented administrator. After spending so much time trying to defeat Reagan, Baker was surprised when he got a call from the Reagan campaign inviting him to be the president's chief of staff.

Reagan needed someone who understood Washington and who could get things done. Everyone knew Baker was right for the job, but Reagan had yet to meet him. Deaver arranged for Baker to join Reagan during a flight on his private plane, and Reagan was impressed with what he saw.

Baker was fifty years old when they met. Despite his graying hair and sagging jawline, he looked far younger than his age. Regular games of tennis had kept him trim, enabling him to continue indulging his appetite for tailored, expensive suits. His kept his hair short and slicked back, making him look at once neat and sinister, like Michael Douglas in the movie *Wall Street*. Everything about his manner and speech and dress conveyed self-possession. He seemed like the type of man who did not ask a question unless he already knew the answer. His meeting with the president-elect was pro forma; he had already won the job, but both men must have known that Reagan needed Baker more than Baker needed Reagan.

After settling the leadership details with Meese, Baker got to work designing the legislative strategy for Reagan's first hundred days. Assembling a team of talented men and women and using the resources and access available to him as a member of the Troika, Baker focused on achieving Reagan's two most important campaign promises—a big tax cut and an increase in defense spending. With an untested Republican president and both houses of Congress controlled by the Democrats, Baker was setting an ambitious goal for himself.

Every call that came in from a congressman was returned personally by Baker; he cozied up to the media; and he organized a legislative strategy group comprising the White House legislative office, the Department of the Treasury and the Office of Management and Budget to ensure that no important congressional ring went unkissed. Importantly, he used Deaver and Nancy to keep Meese's policymaking aspirations in check—so as not to confuse the agenda. By the summer legislative recess of 1981, Baker could sit back and reflect on his extraordinary accomplishments that year. His efforts in those first hundred days helped secure Reagan's legacy in the minds of some as a great American president. And he had done it all with little direction from Reagan.

Nothing in the childhood or early adult life of Michael Deaver indicated that he was on a path to someday serve in the White House as a chief adviser to the president. Unlike his future colleagues, he would not attend an Ivy League school, serve in the military or earn an advanced degree. But what he did possess was just as valuable to a person committed to a life in politics—a genuine likability and an endearing sense of ease.

Growing up in lower-middle-class Bakersfield, California, Deaver was the son of a local civil servant and politician. After a less than remarkable high school career, he attended San Jose State University, where he briefly studied journalism before shifting to what he hoped would be the less academically challenging field of political science. Following graduation, he joined the IBM executive training program before dropping out to play piano in a San Jose bar. Approaching thirty and running out of options, he eventually tried his hand at politics and enjoyed some success as a campaign organizer before joining Reagan's 1966 race for governor.

Deaver walked into the headquarters of Ronald Reagan's campaign unknown to most of the people there. But one of the campaign managers soon recognized his strengths and how to use them. A friendly and pleasant man, Deaver was quick to smile, and, when he did, there was a charming, mischievous sparkle in his eyes. His voice had a beautiful, deep resonance and a calming, folksy cadence. His boyish charm, the campaign manager thought, might win over many voters. But, more importantly, it might win over Nancy Reagan, who was annoying the staff with her frequent meddling and constant nagging phone calls. So Deaver was assigned to "Nancy duty."

Winning her trust became Deaver's route to understanding and befriending her husband. With Nancy's help, Deaver learned Reagan's moods so well that by the end of the campaign, he could read Reagan as well as anyone on his staff. After Reagan won the governorship, Deaver took a job helping run his Sacramento office and eventually became one of Reagan's liaisons to the Republican Party. The job required Deaver to join the governor regularly during his frequent trips around the state on behalf of the party—raising money and supporting candidates. Spending so much time alone with Reagan further deepened Deaver's understanding of the man and strengthened their relationship. Through the years, as Reagan's personal "staff whisperer," Deaver grew to be indispensable to the Reagans, performing important social functions for them. If there was a family crisis or a problem with an employee, Deaver played a leading role in resolving it.

When the Reagans entered the White House in 1980, Deaver strongly considered leaving them to pursue a career in lobbying, but Baker encouraged him to stay on. Baker, although he had just been appointed White House chief of staff, had yet to develop a personal relationship with the new president and hoped Deaver would serve as his liaison to the Reagan family. Baker and Deaver first met during Reagan's unsuccessful 1976 campaign for the Republican nomination for president—Deaver was backing Reagan, and Baker was running the campaign of his rival, George H. W. Bush. Deaver was impressed; Baker, less so. When they met again a few years later, Deaver had changed little.

His mousy brown hair had receded a bit further and his frame had filled out a little more, but his narrow shoulders still gave him the profile of a person who, even in his early forties, looked as though he still had some growing to do. He was still wearing the same baggy suits that probably once belonged to his big brother, and his public comments still displayed the same careless disregard for facts that pegged him as the sort of man who was used to bobbing and weaving through life. But Baker needed Deaver, and so did the Reagans, so Deaver moved his family to DC.

When Baker, Deaver and Meese decided to join forces, Deaver never expected to be an equal, but, being so close to the Reagans, he became essential for the role he played in managing Reagan's relationship with members of the staff. It was a role Reagan himself might have played had he been a stronger manager and more tolerant of the sometimes uncomfortable interpersonal dealings that were necessary. One particularly difficult relationship involved Secretary of State Alexander Haig, who had become an annoyance to Reagan soon after taking office. Reagan wanted him out but could not manage it on his own. The Troika, led by Deaver, took charge, doing for Reagan what most presidents do with great reluctance—pushing out a cabinet officer.

III

To Play the King

Alexander Haig was an intemperate and reckless presence in an administration that prized teamwork, restraint and serenity. Seeming to ignore experience gained over more than a decade of service at the white-hot center of Washington power, he developed a reputation in the Reagan White House for being egocentric and self-indulgent. His actions over the course of his less than two years as secretary of state would do lasting damage to what had been an extraordinary career.

After graduating from West Point, Haig served during the Korean War under General Douglas MacArthur. Later he attended both the Army and the Naval War Colleges and briefly Columbia University before going on to receive a master's degree in international relations from Georgetown. He was a battalion commander in the Vietnam War and received the Distinguished Service Cross, the Silver Star, the Bronze Star and the Purple Heart. Before serving as a four-star general and the seventh Supreme Allied Commander of Europe, he was White House chief of staff to President Nixon. And, if anyone needed further evidence of his mettle, he needed only to remind them that he had been deputy national security adviser to the legendarily difficult Henry Kissinger.

At fifty-seven, Haig had the bearing of a man used to being in charge. He had mastered the duality of seeming both relaxed and intense at the same time. Piercing eyes gave his face a stern, no-nonsense urgency, and even at ease he had an air of authority. He dressed with the careful, deliberate elegance of a man who was probably self-conscious about being short, and he spoke with an affected accent that was designed, perhaps, to convey gravity. He gave the impression of calm insouciance, but in times of stress he buzzed with the coiled energy of a clenched fist.

On the night of Reagan's first inauguration, even before Meese had a chance to step out of his tuxedo trousers, Haig handed him a memo identifying himself as the administration's principal voice on international matters—even in those areas that overlapped with the domestic. Haig remembered how annoyed Secretaries of State Vance and Rogers had been by the constant poaching of National Security Advisers Brzezinski and Kissinger and wanted to prevent anything similar from occurring on his watch. In other hands, the memo might have been received as an earnest and helpful attempt to hit the ground running. But coming from Haig, who was quickly gaining a reputation for being difficult, Meese, Deaver and Baker interpreted it as a power grab.

Having been a chief of staff, Haig was undoubtedly experienced enough to understand how his memo might be misinterpreted, and his instincts must have warned him to tread carefully around the Troika, but something deep within him prevented him from doing so. It was as if he expected them to bend to his needs without his having to return the favor.

Haig's first serious conflict with the Troika was over the leadership of the

White House Crisis Management Team. His infamous memo to Meese envisioned his leadership of the body. Haig had received personal assurances from Reagan that he would be in charge, but as he started seeing signs that Vice President Bush might actually get the post, he complained—first privately, then during a congressional hearing. Deaver was incensed that Haig would go public with what he thought was an internal matter and commented to Reagan soon after the hearing that Haig was a cancer that would have to be cut out.[11]

In Haig's eyes, Deaver was the most frustrating member of the Troika. During the administration's first official visit to Europe, Haig, as secretary of state, expected to be seated close to the president on their airplane flights, but Deaver, who was in charge of protocol and logistics on the trip, saw to it that he rarely was. During ceremonial functions with Queen Elizabeth II and Prime Minister Margaret Thatcher, Deaver never positioned Haig close enough to the center of attention for his liking. Each time Haig perceived a slight, he threw a tantrum. Deaver claimed later (in his memoirs) to have been one of Haig's biggest supporters, but his actions, especially during the European trip, seem to suggest otherwise.

Haig was unaware that Reagan had grown tired of him and that he and the Troika had begun openly discussing his exit. Among his colleagues, Deaver appears to have played the most active role in orchestrating the secretary of state's departure. At first, his actions seemed more intended to urge Haig to get his ego in check, but later, Deaver's behavior became more aggressive.

Hoping to send a clear message, Deaver decided there needed to be a stronger voice in the West Wing on foreign-policy issues in order to compete with Haig's bluster and complaint. Deaver saw to it that Richard Allen, Reagan's weak national security adviser, was replaced with William Clark, who was an old friend of the president's and who had once served as his chief of staff in California. Deaver knew from experience that unlike Allen, Clark was capable of standing up to Haig. At first, Haig and Clark seemed to get along, but their working relationship began to fray once Clark started to make recommendations to Reagan that competed with the advice he was getting from Haig. After that, it was only a matter of time until genuine tensions developed between the national security adviser and the secretary of state.

By the time Haig had begun to add Clark to his list of complaints, Reagan had had enough. When the ax finally fell, the secretary of state seemed to be the only person caught by surprise.

Haig's ultimate removal took place over a couple of days in late June 1982. The combative secretary of state had a habit of threatening to resign during his complaint sessions with Reagan, and the Troika suggested that the president accept Haig's next offer to do so. They did not have to wait long. They arranged for Haig to meet with the president in the Oval Office, where it was expected that Haig would use the opportunity to lodge his usual list of grievances. As anticipated, during a rant about Clark, Haig again threatened to resign. The president's usual approach was to talk Haig back from the ledge, but this time he appeared to let the matter pass.

Then, the next day, following a reception in the West Wing, Reagan asked Haig to join him in his office. Haig was dumbfounded when Reagan unceremoniously handed him a letter accepting his offer of resignation from the day before.

Haig tried to convince the president that his threat to resign had not been serious, but Reagan would hear none of it. In the president's mind, the scene was over. The Troika had written the script and set the stage, and, as directed, Reagan hit his mark, delivered his lines and took his exit.

Haig was left standing alone as Reagan walked immediately into the press room where Baker and Deaver were waiting, having arranged a press conference. With the tone of a man who had just lost his best friend, Reagan announced Haig's resignation. Then, looking to his left, he introduced the public to his new secretary of state, George Schultz.

IV

The Troika: Partner to Power

Much is made of Andrew Jackson's "Kitchen Cabinet" and Abraham Lincoln's "Team of Rivals" as examples of successful White House partnerships. Perhaps it was one of these models that Baker was thinking of when he conceived the idea for the Troika. The difficulties he and his colleagues experienced trying to sustain their three-way partnership demonstrates just how challenging it can be to do so.

The role of the president's right hand may be too personal and demanding for the team approach to work. For a brief period, Baker, Deaver and Meese functioned as Reagan's right hand as well as might be expected of three strong personalities trying to fill a role traditionally held by one person. The team eventually disintegrated when Meese, frustrated by his frequent conflicts with Baker, disengaged. Soon afterward, Deaver regained his interest in working in the public sector, and Baker started putting out signals that he wanted to move to the Treasury Department.

There have been other such right-hand partnerships that, at least briefly, were effective, but none quite captured public attention like the Troika. Two partnerships during previous administrations are worthy of note: Haldeman and Ehrlichman, under Nixon, and Rumsfeld and Cheney, under Ford.

When H. R. Haldeman was chief of staff to President Nixon, he liked to refer to himself as the "president's son of a bitch." He worked closely with John Ehrlichman, an old college buddy who was Nixon's counsel and domestic policy adviser. Their control of access to President Nixon was so complete that White House aides referred to them as the "Berlin Wall." If Haldeman was Nixon's hammer, then Ehrlichman was his "extinguisher" for the way he put out political and bureaucratic blazes. The purpose of their partnership was to protect Nixon not only from outsiders, but also from himself.

The president was so socially awkward that he made even those with whom he had frequent contact uncomfortable. To offset the tension, Haldeman and Ehrlichman would tightly script his social interactions. Equally challenging for the pair was the president's tendency toward capricious decision-making. To prevent Nixon from doing unintended harm, they worked together to slow down the White House working process to ensure that the decisions Nixon made were indeed what he intended. Their briefly successful partnership came to an end when both men resigned because of their roles in the Watergate scandal.

Nixon's successor, Gerald Ford, initially functioned as his own chief of staff, but when he realized how impossible that would be to sustain, he hired Donald Rumsfeld, with Richard "Dick" Cheney as deputy chief of staff. Cheney and Rumsfeld inherited a disorganized White House distracted by bitter rivalries between Ford's staff and the Nixon holdovers. To protect Ford from disputes, Rumsfeld instituted a hierarchical system whereby only nine aides reported directly to the president—and Rumsfeld controlled even their access to Ford. According to historian and presidential scholar Fred Greenstein, Ford's management style was to "steer clear of jurisdictional rivalries, avoid having confidants within his cabinet, have private sources of advice outside the cabinet, and to leave 'management and program implementation to the department heads.'"[12]

Such a leadership approach strengthened the coordination function that Rumsfeld and Cheney performed. With his prickly, demanding personality, Rumsfeld assumed the role of Ford's hammer. Cheney's less challenging disposition complemented Rumsfeld's as they managed the White House together.

The forming of coalitions is a common feature of politics and policymaking, and it is no different at the White House. Reagan's personality and unique management style are the main reasons such an arrangement was necessary, but the willingness of Baker, Deaver and Meese to work closely together and to subsume their individual needs to those of the team contributed to their success. Given the nature of politics and the competitiveness of Washington, it is not difficult to understand why coalitions like the Troika are so rare.

That the Troika survived at all was as much a credit to the commitment of those involved as it was about the public's willingness to tolerate such an arrangement. Historians like Lou Cannon and Hedrick Smith helped make the American public aware of the Troika and its influence, and the public seemed, in light of the obvious shortcomings of the president, generally accepting of its existence.[13]

The Great Depression and the world wars had convinced Americans long ago that no president could do the job without the help of special personal advisers, and as prominent men like Colonel House, Harry Hopkins, Clark Clifford and Sherman Adams rotated in and out of the role, the public came to welcome, and even to expect, their contributions.

The next major iteration of the "right-hand man" occurred some years later, when Bill and Hillary Clinton entered the White House. Many First Ladies have played an important role in presidents' decision-making—Edith Wilson and Eleanor Roosevelt spring immediately to mind—but none was as conspicuously involved as Hillary Clinton. The public expects the president's spouse to be a significant force in his or her life, and few Americans were shocked to hear how influential Abigail Adams, Lady Bird Johnson and Rosalynn Carter were. But those were largely discreet relationships, while the Bill and Hillary partnership was out in the open for all to see.

Bill and Hillary entered the White House a perfectly balanced political partnership, tested by years of close and committed collaboration—a genuine team. When Bill became president, he assigned Hillary responsibility for one of his signature policies—the drafting of the ill-fated comprehensive health care reform bill. Few decisions made a larger impact on the evolution of the role of the president's "right-hand man." After Hillary, it was acceptable for the role to be held by a woman. Had it not been for her trailblazing service, there may have been no Condoleezza Rice, no Valerie Jarrett and no Ivanka Trump.

President Clinton felt confident enough in Hillary's political judgment and abilities to make her the administration's leading voice on health-care reform. His decision would have consequences far beyond policymaking—it would impact how Americans viewed the role of the First Lady, permanently change the political partnership Bill and Hillary had built together and seriously threaten their marriage.

CHAPTER EIGHT

BILL CLINTON & HILLARY RODHAM CLINTON

THE FIRST LADY

Dick Morris, a former key staffer to the Clintons, described their private personalities to biographer Carl Bernstein: Hillary, though she seemed cold, was actually the warm and caring one; Bill, who seemed more congenial, lacked authenticity and often merely reflected other people's emotions back to them. (Photo by Robert McNeely, White House Photographer; Carl Bernstein, *The Making of Hillary Clinton: The White House Years* [Austin: University of Texas Press, 2017])

If I get elected president, it will be an unprecedented partnership, far more than Franklin Roosevelt and Eleanor. They
were two great people, but on different tracks. If I get elected,
we'll do things together like we always have.[1]

—President Bill Clinton

*S*ome Americans are uncomfortable with the idea of their president del-
egating policymaking authority to his wife. They do not mind the First
Lady overseeing "family-oriented" activities such as the Easter Egg Roll or urging
American boys and girls to "just say no" to drugs, but they chafe at the idea of the
First Lady leading anything more consequential. To those Americans, Hillary
Clinton's emergence on the political scene must have been a nightmare.

During the 1992 presidential campaign, the Clintons liked to portray themselves
as a two-for-one deal. If their performance in the first year in the White House is
to be judged honestly, the concerns that some Americans had about their partnership may have been justified. Their misadventures with Congress while trying to
create a health-care reform bill rattled them both and reversed—for a generation—
the general public support for reforming the country's flawed medical system.
Americans would discover years later that many of the difficulties the Clintons
experienced in their efforts to shepherd the bill could be traced back to dysfunction in their marriage and the harmful power-sharing dynamic they had created
together.

After their meteoric rise from the "one-room shack" of a state house in Little Rock,
Arkansas, for a brief time Bill and Hillary reigned in Washington as the quintes-
sential power couple. Of all the First Ladies, Hillary was the first to be openly
and widely regarded as the president's right hand. Other presidential wives may
have performed this function in private, but Hillary did so in the full light of day.
She suffered many of the same criticisms that her predecessors, such as Eleanor
Roosevelt and Rosalynn Carter, endured, but President Clinton paid a price for
giving his wife such a prominent role in his administration. The price was both
political and personal.

After the Clintons failed to enact health-care reform, Bill no longer trusted Hillary's advice quite as completely.[2] Hillary lost confidence in herself and withdrew into a prolonged depression. Bill even suffered his own short bout with depression. Hillary found solace in writing the book It Takes a Village: And Other Lessons Children Teach Us *(1996); perhaps Bill's notorious affair with White House intern Monica Lewinsky served a similar purpose for him. The breakdown of their partnership was as educational for the president as it was for the First Lady. It highlighted their strengths and weaknesses as a team and revealed how unprepared they both had been for the political realities of Washington's particular brand of cutthroat politics.*

Both flawed individuals, the Clintons were each raised in dysfunctional homes and bore the scars of their troubled upbringing into the White House. It is in how they chose to deal with the consequences of their difficult childhoods that one can see the causes that would ultimately lead to their unsuccessful efforts as a presidential partnership.

Not all "right-hand man" relationships are perfect, and the bond of marriage is no harbinger of success, but the Clintons' partnership shows the dangers that can arise when the president's most trusted adviser and policy assistant is his or her spouse. Before she stumbled, Hillary stretched the boundaries of the office of the First Lady farther than anyone in history. She changed forever what it means to be a presidential consort and, in doing so, added yet another chapter to what it means to be the president's right hand.

I

A History of Violence

Noted author and social scientist Harold Dwight Lasswell believed that people who pursue political power are often pursued themselves by deep-seated insecurities.[3] If his theory is correct, the burdens of a dysfunctional personality may help explain why individuals like Bill and Hillary decide to seek lives in politics.

Lasswell's theory might also help explain the Clintons' dysfunction as a couple, their weakness as political partners and even their failure to reform the nation's health-care system.[4] Faced with the conundrum that was the Clintons, Lasswell might look to the trauma they each endured as children to explain their political and personal struggles as adults.

Although it was Bill Clinton who put Hillary on a path to politics, some argue that Bill would never have become president had he not been married to Hillary. A study of his life suggests there is some truth to this assertion. Friends of the Clintons point to the personality traits they shared as clear predictors of their success as political partners. Their shared values and ambitions were just the starting point. Even their individual goals for the future were complementary. "With Bill, you felt he just wanted to be president. Whereas Hillary had this religious zeal."[5] At her husband's side, Hillary added a bit of altruistic gravitas to his naked political ambition and, in the eyes of some, helped soften and legitimize his drive for success. They were suited to each other in more ways as well.

Hillary had more of a killer political instinct than Bill. He tended to avoid conflict, whereas Hillary was drawn to it. Bill preferred discussion and compromise, whereas Hillary's typical response was to square up and fight. Political strategist Dick Morris knew their White House dynamic well: "She has a quality of ruthlessness, a quality of aggressiveness and strength about her that he doesn't have. A killer instinct. Her genre of advocacy is always straight ahead— fight, battle, take the fight to the other side. There's no subtlety, there's none of the nuance that he has."[6]

Hillary had a natural pessimism that Bill lacked. She became his early warning system about whom not to trust. As a former campaign manager of Bill's explained their relationship: "Hillary has much more ability than he does to see who's with you, who's against you and to make sure they don't take advantage of you. He's not expecting to be jumped, but she always is. So she's on the defensive."[7]

To be successful, Bill needed someone with Hillary's qualities and skills. His strengths were her strengths—but, more importantly, in the areas in which he was weak, she was strong. The had both grown up in tumultuous homes, but while Bill's negative childhood experiences had softened him, Hillary's made her tough.

Hillary Diane Rodham was born on October 26, 1947, in the city of Chicago, though she grew up in the middle-class suburb of Park Ridge. Her father, Hugh Rodham, proudly paid cash for their first home after saving for years while living in a cramped Chicago walkup. According to Clinton biographer Carl Bernstein, Hugh was a classic misanthrope: moody, bitter, often demeaning and always judgmental.[8]

He also had a domineering streak. Even with friends, Hugh behaved like a drill sergeant. In fact, during World War II, his job was to oversee the physical fitness of US Navy recruits. In Park Ridge, he had a reputation as something of a loner. He would sit at home by himself most evenings, in front of the television, as life went on around him.

He had been brought up in a family of troubled souls. Once, he walked in on his younger brother who was trying to hang himself in the attic and saved his life just in the nick of time, by cutting him down. His other brother Willard never married and never left home. When their mother died, Willard helped care for their father until he passed. Willard himself died soon after—of loneliness, some family members thought.[9]

Bernstein thought the signs of depression that Hugh and his siblings showed may have been passed on to his children. Bernstein poetically described Hugh's sons as "walking adulthood in a fog of melancholia."[10] Biographer Roger Morris believed the Rodham children suffered borderline abusive behavior from Hugh, of a severity that would have crushed other children.[11] Echoing that sentiment, Bernstein describes how once, when the cap was left off of the family toothpaste, Hugh angrily threw it out into the snow and forced the person responsible for the offense out into the cold in search of it.[12]

Hugh withheld affection from his children and only reluctantly praised their successes. Once, when Hillary came home from school with all As and a single B, instead of lauding her achievement, he criticized her for having not done better. Her brother, a high school quarterback, once threw nine out of ten completions during a single game—a stellar achievement, in any other household. But after the game, Hugh needled his son about not completing that tenth pass. Hugh seemed to expect nothing less than perfection from his children. When Hillary joined the softball team, he took her to a ballpark and stood by unsympathetically, bullying her as she swung at pitch after pitch, trying to learn to hit a curveball.

The Hillary Clinton who rose to be one of the most admired Americans in recent history was tempered like fine steel by her father's constant negativity. If her critics regard her as mean-spirited or bitter, she may have her father to blame. But if people wonder where she got her grace and gritty determination, they have to look to her mother.

Dorothy Rodham's start in life was almost Dickensian for the extent of her suffering. Her parents, barely children themselves when she was conceived, divorced when she was eight. Dorothy was sent to live with her grandparents, who treated her like a servant. She once recalled spending an entire year confined to her room whenever she was not doing chores.[13] When she was fourteen, her grandparents hired her out as a live-in nanny to a nearby family. In return for caring for their young child, she was permitted to attend school, where she finally was allowed to flourish. Dorothy was an engaged and dedicated student. One of her lifelong dreams was to attend college—a goal she would not realize until well into adulthood.

After graduating from high school, Dorothy was invited by her mother (who had remarried) to live with her and her new husband. She hoped her well-to-do stepfather would send her to college, but he never did. Instead, Dorothy was treated no differently than she was when she lived with her grandparents. She left home as soon as she could, at eighteen, and found an office job in the city. Soon afterward, she met Hugh, who was twenty-six and in the navy. He was attracted to her beauty, she to his gruff exterior.

They married in 1942. In 1945, after Hugh was discharged from the service, they moved to the small apartment in Chicago where Hillary was born. By 1950, Hugh had saved up enough money to move the family to an impressive new home in the Chicago suburbs. Despite the difficulties of living with Hugh, Dorothy was determined to make the marriage work, for the sake of her children. Given her selfless commitment to her family, it may be no surprise that it would be Dorothy whose voice resonated the most with Hillary when she was considering divorcing Bill, and it was Dorothy who pressed her to stay in the

marriage.[14] Some might say it was inevitable that Hillary would encounter difficulties in her marriage given that she had such a poor example to guide her.
Dorothy did not have the luxury of family counseling to ease her pain, so Hillary
had to watch for years as her mother suffered emotional and verbal bullying from
Hugh in silence.[15]

Dorothy's love of learning became Hillary's. After a hyperactive high school
career, in which she was a member of the student council, played three sports,
wrote for the newspaper and was a high-achieving Girl Scout, Hillary went on
to study at Wellesley College. By the time she reached Yale Law in 1969, she
was already a national figure. She walked onto the campus known by many of
the women there as a rising young feminist after delivering a famous speech at
her Wellesley graduation for which she was profiled in *Life* magazine[16] as one
of the most notable graduates in the country that year. She was pretty, poised,
supremely confident and a genuine leader. It is no wonder that when Bill Clinton
met her in 1970, he was a little intimidated.

Some of Hillary's friends wondered what she saw in Bill; he was not sophisticated in the way they thought she deserved. But there was an instant attraction—he was whip-smart and boyishly charming. His friend Robert Reich liked to
make fun of Bill's aw-shucks good ol' boy qualities and the way he always seemed
to be telling stories about Arkansas. Yet it was precisely Bill's sense of place that
attracted Hillary to him. Other people she met at Yale carried themselves as if
they wanted to disown their humble beginnings, but Bill was proud of his roots.
Hillary was fascinated by his contradictions—he was part hillbilly, part Rhodes
Scholar. Every time they met, she discovered something new.

Bill Clinton was born William Jefferson Blythe in Hope, Arkansas, in 1946.
(Named for his birth father, William Blythe, he took his stepfather's surname,
Clinton, as a teenager.)

His mother, Virginia, according to some accounts, was a hazardously impulsive young woman[17] whose biggest cares tended to be clothes, makeup and
attracting the attentions of the neighborhood boys. She was bubbly, charming
and outgoing, with dark hair, an open smile and a spicy wit. She liked showy,
cocksure men, and they liked her.

When she met William Blythe for the first time, she was perhaps too over-whelmed by his good looks to notice that he was concealing a secret. Later she would learn that not only had Blythe been married three times, but he was still married to his third wife. It was wartime, and perhaps the sight of Blythe in a uniform clouded Virginia's judgment.

They shared a few passionate months together before his unit was shipped overseas. When he returned for good, he and the pregnant Virginia decided to make a fresh start in a new town. The twenty-nine-year-old Blythe was driving to Arkansas from Chicago to collect his bride when he lost control of his car and crashed. Weak and disoriented, he crawled from the wreckage into the shallow pool of a nearby ditch and drowned.

Pregnant and widowed at twenty-three, Virginia leaned heavily on her mother, Edith, a demanding, opinionated and temperamental woman who would jealously care for young Bill as if he were her own. The infant became a source of tension between mother and daughter, as each thought she knew best how to raise the child. Edith was the type of woman who would have had no problem sharing her doubts about Virginia's skills as a mother. Virginia realized that if she wanted total control over the rearing of young Bill, she would need to find a job and a husband. So, leaving Bill behind temporarily with Edith, Virginia left Arkansas for New Orleans, where she studied nursing. She was working as an anesthesiologist in a nearby hospital in 1948 when she was introduced to a car salesman from Hope Springs named Roger Clinton.

Again, letting her passions cloud her judgment, she overlooked Roger's drinking problem and plucked up her young son from the safe, nurturing home his grandmother had created for him and set him down in the tumult that would come to characterize his youth. Roger Clinton would prove to be a selfish, abusive alcoholic and a destructive risk-taker with a trail of unclaimed children and discarded wives. Young Bill came to call Roger "Daddy," but their relation-ship was always strained by Roger's violent behavior. During one particularly heated argument between Virginia and Roger, when Virginia threatened to leave, Roger took out a handgun and fired it above her head.[18]

Bill Clinton's biographers have pointed to his experiences in that house-hold as what fueled his drive into the hero-worshipping world of politics. Biog-rapher David Maraniss thought Bill fit into a category of children of alcoholics that has come to be regarded as the "family hero." Such children go out into the world to achieve success on behalf of the family in an effort to preserve the family's honor.[19] To say that Clinton was an overachieving student would be a gross understatement.

Aided by an almost photographic memory, his mother's cheekiness, charm and good looks, he was popular with the ladies and held so many academic and extracurricular honors that his high school principal barred him from running for class president so that other students would stand a chance. His gifts carried him forward on a wave of achievement, taking him first to Georgetown, then to Oxford as a Rhodes Scholar and then on to Yale Law School, where in 1970 he was stopped in his tracks by the makeup-less, bespectacled young Hillary in clunky suede boots, tight jeans and an oversized sweater.

Hillary was unlike any woman Bill had ever dated. He preferred the bubbly, big-haired type like his mother—ladies who got along to get along. Few people would describe the young Hillary as such a lady, but Bill was drawn to her nonetheless. He liked her directness and appreciated her brutal honesty. His mother did her best to deflect Bill away from the "homely, opinionated" young Hillary, but Bill would have none of it. He made it clear to his mother that if he married anyone, it would be Hillary.[20]

In the beginning, neither Bill nor Hillary was sure they would be a lasting couple. They each appreciated the other's gifts and recognized that their combined strengths might make for a formidable partnership, but Bill worried that, considering all that she could achieve on her own, small-town life in Arkansas might not be enough for Hillary. He knew that regardless of whether she joined him, he would be returning to Arkansas to begin a career in politics. He wanted her to come along but would have understood if she refused.

For Hillary, choosing to follow Bill would come with significant costs. She loved him, and she was convinced that he had the makings of a leader, but the realist in her knew that the path he had chosen might not work out. If she married Bill, she would have to stay with him whether or not he was successful. Had he been from somewhere rich in opportunities, such as New York City, the prospect might have seemed less risky. But by linking herself to a son of far-flung

Arkansas, she was potentially and perhaps irrevocably diminishing her chances of achieving success in her own right.

The 1970s were a tough time to be a career-minded American woman, but even women like Hillary, whose academic and professional achievements opened up opportunities unavailable to most, had a lot to lose if they made the wrong choice. Although more women than ever were entering into important positions in government, law and the corporate world, these opportunities were clustered in heavily populated areas where people had progressive attitudes. The South was a different story.

Hillary also had doubts about whether Bill would prove faithful. He had grown up in a household where infidelity was not uncommon. His mother and stepfather had each accused the other of stepping out on their marriage. Even as she aged, Virginia never let go of her party-girl attitude, and there was more than one man with whom Roger accused her of being overly friendly. Some, perhaps even Hillary, believed that growing up in such an environment was one of the reasons that Bill had a reputation as a bit of a womanizer. Hillary herself was not totally convinced his behavior would change once he was married.

For all these reasons, paralyzed with doubt, for two years Hillary strung Bill along while she weighed her options. To give herself time to think, she deferred graduation from Yale Law for a year so that she and Bill could spend more time together. She filled her time volunteering on George McGovern's presidential campaign and studying childhood development. Together Bill and Hillary graduated in 1973, and, during a trip to London that spring, Bill popped the question. But Hillary was still unsure. Since she could not make up her mind, Bill, who was planning to take the Arkansas bar exam, suggested that they take the exam together—just in case. She took the DC bar exam as well—just in case.

Bill knew that Arkansas would be a challenging place for someone with Hillary's personality. She could be a bit aggressive—a quality that was seen as unladylike in the Ozarks. He seemed to also worry about his ability to be faithful to her, given his wandering eye. "For the longest time, I'd thought I'd never get married,"[21] he once confessed. He liked his freedom, but he consoled himself with the belief that a marriage to Hillary "might not ever be perfect, but would certainly never be boring."[22]

Bill's family made no secret of their disappointment in his choice of Hillary.

They were used to seeing Bill with beauty-queen types, and the Hillary Rodham of the early 1970s looked like a throwback to the 1960s. One of her oldest friends, Sara Ehrman, described the first time they met.

"She had brown hair, brown glasses, brown top, brown skirt, brown shoes, brown visage, no makeup."[23] She had long, frizzy hair and she wore thick, heavy glasses that were her only sartorial flourish. She changed frames the way some women might change shoes. On warm days, when she preferred a T-shirt and sandals and hip-hugging blue jeans that showed off her girlish figure, it was easy to see why Bill was such a persistent suitor. But she was not just pretty; she was confident. When the petite young Hillary entered a room, she did so with an attitude bordering on cockiness. She walked straight up to a person and looked them dead in the face. Women did not do that in the 1970s.

Hillary's decision to finally marry Bill may have had more to do with the fact that she had failed the DC Bar than how she felt about Bill. She had passed the Arkansas Bar with ease, but the DC Bar was considerably more difficult. She was so embarrassed she kept her failure a secret, from even her closest friends, for decades.

Sara Ehrman could not believe the news when Hillary told her she would be moving to Arkansas. "No one moves TO Arkansas," she said.[24] Hoping to discourage her, she offered to drive Hillary to Fayetteville, where Bill was living, and took every opportunity along the way to persuade her not to stay. Hillary may not have been totally convinced that life in Arkansas was right for her, but she was sure that she would give it a chance. Nothing her friend could say would change her mind.

She was in love with Bill and moved by the clarity of his vision for his life. One day they were traveling past a home in town that Hillary told Bill she admired. The next time she saw it, Bill was escorting her over the threshold. He had secretly bought the home. It was too big for him to live in alone, he told her. He asked her to join him there, and this time she said yes. Their marriage would end up being far more challenging than either of them anticipated.

II

A Dangerous Pattern Emerges

The close political partnership for which the Clintons are known today took many years to develop and involved some significant defeats, beginning with Bill's first congressional race in 1974. Hillary played a persistent, though marginal, role in the campaign. From a phone booth outside of her office in Washington, DC, where she was working on the committee to impeach President Richard Nixon, Hillary would call Bill's campaign office almost daily with unsolicited advice. Because she was the boss's girlfriend, her suggestions were tolerated, but they were not usually followed. It was not until after Bill's 1982 campaign for reelection as governor that Hillary became a leading, rather than contributing, influence on Bill's campaign decisions.

As governor of Arkansas, Bill Clinton went into his reelection campaign filled with optimism. He achieved a number of successes in office that he hoped his fellow Arkansans would remember fondly on Election Day. There had been a few significant missteps regarding an unpopular road tax, but for the most part he felt good about his accomplishments. When his opponent, Frank White, beat him by thirty thousand votes, how the Clintons chose to deal with the defeat showed the differences in their personalities and influenced how they would function as a team in the years to come.

For days after his loss, Bill walked the streets of Little Rock in a fog, asking everyone he knew, over and over, "What did I do wrong?"[25]

The most frequent criticism he received was that he had tried to do too much too fast. He had championed education reform, regulatory reform and a statewide road improvement project that he hoped to fund with a new car registration tax. In his campaign for reelection, as he greeted factory workers each morning looking for votes, workers passed him by angrily declaring that he would never get their vote because he had raised their taxes. His opponent, White, pounded him about the car tax but got even more traction out of an explosive immigration issue—many Arkansans were irritated about the growing number of Cuban refugees being settled in the state. White ran campaign ads accusing Clinton of putting the safety of state residents at risk for the sake of foreigners.

Clinton's relative youth was also used against him. White, a late-middle-aged Little Rock banker, changed his party affiliation from Democrat to Republican simply for the chance to run against the younger Clinton. He told campaign audiences that Bill could not possibly relate to the problems of ordinary Arkansas workers because the recent Oxford and Yale grad had never held an actual job.

Despite White's growing support and the pummeling Bill was getting in the press, the polls indicated that Bill was on track to victory. Hillary had been too distracted by the birth of their daughter Chelsea to pay much attention for most of the race, but in the final days she realized that the reports she was getting from her own sources didn't match what Bill's advisers were telling him. She reached out to pollster Dick Morris for advice, but it was too late. When Election Day finally arrived Bill had to face the fact that he had suffered an embarrassing defeat, by a significant margin, in a statewide race, to a man who had never held elected office.

Hillary blamed herself. For years, she had ignored complaints about her plain appearance, East Coast establishment sensibilities and unusual fashion sense. Many Arkansans were confused by her insistence on using her maiden name in a state where such a practice was unheard of. Hillary realized that, because of her refusal to try to fit in, she bore some responsibility for Bill's loss. So she decided to change her appearance.

Gone was the hippie-inspired, free-flowing hairstyle. She replaced it with a short, sensible bob with blond highlights. Her thick, "Soviet party boss" eyeglasses were swapped out for contact lenses. She abandoned the boxy pantsuit uniforms she had taken to wearing in favor of soft, feminine dresses. She started wearing makeup, affected a Southern twang and changed her name to Hillary Rodham Clinton. Then she turned her attention outward.

She fired members of Bill's campaign staff and replaced them with old colleagues. She convinced Bill to reach out to the legendarily difficult Dick Morris for help. Morris had helped Bill before but been let go because most of Bill's campaign staff found him too prickly to work with. Those staffers were dismissed, and Morris was invited back. Next, Hillary turned her sights on Bill.

She convinced him to pick himself up, lick his wounds and run again—not in four or six years as others had suggested, but right away. For the first time, she would take active control over his campaign.

The Clintons' political partnership came into full bloom during the race to unseat Frank White as governor in the next election, in 1984. Bill played the candidate; Hillary played the strategist. The arrangement enabled Bill to give free expression to his welcoming, amiable side, and Hillary became his attack dog. When Bill balked at using negative ads against his opponent, Hillary forced him to accept their necessity. She took on all challengers and personally attended White's campaign rallies, where she stood in the audience and challenged any misrepresentation of her husband's record. She decided whom to hire and whom to fire. No significant media buy or major purchase took place without her sign-off. She shaped Bill's strategy, edited his speeches and approved his schedule. Dick Morris recalled a comment Hillary made to him about her role during the campaign: "[Bill] is too nice to manage his own life. He doesn't understand how venal people can be. He's not tough enough. I've got to move in and take this over."[26]

On Election Day, Clinton defeated Frank White by ten points. Losing that first reelection campaign had taught him many important lessons—not just about himself as a person, but also about himself as a politician. This time in office, he focused on shepherding a single, signature issue. Two years in the political wilderness had also taught him much about Hillary. He came to believe she was essential to his success. He was convinced that she possessed important skills and qualities that he did not and on which his continued success might depend. When reporters asked Governor-elect Clinton what he would focus on in the coming term, he was proud to say education reform. And he was equally proud of his pick to lead the effort: his wife, Hillary Rodham Clinton.

After Bill's victory, the Clintons might have thought they had stumbled upon the formula for political success, but their victory came at a price. During the campaign, a dysfunctional and self-reinforcing power-sharing dynamic emerged in their relationship.

Bill had become deeply and unhealthily dependent on Hillary, and she developed a sense of entitlement for having helped turn his career around. She felt she had earned the right to be regarded as a partner to his power. Placing her at the helm of his signature program was an expression of their new power-sharing arrangement. And, for a while, their partnership worked.

After winning a string of reelection races, they were heralded as the future of the Democratic Party. Their defeat of George H. W. Bush to win the White House in 1992 only strengthened their commitment to their partnership. As they arrived in Washington to claim their prize, they would learn the hard way that there were limits to their success—as they watched the explosive consequences of their joint decision-making imperil all that they had built.

III

The First Lady

As the saying goes, a chain is only as strong as its weakest link. The Clintons' dysfunctional marriage, laid bare by the stresses of the office, exposed their weaknesses both as individuals and as a team and contaminated their policymaking in the process.

Looking back on the Clintons' health-care reform efforts, one sees that failure was not always inevitable. Early on, polls showed a healthy public appetite for reform, and serious bipartisan opportunities emerged throughout the process that would have made possible some approximation of what the Clintons sought if they had only been more open to compromise. But compromise was not part of their vocabulary in those days. Ultimately, their efforts to reform the health-care system were undermined by intense secrecy, their personal power-sharing arrangement and their insistence on treating health-care reform like a war in which everyone was either friend or foe.

Hillary's dream of reforming health care met its official death on August 26, 1994. That was the day when Senate Majority Leader George Mitchell decided that there was neither the political will nor the time to move a bill to the Senate floor before Congress adjourned. After all the Clintons had suffered in their fight to draft the bill, Mitchell's decision was probably welcome news.

The Clintons entered the White House steadfastly determined to accomplish what had eluded so many other presidents that century.[27] With majorities in both chambers of Congress and with supportive poll numbers, the prospects of reforming the nation's health-care system seemed bright. But, from the start, the Clintons experienced problems—some of which were of their own making.

It was Hillary's idea to make health-care reform one of the main legislative goals of Bill's first year in office. Before the inauguration, she had expressed interest in having some sort of leadership role in the government, and after her wish to be White House chief of staff or US attorney general fell through, she proposed taking the helm of some important policy initiative instead. She wanted a high-profile role to play, comparable to the leading role she had played in the campaign. Bill agreed. He felt he owed her big for helping him win the presidency, and if health care was what she wanted, he was happy to oblige. Having witnessed her leadership of the Arkansas education commission a decade before, he had little doubt that she possessed the skills to see it through.

The National Task Force on Health Care Reform was officially announced by the president on January 25, 1993. Chaired by the First Lady, the commission was mandated to issue a report with legislative recommendations within the first hundred days of the administration. The president chose his close friend and fellow Rhodes classmate Ira Magaziner to be Hillary's deputy. The wealthy New York business consultant would join his notable organizational skills with Hillary's to get a handle on an industry that, in dollar terms, represented a sixth of the nation's economy.

The colossal scale of the enterprise was painfully clear from the start. Originally established with twelve people, the task force grew quickly to more than five hundred committed, if befuddled, advisers. Hillary parsed the number into twelve "cluster teams" and thirty-eight "sub-groups." Each group was charged with the task of examining one of seven important problems, crafting a solution and then presenting it to the other groups for review. All the best ideas would be gathered into a draft piece of legislation and presented to Congress for consideration before the summer recess.

To prevent leaks, Hillary insisted that all task-force meetings take place in secure conference rooms on the White House campus. Members were not permitted to speak to the press, their names were not made public—even to the other members of the task force—and discussion documents were carefully numbered and tracked. Senator Jay Rockefeller, a key figure involved due to his Democratic leadership of the Senate committee of jurisdiction, pronounced the operations of the task force more complicated than the invasion of Normandy.

Even working eighteen-hour days, seven days a week, the task-force members had difficulty crafting the legislation in time to meet Clinton's hundred-day deadline. Hillary put on a brave face, attending as many meetings as she could and building up a command of the subject matter that few could challenge. She met individually with federal and state officials, gave speeches across the country and testified in front of Congress, all in an effort to build support for the initiative. Under the best conditions, her energy, professionalism and commitment would have foretokened success, but dark clouds soon began to gather.

On February 25, a month after its establishment, the task force was sued by the Association of American Physicians and Surgeons. AAPS argued that the deliberations of such an important public issue as health-care reform, which involved such a large swath of the economy, should not be closed to the public. They sued for the opportunity to shape any resulting legislation.

Hillary had convinced those around her that to open her reform efforts up to debate would only slow down the process. She argued that the interest groups would have a chance to make their views known after the draft legislation was complete. Besides, she urged, groups like AAPS were just organs of the Republican establishment, and, since Democrats held the reins in both chambers, there was no need to be bipartisan on the front end. The Republicans would just have to grin and bear it until the draft was done. Then they could criticize the bill all they wanted.

AAPS also expressed concern that the First Lady, someone unaccountable to the voters, should have control over such an important government initiative. President Clinton had gone to pains to assure Americans that he was in complete charge of the health-care effort, but his promises were not enough. Everyone knew who was really in charge.

The following month, a district judge ruled that the proceedings of the task force must be open to the public.[28] An exception was noted for any work product generated specifically for the advice or personal use of the president, but all other informational matters, including the identities of the participants, had to be made public.

As details about the task force began to emerge, and the medical community came to understand the full scope of Hillary's ambitions, they were alarmed. Pooling their resources into a well-funded and carefully organized campaign, they focused on convincing the American public that the Clintons intended to destroy health care as they knew it.

The Health Insurance Association of America bypassed the administration and went directly to the American people with a slick TV campaign in which they introduced the public to "Harry and Louise," a fictional married couple who sat at the kitchen table after dinner struggling to understand the details of Hillary's health-care proposal. The ads accomplished what Hillary, despite her energetic efforts, could not: they explained the reforms to the public in simple, easily digested terms. Each night, during commercial breaks in their favorite shows, American families listened as "Harry and Louise" discussed the most troubling details of the Clinton plan.

As opposition to the bill grew, House Majority Leader Richard Gephardt, a Democrat, suggested to Hillary that she could ease the bill's passage by attaching it to the budget bill the president was currently drafting. Budget bills face comparatively less scrutiny in the congressional legislative process. Given the growing opposition to Hillary's bill, Gephardt thought it was far too controversial to pass as a stand-alone measure—even in a Democrat-controlled Congress. Inserting the bill in the president's budget would avoid a filibuster in the Senate, thereby easing its passage in the House. Hillary agreed. She conveyed the suggestion to the president, who understandably hesitated, fearing the safety of his own bill. Seeing that this was probably her best option, Hillary persisted. She might have succeeded in convincing him had Senator Robert Byrd of West Virginia not rejected the idea out of hand on the grounds that it would violate his famous "Byrd Rule."

The "Byrd Rule" is a long-standing tradition governing the treatment of budget bills. Under the rule, such bills, unlike other pieces of legislation, do not require the support of sixty senators to compel a floor vote. Instead, only a simple majority is required. But the Byrd Rule also mandates that such budget bills may not include "extraneous" matters—provisions that lay outside the purview of the committee of jurisdiction. Given that health-care legislation flowed through a different committee than the Budget Committee, Senator Byrd interpreted Hillary's bill as non-germane. He threatened to oppose any effort to attach Hillary's bill to the president's budget. His threat destroyed her best chance to move the legislation intact and without having to compromise on any of its elements.

As Hillary weathered the disappointing news, the "Harry and Louise" train kept chugging along, picking up converts along the way. To counter its popularity, Hillary came up with the idea of fashioning her own campaign, in the form of a nationwide bus tour modeled on the Freedom Rides of the civil rights movement.

The Health Security Express was actually a series of coordinated bus tours commencing in different regions of the country and timed to coincide with the congressional floor debate on the health-care bill. Cabinet officials and even the president himself spoke at the rallies, but at each stop, they encountered better-organized protesters rallying against them. During one of the tours, a bus funded by AAPS trailed Hillary's bus, stopping wherever she stopped. This embarrassed her, as it was intended to, to the point where she canceled some of the rallies.

Even with such well-organized opposition, health-care reform might still have succeeded, given the number of viable bipartisan alternatives proposed by others at the time. A spate of sympathetic congressmen and senators came forward with their own versions of Hillary's plan that, though they covered fewer people than Clinton intended, would have been a good start.

Not only did Hillary refuse to support the alternatives, she vilified their proponents for even suggesting that compromise was necessary.[29] For Hillary, it was all or nothing. Believing she held the moral high ground, with the long-term interests of the nation at stake, she refused to even meet on the subject. When an offer was made to cancel the "Harry and Louise" commercials in return for a place at the negotiating table, she refused.

So, in the summer of 1994, almost two years after the initiative began, health-care reform died unceremoniously. Not only did the biggest, highest-profile initiative of the fledgling Clinton Administration go down in flames, it became a rallying point around which Clinton's Republican enemies organized to take back the US House of Representatives. This key defeat would introduce a series of painful disappointments for the Clintons in the years to come—including an effort to impeach the president.

Though Hillary was the lead, the failure of the health-care initiative was as much the president's fault as it was her own. Even though it was his name on the legislation and his legacy at risk, the president might have done more to persuade Hillary to commit to the compromising necessary to save the project. Master politician that he was, he certainly recognized early on that the initiative was in danger, but he could not seem to change course or rein in Hillary's outsized ambitions.

Perhaps he was unwilling to challenge his wife at a time when they both were under attack from so many outside forces. Troopergate, Travelgate, Whitewater and the death of their friend Deputy White House Counsel Vince Foster were just a few of the difficulties they labored under to craft the bill. So many pressures on them as individuals, as a married couple and as a political partnership must have made it difficult for Bill to trim his wife's sails.

Outside pressures were only part of the reason the Clintons' reform effort failed. The challenges they faced as a married couple also took a toll. The first year of the administration was filled with political and strategic missteps, the provenance of which might be directly traced to the dysfunction in their personal relationship.

Clinton devotees are notoriously tight-lipped when it comes to the Clintons' marriage, but Dick Morris, the controversial politico and one of Bill Clinton's closest behind-the-scenes advisers in Little Rock and later in Washington, let some details escape. His personal observations on the Clintons' relationship offer valuable insights into how the pair operated and related to each other.

In his description of the Clintons, Morris suggested that guilt was a driving psychological influence in their marriage: guilt on Bill's part for his seeming inability to restrain his hormonal urges and Hillary's use of guilt as a means of control. The Clintons described by Morris were two emotionally stunted individuals who used demonstrations of love as others might use currency. If Bill Clinton needed someone, according to Morris, he would shower that person with attention. Otherwise, he could be elusive and emotionally distant. Morris believed Hillary's psychology responded to this emotional roller coaster–perhaps because of a similarly parsimonious nature in her own father. Morris also thought Hillary craved coming to Bill's rescue:

I think the big frustration of their marriage is that she's married to the most elusive, withholding, anal-retentive man you can imagine. He uses denial of affection as his method of getting people to do what he wants them to do—the ones he's close to—rather than to praise or give affection. I believe that it's a relationship in which she is . . . addicted to him. And she adores him. She's the best thing that ever happened to him. But he's very remote. And when he requires rescue she gets more attention, more affection, more love, more of the caring that I believe she craves from him, and also more power than she otherwise would get.[30]

Bill must have known that his complicated relationship with his wife affected his ability to manage her effectively and dispassionately as a member of his staff. But when she requested to helm his health-care initiative, he could not deny her.

Hillary's goal was a noble one: to make health care more affordable and available to the majority of Americans by combining federal and state participation with private-sector involvement. She hoped the end product would be a less costly and more efficient form of Medicare or Medicaid, covering everything from mental health to prescription drugs. Convinced the public was with her, Hillary charged forward, ignoring criticism even from within her own ranks. Refusing to kiss the rings of Washington power brokers and freezing out the media, she enveloped herself and the president in an echo chamber.

Though Hillary was in effect an employee of the president, in his eyes, he and Hillary were equal halves of a whole—"two for one." Not only did he believe she was partially responsible for his ascendency, on more than one occasion, he admitted that he believed Hillary was the one with the real talent in the relationship. Their experiences together had reinforced his belief that her participation in his career was a major reason for his success. This is to say nothing of the numerous times she literally pulled him back from ruin. And, of course, she was the mother of his child. Viewed from that perspective, Bill owed Hillary far too much to have any real hope of effectively managing her the way he might manage another staff member.

It also did not help that Bill was by nature conflict-averse. As mentioned, Hillary was drawn to a fight, whereas Bill preferred to find common ground in a conflict. This difference in their personalities served them well as long as they functioned as a team, but whenever they were up against each other, this dynamic put Bill at a disadvantage. He may have been reluctant to criticize Hillary's role on the health-care task force for fear of igniting an argument.

Making matters worse for Hillary, the president's senior aides were equally reluctant to challenge the First Lady. Health Secretary Donna Shalala, Treasury Secretary Lloyd Bentson, Communications Director George Stephanopoulos and Chief of Staff Mack McLarty all had major concerns about the initiative, but they quickly learned never to openly express doubts about Hillary's leadership, for fear that she might turn on them. Instead, the president's economic advisers voiced their concerns in private. They complained that Hillary's reform bill was "[b]loated with over-regulation, too ambitious in concept and too difficult to maneuver politically."[31] Even in the face of these strong criticisms, the president would not act—perhaps out of a sense of loyalty to his wife.

The size and scope of the legislation turned out to be major impediments to its success, but those problems were minor in comparison to the strategic miscalculations the Clintons made. All legislation bears flaws of some kind, but it might still become law if it is deftly maneuvered through the legislative process. Hillary made two crucial mistakes in this area from the start.

The first was her insistence on secrecy. Hillary justified her secrecy by insisting that in order to keep the process efficient she needed to conceal the debates, the identities of the participants and details of the meetings. On paper, secrecy may have seemed wise. Hillary was trying to prevent her opponents from getting information they might use to attack her. But, in the process, she unwittingly denied her allies in Congress the information they needed to buttress her defense.

Hillary's second crucial mistake was to be insensitive to the strategic reality that she needed to include Republicans in the shaping of the bill. Although many Republicans were against health-care reform, there were some who sympathized with her mission, and their support could have been mobilized to soften the opposition among their colleagues as well as among the few Democrats who opposed the bill.

Of course, the president had to accept some of the blame for how things turned out. Had he been a better manager and insisted that Hillary concede at key points along the way, he might have been able to salvage a stopgap solution, laying the groundwork for a gradual expansion of their plan later. Yet he supported the ring of secrecy Hillary created around herself and approved tactical decisions that his political instincts must have recognized were errors.

All presidential partnerships have their difficulties, but husband-and-wife teams in the White House bear a special set of challenges that can hamper the effectiveness of this special partnership. Having worked so successfully with Hillary in Arkansas, the president expected the same fluidity to exist in Washington. But DC is not Little Rock. If there is truth in President Barack Obama's comment that the presidency accentuates the qualities—good or bad— of the person who holds the office, the same might also be said of a president's relationships.

IV

Hillary Rodham Clinton: Partner to Power

The act of criticizing the president for permitting his wife to play too prominent a role in his policymaking may go back as far as Abigail Adams, the nation's second First Lady and arguably the first to function in the role as it is understood today.

Most of the assistance Abigail provided her husband was discreet. She would give him thoughtful advice behind the scenes or in their correspondence. In the days when John Adams was serving in the Continental Congress, for example, Abigail would include in her letters to him news about how the people in Massachusetts were viewing his efforts in Philadelphia. She would help interpret the local news for him and offer ways he might use the information to inform his conduct in the Assembly. She continued to act as his "eyes on the ground" when he was appointed ambassador to Paris. Later, when Adams became president, he consulted Abigail on his appointments, allowed her to read and comment on secret diplomatic dispatches and involved her in important domestic-policy decisions. Abigail was a leading influence, for example, on Adams's decision to support the controversial Alien and Sedition Acts.

By the 1840s, the public was more receptive to First Ladies openly advising their husbands. But, had the public been fully aware of the extent of the working partnership between President James K. Polk and his wife, Sarah, they might not have been so welcoming. From the very beginning of Polk's career, Sarah was involved in all aspects of his political life. When he ran for Tennessee governor and the US House of Representatives, she was his closest campaign adviser. In the White House, they literally worked side by side in the 1845 equivalent of the Oval Office. Polk later confessed that he rarely consulted his cabinet on issues; he relied instead on Sarah. One of their greatest achievements together was the expansion of US borders to stretch from the Atlantic to the Pacific—absorbing the Oregon, California and Texas territories along the way. Sarah was also the president's chief surrogate. She represented him at so many official and political events that his vice president, George Mifflin Dallas, once complained that she had more influence in the nation than he did.

In the early 1900s, politicians' wives were expected to actively and publicly support their husbands' careers, but Nellie Taft was more engaged than most. William Howard Taft probably would not have become president without her. It was true he was ambitious, but he would in all likelihood have been just as happy if he had never been elected president. His wife pushed him and took charge of his career, facilitating his election to the office. After his stints as secretary of war and governor of the Philippines (both jobs he had not actively sought), Taft considered retirement, but Nellie saw an opportunity to capitalize on his national profile. In a private meeting, she pressured outgoing President Theodore Roosevelt to support Taft's nomination for the presidency. Roosevelt agreed, and once Taft was elected, Nellie scaled back her involvement in his political affairs and settled into the more traditional role of a First Lady.

In the 1940s, Eleanor Roosevelt was often regarded as the most influential First Lady in history. Hillary Clinton has many times been compared to Eleanor Roosevelt, even by her husband (see the opening quotation of this chapter). Like Eleanor, she ended up in politics because of the man she married, and both women were dedicated to social causes. But the Roosevelts were not a White House team the way Bill and Hillary were. Times when the Roosevelts worked closely together politically were rare.

The first First Lady in the modern era to play an open and indisputably consequential role in the political affairs of a sitting president was Rosalynn Carter.

President Jimmy Carter once said of his wife: "There's very seldom a decision that I make that I don't first discuss with her . . . very frequently, to tell her my options and seek her advice. She's got superb political judgement. She probably knows the human aspects of the American people and their relations to the government better than I do. We have an absolutely unconstrained relationship, an ability to express our doubts and concerns to each other."[32] In a first for a presidential spouse, Carter appointed Rosalynn his special envoy to Latin America. In addition to helping ensure good relations with the region, Rosalynn was charged with encouraging Latin American leaders to improve their human-rights records. Carter leaned on her much the same way Polk had leaned on his wife. They discussed many major presidential decisions—especially on domestic affairs—and met at the end of each day and during their weekly lunches to discuss Carter's work. Rosalynn's sphere of influence spanned the domestic as well as the international. She headed a mental health commission for the president and even attended and advised him during the Camp David Accords. Her role as one of Carter's key advisers was not welcomed by all Americans. Although most had no idea that she sat in on cabinet meetings and participated in the negotiations at the Mideast peace talks, during her well-publicized tour of Latin America some accused her of overstepping her role. They questioned her qualifications and wondered why she was involved in such an important way in the country's foreign policy. Perhaps because of those criticisms, the First Ladies who followed her tended to stick to the more traditional aspects of the role. That is, until the Clintons arrived.

President Clinton was a trailblazer. He not only permitted his wife to serve openly in a position of genuine power, but also was among the first presidents to allow his vice president a powerful and public role.

In past administrations, for a host of reasons, presidents regarded their vice presidents as competitors and denied them full entry into their inner circle. This was not the case with Bill Clinton and Al Gore. Gore agreed to share Clinton's ticket with the understanding that he would play a leading role in the administration. At least in the beginning, they worked so closely together that their partnership made a lasting impact on the public's perception of the relationship between presidents and their vice presidents. When, during George W. Bush's 2000 presidential campaign, vice-presidential candidate Dick Cheney was promoted as Bush's right hand, many Americans welcomed him in the role, perhaps in recognition of the successful partnership between Clinton and Vice President Gore.

Dick Cheney became the most powerful vice president in American history. His managerial, organizational, congressional and White House experience made him a formidable force in the executive mansion. Though he would become a controversial figure after 9/11, his gravitas, vast experience and accountability made him not only an invaluable assistant to President Bush, but also a welcome change from the long line of shadow men who preceded him.

CHAPTER NINE

GEORGE W. BUSH & DICK CHENEY

RECONSIDERING THE VICE PRESIDENT

Starting in February 2001 and on at least five occasions
leading up to the spring of that year, Vice President Cheney,
one of Bush's principal advisers on intelligence matters in the
White House, was warned by national security staff that al
Qaeda was a clear and present danger to the US. Though he
was repeatedly encouraged to consider a military response
against the growing terrorist organization, he chose to
prioritize other matters. (George W. Bush Presidential Library)

Part I

> I didn't pick Dick Cheney because of Wyoming's three elec-
> toral votes.[1]
>
> —President George W. Bush

*A*t 10:15 a.m. on the morning of September 11, 2001, as the president of the United States cruised safely forty thousand feet above the US aboard Air Force One, watching looping news footage of a passenger plane flying into the Twin Towers, Vice President Cheney was issuing orders in the Presidential Operations Emergency Center deep beneath the White House. A military aide interrupted the vice president to inquire what to do about a suspicious passenger plane heading toward Washington that was suspected of being hijacked. Without skipping a beat, taking a breath, or consulting the president, Cheney ordered the plane shot down. The fact that he was not in the military chain of command and therefore lacked the constitutional authority to issue such an order did not seem to matter.

This chapter tells the story of the first months following 9/11, as President George W. Bush responded to the greatest national security crisis the country had experienced since Pearl Harbor. It is also the story of Dick Cheney's highly controversial tenure as Bush's right hand.

As the events of 9/11 unfolded, George Bush could not help but feel concerned about his performance. He was perhaps the least prepared president to face such a crisis in the history of American commanders in chief. His only significant foreign-affairs leadership experience up to that point had been at the head of a trade mission to China while governor of Texas, and his only military service was performed in the skies above Houston as a member of the Texas Air National Guard. He knew little of the inner workings of Washington, and his only executive experience as an elected official was holding perhaps the weakest governorship in the nation. Franklin Roosevelt had been president for almost eight years when the bombs started falling on Pearl Harbor; Bush had been president for not even one.

In many ways, Dick Cheney was the opposite of George Bush. Unlike the president, almost from the beginning of his career he had held a series of consequential posts in the federal government. And while he had not personally worn the nation's military uniform, he had served as secretary of defense during the first Gulf War. He understood Congress as a former high-ranking member of that body, and he understood the White House as a former chief of staff. On paper at least, Bush could not have picked a better person to serve at his side at such a challenging time. For critics of the Bush Administration, however, Cheney came to represent the dangers that can arise when a president allows an adviser too much power.

As Bush's right hand, Cheney played a pivotal role in many of the controversial decisions that characterized the nation's response to 9/11: his was a leading voice promoting what is now known to be a fictitious premise surrounding the call to unseat Iraqi president Saddam Hussein; Cheney pushed for the use of "robust interrogation" methods at secret CIA "black sites" abroad; it was Cheney's idea to forbid terrorism suspects access to US courts; and Cheney was among the strongest advocates for the establishment of a detainee facility at Cuba's Guantanamo Bay.

Even in the face of the vice president's considerable experience, Bush had doubts about deferring so readily to Cheney's leadership. But at the time, with questions swirling around the visibly unsteady new president, Cheney seemed to have all the answers. To the disappointment of many—including, eventually, the president—too many of the answers turned out to be wrong. After spending his first term giving his vice president a wide berth, Bush spent his second term marginalizing him.

I

Bush/Cheney 2000

Bush's personal story has a familiar arc: The son of wealth and privilege wanders aimlessly through life for decades, indulging his whims and rarely applying himself to any channeled aspiration. He stumbles from one professional failure to the next, experiencing a couple of brushes with the law along the way, until he suddenly finds his footing. Where Bush's story deviates from that well-known narrative is that he was able, in the span of a decade, to transform himself from a failed businessman and semi-professional alcoholic into a serious candidate for the presidency of the United States. What becomes clear in hindsight is that it was inevitable that he would become a national political figure. The events, influences and conditions in his life all pointed him in that direction. But he resisted as long as he could.

George Walker Bush, or George Jr. as he was often called, was born in New Haven, Connecticut, in 1946. His father, George Herbert Walker Bush, who was studying at Yale at the time, was the second son in an old and noble American family.[2] The Bush fortune, amassed in the 1920s by family patriarch Samuel Bush, would afford generations of Bushes access to the country's finest schools and most exclusive clubs. It also financed the huge family compound on the southern coast of Maine overlooking the Atlantic where the growing Bush brood gathered each summer to count their blessings.

Samuel's son Prescott would become a partner in the most prestigious investment bank on Wall Street and later US senator from Connecticut. His Senate seat would come in handy when grandson George Jr. decided to "swing for the fences" and apply for a place at Yale, where he had neither the grades nor the history of accomplishments to justify admission. His high school counselors advised him to consider a less competitive ZIP code, but George Jr. knew, even at his tender age, that such advice ignored his greatest asset.

His beliefs were confirmed as he opened his Yale acceptance letter that spring. Forever after, whenever he encountered a bump on the road of life, he would fall back on the family name.

In 1948, after graduating from college, George Sr. shuffled young George Jr. and wife Barbara off to Midland, Texas, where he hoped to find success in the oil business. He might have transitioned into finance, as so many other Bush family members had, but he wanted to make it on his own steam. At the time, oil prices were rising, and huge opportunities awaited those brave enough to try their hand at "wildcatting"—the highly risky field of oil exploration. His father's adventurous spirit and appetite for risk would make a lasting impression on young George Jr.

In small-town Midland, the Bush family folded comfortably into the local community. George Jr. and his siblings attended the public school, presented themselves scrubbed and oiled each Sunday at their neighborhood church and spent their Friday evenings with the rest of the crowd rooting for the local high school football team. The cowboy-boot-wearing, wise-cracking, swaggering "George W" who would someday become president was formed on the dust-strewn, rolling landscape of 1950s West Texas. Even after his father struck it rich and moved the family into a large home in an exclusive Houston suburb, young George clung stubbornly to his frontier sensibilities.

Because his father was away often, as the eldest of six, George was expected to help his mother with his younger brothers and sisters. He spent long periods alone with his mother, forming a deep bond with her. In course, he inherited her sarcastic nature, many of her mannerisms and her sharp tongue. In later years, George would fondly introduce himself at campaign events by saying that he inherited his father's eyes, but he got his mother's mouth. The bond between him and his mother grew tighter in the long, sad days they spent together after the death of his sister Robin from leukemia. George was eight at the time. After Robin's death, when area boys asked him to come out to play after school, George would often beg off, saying he had to take care of his mother. Barbara would confess years later that young George helped keep her sane through that dark period.[3]

Robin's death came as a complete shock to George. Biographers have speculated that her passing had a lasting effect on George's personality—making him acutely aware at a young age of the fragility of life. It might also have influenced the pattern of reckless behavior he would exhibit in his early adult life.

For the most part, however, his was a relatively charmed childhood. He faced no significant personal challenges until he was sent off, at age fourteen, to an exclusive boarding school in Andover, Massachusetts. Years later, Bush would pronounce his four years there as the hardest he had worked in his life before he ran for president.

George was poorly equipped for the academic rigors of Andover, and he struggled, but he was well liked and got on with the other boys. Being a Bush, he was of their world, but his West Texas strut and folksy manner set him apart. For much of his life, he would straddle the line between insider and outsider, leaning to one side or the other to suit his needs.

His difficulties as a student were not about intelligence. As he proved throughout his later life, he had the discipline and capacities to rise to demanding mental challenges. When he applied himself, he often succeeded; the problem was finding the will to buckle down and face the task. Although he could eventually count himself among the best educated presidents in American history, his lack of interest in his studies, beginning at Andover, would forever saddle him with a reputation as an intellectual lightweight.

To everyone's surprise, George Jr. graduated and was accepted at Yale, where he promptly gave new meaning to the idiom "Gentleman C." Despite his marginal academic performance and a reputation for overindulging in the ample diversions of campus life, he was tapped to join the prestigious Skull and Bones society. He would be the first to confess that his admittance was more in deference to his father and grandfather than to any individual achievement on his part. Bush's years at Yale flowed over him like a rippling wave of Milwaukee's finest. After graduation, he would never set foot on campus again until he was invited back as president to give the commencement speech. He was happy to reassure the graduates, as he acknowledged fellow attendee Vice President Cheney in the audience, that they too could rise from being a C student to become president. In his memoirs, Bush confesses that he accomplished little as a Yalie. After they handed him the diploma, he turned his back on the institution.

In the 1960s, while Bush was skipping class, halfway around the world other young men were dying in Vietnam. To avoid the draft, Bush used his family connections to acquire a coveted slot in the Texas Air National Guard, where he hoped to apply himself to the task of dutifully patrolling the "hostile skies" over Dallas. After a year of training, he settled into a life that looked little different than the one he had lived in New Haven. As long as he logged the requisite number of flight hours, he was free to do as he pleased. When he wasn't in the cockpit, he was partying with friends. Bush would serve in the Guard with mixed reviews for five years, transferring briefly to serve in the Alabama Guard while he worked on a political campaign there. He would eventually resign his commission to accept a seat in the 1975 class of the Harvard Business School.

The Harvard admissions office seemed not to care that Bush had so little business experience. A Yale diploma and a father serving as US ambassador to the United Nations certainly must have helped move his application along. Nonetheless, the news that he had been accepted at Harvard was something of a shock to his family. After his lackluster undergraduate career and uneven achievement as a Guard pilot, the Bush family could not be faulted for underestimating young George, who, it was becoming clear, had a drinking problem.

True to form, Bush was far short of a stellar student at Harvard. According to his classmates, he would often show up to class in cowboy boots and a leather National Guard flight jacket, with a mouth full of tobacco juice. Some also noticed his tendency to overindulge at local bars. After graduation, Bush landed dozens of job interviews but received no offers. He went back to Texas broke and jobless, but he was not worried. As a Bush, he knew, he would be fine.

While Bush was trying to figure out his next steps after Harvard, the man who would one day help him make history was undergoing a transition of his own. In 1975, Dick Cheney, despite having been a resident of Washington, DC, for only six years, was enjoying an extraordinary run of success. He had arrived in the city on a political science fellowship, hoping to land a short-term job with a member of Congress before returning to Wisconsin to complete his PhD. Whether he worked for a Democrat or a Republican did not matter to Cheney at that point. He had not yet developed a firm political leaning. By the time he and Bush met in the mid-1980s, however, he would be a standard-bearer for the Republican Party—espousing a political philosophy so conservative that those on the left often compared him to Darth Vader.

The first son of an enlisted navy man, Richard Bruce Cheney was born in Lincoln, Nebraska, four months before Pearl Harbor. His mother, Marjorie, and her family raised Dick Jr. while Dick Sr. was away during the war. When Dick Jr. was thirteen, his father moved the family to Casper, Wyoming, so he could take a job working for the US Department of Agriculture as a soil conservationist. Dick Sr. struggled to provide for his family on his small salary as a civil servant. He had hoped to take advantage of the GI Bill and attend college after the navy, but family commitments intervened.

The Cheney home was a modest one, even by Casper standards. The family car was an old Buick coupe without a rear seat, and Cheney and his younger brother had to fight over who got the better of two wooden boxes to sit in on long drives. In the summer, if Cheney's mother could not pack food for family trips, she kept careful records of their purchases on the road, to stretch their limited funds. Not much has been written about Cheney's relationship with his father. His official biographer, Stephen Hayes, struggled to show a close bond between them in his 2007 book, *Cheney: The Untold Story of America's Most Powerful and Controversial Vice President*. More is made of Cheney's relationship with his mother.

If Cheney inherited his laid-back attitude from his father, he got his competitive streak from his mother. In the 1930s Marjorie Cheney had been a member of a nationally ranked women's softball team called the Syracuse Bluebirds. As a boy, if Cheney wanted to play catch, he asked his mom.[4] She was the one who taught Dick and his brother to hunt and inspired his lifelong love of fishing.

Dick was a good student, but he was a better athlete. His high school transcript reflects his stint as senior class president, but Cheney later described his campaign as more of an afterthought than the subject of any serious effort.[5] Growing up in the 1950s, he liked to have as much fun as any boy his age. There were tongue-wrestling contests at the local make-out spot, where the occasional can of malt liquor was consumed. The problem drinker Cheney would become would not emerge until years later, after he was stripped of his scholarship by Yale administrators and asked to withdraw for poor academic performance.

Cheney had not planned on attending Yale. Like his captaincy of the football team and the class presidency, it sort of fell into his lap. Things had a habit of doing that for Cheney. To hear him tell it, he had not given much thought to college at all until a wealthy local man, and regional recruiter for the university, offered him a scholarship. The man had hoped to award it to Cheney's girlfriend,

Lynne Vincent, who was one of his favorite employees. However, since Yale did not admit women in those days, he did the next best thing and gave the seat to Cheney, the man he correctly thought would someday be Lynne's husband.

Cheney never seemed to find his place at Yale. He made friends and enjoyed campus life, but he struggled academically. After a difficult first year, he was not surprised when over summer break he received a notice that his scholarship had been revoked. He was welcome to return in the fall, but he would have to pay his own way. Cheney labored over the decision of whether to return. Though Yale tuition would be a hardship for the family, he felt a special burden to continue his studies for their sake. For the son of a man who had to abandon his own dreams of attending college, a chance at an Ivy League diploma was hard to pass up.

Sadly, Cheney's return trip to New Haven yielded the same result, and he received another letter. This time it was suggested that he take some time off to consider whether Yale was the right fit for him. He spent a semester laying cables for a Wyoming power company, drinking beer with friends and saving his money for one last try. He returned to New Haven in the spring semester, brimming with new confidence and commitment, but the result was the same. The next letter brought Cheney's academic career at Yale to an end.

Depressed and disappointed, he spent his days laying power cables, and his nights of drinking grew rowdy enough to land him in jail on more than one occasion. Hoping to arrest a developing pattern of bad behavior in the man she hoped to someday marry, Lynne delivered Cheney an ultimatum. Whatever she said to him that day was strong enough to motivate him to pull himself together. He committed himself to Lynne and to finishing his degree at the University of Wyoming. After graduation, they married and moved to Wisconsin, where Cheney was admitted to a PhD program and where Lynne also studied. They were on the way to settling into quiet lives as college professors when Cheney received word that he had been awarded a fellowship in Washington. His decision to accept would permanently alter the course of both their lives.

Two important developments occurred for the Cheneys that would have an impact not just on their lives, but also on the life of George W. Bush. First, Cheney got a job working for a Republican congressman who would eventually introduce him to his friend, Congressman Donald Rumsfeld. Second, six months later, when Cheney had the opportunity, he chose not to accept a job working for

Senator Edward Kennedy; had he done so, given that he had yet to determine his political identity, he might have become a Democrat. Instead, he ended up working for conservative Rumsfeld, who had recently left his seat in Congress to head the Office of Economic Opportunity in the Nixon White House.

The OEO had been created by President Lyndon Johnson as a part of his Great Society initiative, but Richard Nixon came into office determined to dismantle it. It was Rumsfeld's task as its new director to work his way out of a job by destroying the agency from within. Cheney was brought to Rumsfeld's attention as someone who had the skills and the discipline to aid him in the task. Years later, Cheney would pronounce Rumsfeld the most difficult boss he ever knew: He was insulting, terse and demanding. He had a habit of sending reams of memos—"snowflakes"—to employees in which he criticized their work and even their personal character. Rumsfeld was a hard-driving, mean-spirited taskmaster. They could not have known it at the time, of course, but in a few short years he and Cheney would be the closest of partners, occupying the upper echelon of Washington power. Rumsfeld would be White House chief of staff, and the thirty-three-year-old Cheney would be his deputy.

After Harvard Business School, Bush decided to follow in his father's footsteps and try his hand at the oil business. He had a rough start at first, squatting in a friend's alley apartment and mooching off members of the country club, but he was slowly able to make a little money buying and selling oil leases. Taking another page out of his father's book, he would eventually schedule a trip back east to ask friends and family for funds to start his own drilling company. He named the company Arbusto, Spanish for "bush." Years later, during his run for Congress, his opponent could always get an easy laugh at campaign stops by referring to the failed company as "Are-bust-o."

He moved into an apartment building in Houston popular with young singles and started making the rounds. His future wife, Laura, lived in the same complex, but they never met. As a local public school teacher, Laura Welch could hardly be expected to keep Bush's bachelor's hours. By the time they did meet, they were both in their thirties and ready to settle down. They went out for dinner and, though their personalities contrasted—he was restless and impatient, she was calm and passive—they knew they were right for each other. Within months, they were married and Bush was running for Congress.

To his friends and family, it was a surprise that Bush would enter politics. But in retrospect, all the signs were there. Bush had been working on campaigns since he was a boy, first in support of his father and later in support of others. He had transferred to the Alabama National Guard just so he could help run a Senate campaign there. Campaigning was in his blood, and he had the perfect temperament for the profession. He was folksy, naturally friendly and approachable. He was well educated, handsome and politically connected. Most of all, as a Bush, he could tap into huge pools of campaign funds. Despite having never run for office before, he won his congressional primary easily and lost the general by only six and a half thousand votes. A solid first effort.

Over the next ten years, Bush would grow increasingly involved in politics. When his father ran for president in 1988, George Jr. moved Laura and the kids to Washington so he could work alongside his father's campaign manager, Lee Atwater. They became close friends, and Atwater gave Bush valuable insights into the mechanics of campaigning. Bush would use what he learned to run four victorious campaigns of his own—for Texas governor in the 1990s and for president in the 2000s.

While Bush was building his political career in Texas, Cheney was a thousand miles away, busily attending to the coattails of Donald Rumsfeld. After the Office of Economic Opportunity, Nixon appointed Rumsfeld director of the Cost of Living Council, and Rumsfeld took Cheney along. When Nixon won reelection, Rumsfeld was appointed ambassador to NATO. He invited Cheney to join him in Brussels, but, this time, not wanting to disrupt the routine of his young family, Cheney declined. It would not be long before their paths reconnected.

When Nixon resigned in the aftermath of Watergate, incoming president Gerald Ford recalled Rumsfeld from Brussels to direct the transition team. Cheney was asked to pick Rumsfeld up from the airport on his arrival in Washington, and by the time the two arrived at Rumsfeld's door, Cheney had been offered a spot on the team.

The leap for Rumsfeld to White House chief of staff was an easy one. When

Ford asked, Rumsfeld accepted on the condition that Dick Cheney be made his deputy.

Spending so much time with Rumsfeld in Washington not only influenced Cheney's career, but also shaped his political ideology. It was under Rumsfeld's tutelage that he came to believe that government was the source of, not the solution to, most people's problems. At Rumsfeld's side at the OEO and CLC, Cheney came to share Rumsfeld's view about how inefficient government could be. "The entire experience created strong feelings that I have to this day about the government trying to interfere in the economy—it moved me pretty radically in the free-market direction, the importance of limited government."[6]

Rumsfeld also helped teach Cheney the art of bureaucratic knife fighting. One of the reasons President Ford had brought Rumsfeld aboard was to ease out the Nixon holdovers. Soon after his arrival, Rumsfeld started with the domestic-policy staffers. Ford wanted to hold off on firing the foreign-affairs staffers, for fear that it might have consequences for international relations, but as the 1976 presidential primaries approached, Ford decided he needed to appease the ultra-conservatives in his party and move more aggressively against unwanted senior foreign-policy staff. Over the course of a week, Ford replaced his vice president, defense secretary, CIA director and national security adviser, in a string of mass firings dubbed by the press the "Halloween Massacre." Only Secretary of State Henry Kissinger survived. Under Nixon, Kissinger had held the dual posts of secretary of state and national security adviser. Ford kept Kissinger at the State Department but stripped him of his NSC portfolio. Instead, he assigned this sensitive White House post to someone he considered to be his own man, Brent Scowcroft. The CIA directorship was given to his friend George H. W. Bush, Rumsfeld was appointed secretary of defense and Cheney was promoted to become the youngest White House chief of staff in history.

It is inconceivable that President Ford would have made such significant changes without Rumsfeld's recommendation and the help of his sharp elbows. Vice President Rockefeller certainly had his suspicions about Rumsfeld's involvement. He once told Ford that he thought Rumsfeld's decision-making at the time seemed geared toward making the environment more hospitable to his own ascendency. Pushing out Rockefeller, getting his own man placed as chief of staff and marginalizing Bush at the CIA would open up opportunities for Rumsfeld down the line—in case he wanted to get on the presidential ticket. Dick Cheney sat center stage as all of this played out. (The lessons he learned would come in handy when, during the first Bush Administration, he sat over at the Pentagon and struggled for primacy with Secretary of State James Baker. By the time he sat at George Jr.'s side in the Oval Office a decade later, Cheney had certainly honed his skills as a bureaucratic in-fighter.)

Another event that would have far-reaching consequences for Cheney involved Congress's systematic weakening of the office of the presidency in response to what had been seen as executive overreach by President Nixon. As President Ford issued multiple executive orders in an attempt to reclaim powers stripped from him by a Congress angry about Nixon's abuse of office, Cheney developed strong views about the relationship between the executive and legislative branches, views that would inform his decision-making for decades.

President Ford's 1976 loss to Jimmy Carter separated Rumsfeld and Cheney again. Rumsfeld turned his thoughts to greener pastures, and Cheney became a successful Wyoming congressman. He completed five terms, rising to the office of Minority Whip, before leaving to serve as secretary of defense to George Sr.

It might be a stretch to suggest that Cheney was ideologically transformed by his association with Rumsfeld, but he was certainly heavily influenced. If Cheney's personality combined his father's laid-back style with his mother's competitive drive, Rumsfeld should be credited for bringing his competitive side to dominate. If recent biographical sketches of him are to be believed, the young Cheney would have been happy simply to have married Lynne and been a college professor. Working with Rumsfeld seemed to bring out Cheney's intensity. The Cheney that Rumsfeld helped create worked six days a week, fueled by pots of strong black coffee and cartons of Marlboro Reds. He was sensitive to people's feelings, but he also was a killer when he needed to be. He was ambitious, but not ostentatiously so. He was discreet, loyal, good with details and calm under pressure—just the sort of person one might look to in a crisis.

George W. Bush first met Cheney during a visit to the office of the then Wyoming congressman in 1987. In advance of the Republican primaries, Bush was doing the rounds on Capitol Hill, seeking support for George Sr.'s presidential bid.

Cheney was a rising star in the House of Representatives at the time and avoided expressing open support for Bush's father, for fear of offending the other candidates in the race. He and George Jr. would cross paths again when Cheney was named defense secretary in 1989. When George Jr. ran for governor, Cheney was happy to write him a check, but the pair did not actually start working together until Bush was planning his own run for the presidency in 1999 and tapped Cheney to be his vice president.

If Cheney is to be believed, he did not want the job. He told Bush that there were many reasons his candidacy would not help the Bush ticket. He and Bush both lived in Texas, and the Constitution forbade the presidential and vice presidential candidates from being from the same state. Even if Cheney changed his residency back to Wyoming, the state only had three electoral votes, which was hardly anything to get excited about. Cheney also cited his run-ins with the law as a youth, his dismissal from Yale, his heart attacks and the fact that he had a homosexual daughter as reasons Bush might want to inquire elsewhere. Bush accepted Cheney's reservations and instead asked him to lead his search committee for a vice president.

Biographers have speculated that Cheney accepted the job of Bush's head-hunter because he had changed his mind about running and saw the opportunity to oversee the selection process as a way to shape the outcome to his advantage.[7] Only Cheney knows the truth, but if it was an act, then he certainly put on a good show. A number of extraordinary candidates were assembled and thoroughly interviewed, including Senators Lamar Alexander, John Danforth, Bill Frist, Chuck Hagel, Congressman John Kasich and Governors John Engler and Tom Ridge. Cheney also considered Senator Connie Mack of Florida but quickly moved on when the senator threatened to never speak to him again if his name appeared on the list.

The tax returns, health records and personal information of each candidate was gathered into binders for Bush to review. Cheney took a leave of absence as CEO of Halliburton, where he had gone to work after leaving his post as secretary of defense, to lead a team consisting of his daughter Liz and David Addington, one of Cheney's former DoD lawyers. Cheney and his wife flew down to Texas on a hot summer day to have lunch with Bush and Laura so that he and Bush could discuss the candidates privately. After reviewing the binders, Bush asked Cheney to reconsider his offer to run with him. This time, Cheney accepted.

For Bush, what made Cheney an ideal candidate was the fact that he seemed not to want the job to begin with. There were downsides to selecting Cheney, but to Bush's mind they were minor. Cheney's history of drinking and his failing out of Yale were both matters to which Bush could relate personally. Cheney's health history was serious, but neither Cheney nor Bush was overly concerned about it. A key deciding factor for Bush ended up being the issue of loyalty.[8] As Bush reviewed the list of candidates, he could see that they were all superior public figures, but he worried that he might have to compete with them while in the office. Because Cheney had no aspiration to be president, Bush was convinced that he would be the most loyal.

A final selling point for Bush was that Cheney possessed the qualities and skills that seemed to match his own personal deficiencies as a candidate. If a crisis ever arose during his presidency, Bush knew he could rely on Cheney's loyalty and experience. Of course, Bush was fully confident that he had the tools to be an effective president, but he must have figured it wouldn't hurt to have someone like Cheney on hand if things suddenly went sideways.

II

The Prince of Darkness

When the US was attacked on 9/11, Bush must have imagined that he had the perfect person to be at his side, but even with Cheney's gold-plated resume, it was not a foregone conclusion that he would play the role of right hand to the president during the crisis. Bush had assembled a gifted team of advisers, and he might have chosen any one of them instead.

Bush might easily have tapped his close friend and national security adviser, Condoleezza Rice, to be his right-hand woman. They worked, exercised and even vacationed together. Other than Laura, Rice may have been the president's closest friend in the White House. And, having worked for the National Security Council for George Sr., Rice had the requisite background in foreign affairs. But even with her experience, Bush knew that Rice did not compare to Cheney at stirring the heavy tectonic plates of government. And, though Rice was not new to government service, tactically she was no Henry Kissinger.

Later, long after George W. Bush had left the White House, George Sr. shared with his son the disappointment he had felt about Rice as an adviser.[9] As the elder Bush recalled, Rice had not been much of a bureaucratic warrior in comparison to Rumsfeld, George Jr.'s secretary of defense; Cheney, his vice president; or Powell, his secretary of state. They were masters of the rapier arts, with decades of bloody government battles behind them and the scars to show for it. The more conciliatory Rice was completely out of her depth in their company.

In light of Rice's inadequacies, Cheney eventually emerged as the best partner to power out of Bush's senior staff. Despite their strengths, having Rumsfeld or Powell serve as right-hand man was out of the question. As a result of the long, slow-burning conflict between Rumsfeld and Bush's own father— George Sr. long suspected that Rumsfeld had exiled him to the CIA during the Ford Administration to prevent him from emerging as a viable candidate for the vice presidency when Ford ran for election in 1976—Bush's relationship with Rumsfeld was strained. And though Powell, a man with a stellar reputation in Washington, would have been a masterful right hand, he and Bush were not close; also, importantly, Powell did not share Bush's philosophy about how to pursue al Qaeda.[10] Chief of Staff Andrew Card was well placed to be an effective right hand, but he was generally regarded as too nice. So, that left Cheney. Only he had the strategic relationships, the political reputation, the deep bureaucratic experience and the pugilistic skills to effectively serve the president in the challenges ahead.

Although they worked together closely, the relationship between Bush and his vice president was not a seamless one. Describing their friendship, Bush once said of Cheney, "We run in separate circles. Dick goes home to his family, and I go home to mine. I wouldn't call him a very social person. I'm certainly not a very social person either. So we don't spend a lot time socially together."[11] But Bush had tremendous respect for Cheney and viewed him as a mentor of sorts. Their respectful, often formal professional relationship worked well for them both. And, importantly, their partnership was aided by a shared determination to do whatever was necessary to avenge the victims of 9/11.

When he entered the White House, Cheney may not have planned to position himself to be Bush's right-hand man, but his efforts in the early days of the administration essentially guaranteed that regardless of how the power centers developed, he would be an important player in the West Wing. Remembering from his days as chief of staff how poorly Vice President Rockefeller had been treated during the Ford Administration, Cheney had already started crafting a number of levers of influence with President Bush. In an interview, historian Ron Suskind captured Cheney's efforts:

> During the transition, you see Cheney essentially sort of mapping territory. Certain people like [Treasury Secretary] Paul O'Neill or [Secretary of State] Colin Powell are like, "What's he doing?" Cheney was essentially creating the architecture in which George Bush would live as president. . . . Cheney would provide the framing and cosseting of Bush in terms of what Bush would have available to him.[12]

As the leader of Bush's transition team, Cheney ensured the placement, throughout the government, of people he knew would be friendly not only to Bush, but also to himself. In a similar vein, Cheney organized the vice-presidential White House staff to mirror the presidential staff. For each one of Bush's key White House advisers, Cheney had a counterpart on his staff who worked closely with the president's team. And to guarantee their access to information and resources, Cheney made sure that his advisers were given the title of "assistant to the president," the same as those on Bush's team.

Cheney requested, and was granted, carte blanche access throughout the government, making him a sort of roving counselor, able to attend any meeting he pleased—including any meeting that the president attended.

Understanding more than most the importance of proximity to the Oval Office, Cheney made his West Wing suite his primary work space. Vice presidents traditionally had an expansive sequence of rooms overlooking the West Wing in the Old Executive Office Building next door. Cheney retained those offices, but they were not where he reported to work each morning.

From the very start, Cheney cultivated the expectation that he would not be a merely ceremonial vice president in the mold of Lyndon Johnson or Dan Quayle.[13] He would be a key decision-maker, more like Al Gore or Walter Mondale.

Bush and Cheney may not have been close personally, but from the very beginning they functioned well as a team. Before 9/11, Bush made tax cuts and education reform the main priorities of his first term. He chose to handle education reform himself, given his experience working on such issues in Texas. To Cheney he gave the responsibility for crafting his major-tax-cut bill. Cheney was also made chairman of the president's controversial Energy Task Force, which was charged with creating a national energy policy aimed at reducing America's reliance on foreign oil. In characteristic Cheney fashion, the vice president kept the work of the task force so secret that Congress and the Government Accountability Office eventually had to sue the president for details of its proceedings.

Bush also made Cheney his enforcer. When the president decided that Treasury Secretary Paul O'Neill was not working out, he had Cheney deliver the message. According to O'Neill, he was meeting with his staff when he received an unexpected call from the vice president. Cheney told him, cryptically, that the president had decided to make a change in his economic team. After a brief pause, he added that O'Neill was the change. Then he concluded the call.

Bush also took the unprecedented step of giving Cheney sole responsibility for intelligence matters. During his interview for the PBS series *Frontline*, former *Washington Post* journalist Barton Gellman expressed surprise at Bush's decision:

> When Bob Graham became chairman of the Senate Select Committee on Intelligence, he went in a normal sort of courtesy visit to see Bush in the Oval Office. And some time during that first—and only—meeting, Bush told him, "Dick Cheney's going to be your point of contact in the White House. He has the brief for intelligence."[14]

Gellman was surprised to hear that the president would prefer not to take the lead on something as consequential and sensitive as intelligence matters. He could understand Bush might want to have Cheney's considerable expertise in the room during briefings or discussions on intelligence, but to delegate responsibility for the whole portfolio seemed bizarre.

Cheney organized an impressive constellation of resources for himself in the West Wing that essentially guaranteed his status as a key player, but perhaps the greatest source of his power was his understanding of Bush.

Being the president's right hand is about more than having access to the president or sharing his or her mission. As mentioned in other chapters, it is also about understanding the president's thinking. In Cheney's case, it was about fully sympathizing with the president's reasoning for doing whatever it took to protect the nation. Cheney understood Bush's need to have every tool available to him in the fight, and it became his mission to help Bush acquire those tools by any means.

Cheney was such a visible and active vice president that many in the media began to speculate that he was playing puppet master to Bush. David Frum, a White House speechwriter at the time, suggested that Cheney's influence over the president was as invisible as it was powerful. He compared watching Cheney in the role of vice president to seeing "iron filings moving across a table. You knew there was a magnet under the table moving things, but you did not see the magnet."[15] In reality, however, Cheney was only doing what Bush would have done himself had he the time and experience to do so. At one time or another, Sherman Adams, Clark Clifford and Alexander Hamilton were all accused of leading the president around by the nose, but evidence shows that, in every case, it was a false assumption. Like Cheney, each of those right-hand men had been acting in concert with his president.

In the aftermath of 9/11, Bush and Cheney expressed two main goals: to pursue those responsible for the attacks and to prevent any future attacks. These efforts would require strengthening the presidency in ways not seen since the days of Franklin Roosevelt. The lengths to which Bush and Cheney were prepared to go to achieve their goals would inspire criticism even from many of the president's closest advisers.

Many Americans were alarmed to read in the papers that Bush wanted to monitor and analyze their communications for reasons of national security. In addition, he wanted the authority to determine unilaterally the treatment of al Qaeda fighters captured on the battlefield, where they would be held and how they would be tried—even whether any hypothetical prisoners who were Americans would enjoy protections under US law or whether they would be regarded as stateless war criminals. Some of these powers Bush already possessed. The others would become a source of tension between him and Congress.

When their initial efforts to involve Congress in the decisions surrounding these controversial authorities did not have the desired outcome, Bush and Cheney decided they did not need congressional approval anyway. After all, this was a time of war. Cheney's many years of high-level government experience had convinced him that in wartime the president possessed almost absolute power.[16] He urged Bush to bypass Congress altogether and instead to work within the executive branch to secure the authorities he needed. The Office of Legal Counsel within the Department of Justice became the vehicle Cheney used to get legal cover for all the new powers Bush would exercise. The OLC drafted legal opinions for the White House that effectively made it unnecessary for Bush to seek the advice or consent of anyone outside of the executive branch.

In one area in particular, Cheney knew he would have great difficulty winning congressional approval—the wiretapping of American citizens. He knew the government possessed the means to locate and prevent the growth of homegrown terrorist cells with the use of the National Security Agency, but he also knew it was illegal to record and analyze the domestic communications of Americans. The vice president's office pressured the OLC to draft a memorandum granting the president the authority to use the NSA for this purpose, removing Congress from the process. The OLC complied, by interpreting Article II, Section II, of the Constitution as granting the president, in times of war, special "plenary powers" that enabled him to act almost without limitation in order to ensure the security of the nation.[17]

As Bush and Cheney responded to each emerging challenge together, they developed a tight working rhythm. One particular incident involving Cheney's lobbying of Bush to accept his recommendation for the treatment of enemy combatants illustrates their process and what each of them brought to the table.[18]

When Cheney wanted to create a military commission to try non-American combatants captured on the battlefield, he first approached Bush privately. Cheney thought that enemies of the state should not be permitted to access American courts, enjoy the protections of the Uniform Code of Military Justice or the benefits of the Geneva Convention. Cheney envisioned addressing this problem by creating a secret military court. After discussing the matter broadly with Bush, the vice president worked with OLC to draft a short memorandum describing how the commission might work. Later, during one of their weekly lunches, Cheney discussed his idea with Bush in greater detail. Observers remember Cheney arriving for his lunch with the president that day carrying a single sheet of paper and emerging afterward with that same sheet. Cheney had condensed the functions of the commission he envisioned into a short outline and presented the document to Bush for his review. After lunch, Cheney walked down the hall to his office and had the outline fleshed out into a four-page executive order that determined how all prisoners, including Americans, would be treated if they were designated "enemies of the State." Cheney and Bush discussed this sweeping and highly controversial new authority alone, without advice from Rice or Powell or Rumsfeld. Just Bush and Cheney, sitting alone in the president's private dining room.

When Cheney left that lunch with Bush, his thoughts were not about seeking out the president's national security team for comment; he was focused on swiftly translating the outline into an official document before the president left for a weekend trip. Cheney worked only with his own lawyers on the document. The secretary of state, the secretary of defense and the national security adviser heard about it later, the same way most Americans did—from the news media. As Marine One landed on the lawn outside of the Oval Office, the final copy of the executive order was rushed to Bush for his signature. The president quickly reviewed the text, signed the document and left for the day. This is how Bush and Cheney functioned. Bush relied on his vice president to handle this very sensitive matter, and he valued his work so much that, though the effort should perhaps have included the participation of the other key members of the cabinet, Cheney was permitted to do an end-run around them. This incident might give credence to the notion that Cheney had Bush on a leash. But anyone who knew President Bush knew that he was not the type of person who could be easily finessed.

White House staffer Matthew Dowd once commented, "If you spend any time around President Bush, you quickly realize he's not a guy who can be led around in that way, not at all." General Richard Myers, who served as chairman of the Joint Chiefs of Staff, shared Dowd's view. "This whole notion that the vice president was the puppet master I find laughable. He was an active vice president because I think he was empowered, but he wasn't a dominant factor. The alpha male in the White House was the president."[19]

Despite Cheney's considerable advantage of experience over Bush, he did not dictate to the president; he made recommendations. He saw his job as providing Bush with options. And since Bush wanted every legal authority available to him to pursue al Qaeda, Cheney worked to secure those authorities.

Cheney was chosen as right hand not only because his distinguished credentials compensated for Bush's shortcomings or because of his nuanced understanding of the process and inner workings of the federal government; he was chosen because he and Bush were of a similar mind on most matters, including presidential power and leadership. Each man knew his place and performed his assigned role.

Unlike Cheney, others around Bush tried to steer him in directions he did not want to go. Powell and Rice, for example, pressed him repeatedly to be more mindful of US allies when he made decisions. What they failed to fully understand is that in the early period of the "war on terror," Bush was genuinely willing to fight al Qaeda alone if necessary—he was not concerned about US allies such as Europe. He welcomed their support, but it was not Europeans who had elected him to protect their children at night.

The advisers who were successful with Bush were the ones like Cheney, who focused on executing his wishes instead of on guiding him down paths he did not want to follow. Pursuing al Qaeda would require more than a sophisticated manipulation of the levers of government. The person at Bush's side would need to be truly committed to Bush's vision. Bush wanted an aggressive use of all executive authorities available to him to fight al Qaeda. Cheney, as a committed right-hand man, devoted himself to delivering those powers.

III

Reconsidering the Vice President

Cheney's tenure as Bush's right hand, like all such relationships, eventually ran its course. As he grew more comfortable in his role as president, Bush came to rely less on Cheney and more on his other advisers—most notably Condoleezza Rice. The change in the Bush-Cheney partnership was gradual. Bush's working style would play a role in creating some of the distance, but a series of significant actions on Cheney's part, including his unwelcome pressuring of the president, may also have contributed.

A member of the boomer generation born after World War II, George Jr. had never experienced anything like 9/11. As he contemplated the extraordinary challenges ahead, he appreciated having someone of Cheney's wisdom and experience to guide him. But as the crisis matured, Bush discovered that, in many ways, Cheney was just as in the dark as he was.

After an initial spike, Bush's approval ratings began to decline sharply as Americans increasingly blamed him for pulling the country into a conflict with no end in sight. He grew to regret having been convinced by his vice president that invading Iraq would be a quick and relatively painless endeavor. Cheney, basing his recommendations on his own experience having led the fight against Iraq as US secretary of defense in the 1990s, insisted that stabilizing Iraq after Hussein's removal would be swift and the Iraqi people grateful. He was wrong on both counts. Each time Cheney's assertions were proven incorrect, Bush's doubts about his vice president grew.

For Bush, who prided himself on his instincts and who had initially resisted when Cheney and others tried to convince him to target Saddam Hussein, the failure to find the much-publicized "weapons of mass destruction" after the invasion convinced him to put more faith in his own gut. Bush had agreed with Cheney's assessment that intelligence reports seemed to indicate that Hussein had actively pursued weapons of mass destruction, but Cheney kept pushing Bush for action. He reminded the president that Hussein had used chemical weapons on his own people. And although no clear corroborating evidence existed, Cheney was convinced that the Iraqi president had not followed through on his UN obligations and destroyed the country's stockpiles of weapons. If he still had them, Cheney argued, what was to stop him from selling them to the highest bidder?

Further, although initially Bush agreed with Cheney that Hussein was a destabilizing force in the region and must be stopped, he would eventually regret letting himself be convinced that Hussein's activities made him an immediate threat to the national security of the United States. Cheney insisted that, were

Iraq destroyed, the US could establish in its place a friendlier government—an island of democracy in a tempestuous sea. Knowing little of regional history, Bush accepted Cheney's recommendation. Later he would learn that Hussein was nowhere near the danger Cheney had made him out to be.

Cheney also convinced Bush that Iraq's oil should be a source of concern and an additional reason to neutralize Hussein. He convinced Bush that the country's proven reserves gave the Iraqi president the means to fund terrorist activities around the world. Furthermore, oil wealth equipped Hussein with the resources to do harm to US economic security. At any time, Cheney argued, Hussein could use Iraq's oil to apply pressure on international markets and, by extension, on the US economy. There was no immediate evidence that Hussein was planning such an act, but Cheney believed it was possible, and he urged Bush to act.

The cooling of the relationship between Bush and Cheney was not all Cheney's fault. Bush's working style made him an easy target for the kind of hyperbolic advice that Cheney and others were adept at providing. As a self-styled man of action, Bush appreciated the argument that, in the wake of 9/11, the world had to see that Americans would not permit such horrific acts to go unpunished. Cheney, and particularly CIA Director George Tenet, argued that someone had to pay. Given Hussein's aggressive past behavior, he was a compelling target.

Bush also resonated to the argument that, visually, Iraq was a more attractive target than other countries that harbored terrorists. Unlike Afghanistan or Somalia, Cheney argued, Iraq possessed imposing physical structures that would present a striking image on American TV screens. Why send American pilots to flatten sand castles in Somalia, when the high-rises of Baghdad awaited just over the horizon?

Such arguments had weight with Bush when the hostilities were in the early days or while the war was going well, but as conditions on the ground worsened and bodies of American soldiers began streaming into Dover Air Force Base, Bush's reservations about Cheney's advice multiplied. By the beginning of his second term, as he drew closer to the end of his time in office, Bush started to consider his legacy. Did he really want to be remembered as the president who mired the nation in a decade-long war, bankrupted the country or isolated the

American people from allies abroad? All of these scenarios were starting to look possible. Bush decided to change course, and, as a consequence, his relationship with Cheney changed.

Bush began to ignore Cheney's insistence on war and began to open himself up to the recommendations of advisers such as Rice, who were recommending diplomacy over combat. Rice's appointment as secretary of state after Powell's departure signaled a clear shift in the president's approach to the war. In his first term, and with Cheney's help, Bush had laid the foundation for the global "war on terror." In his second term—this time, with Rice's leadership—he began to rebuild America's international alliances. Whereas in his first term, Bush had joined Cheney on the march to war, in his second he chose to follow the beat of his own drummer.

IV

Cheney: Partner to Power

Cheney was not the first vice president to function as a right-hand man. That distinction belongs to Martin Van Buren. Van Buren was the first vice president to have been personally chosen as a running mate by a presidential candidate—in this case, Andrew Jackson—and the first to be included as a member of the president's inner circle.

President William McKinley seemed to follow Jackson's example when he relied on Vice President Augustus Hobart as his "assistant president." Van Buren and Hobart represent points on a timeline of progress that has made it possible for vice presidents like Cheney to exist today. The transformation of the vice presidency from the marginal role it was during the Washington Administration to the central one it has become is the result of environmental, institutional and personal influences on the office.

The explosive growth of the federal government beginning in the 1930s and the attendant pressures on the presidency rank high among the environmental influences that have shaped the evolving perception of the vice president. Starting with FDR's administration, these factors made it necessary for someone of the most senior rank to be available to speak and act for the president in times of crisis. FDR wanted to been seen as responding to the problems of suffering Americans with the full resources of the government, and as he leaned on Vice President John Nance Garner during his first term, he was unwittingly expanding the duties of the office of the vice presidency in the public's understanding.

Another environmental factor, the growing popularity of television and radio, further raised the profile of the vice presidency—particularly after 1976, when official debates among vice-presidential candidates began to be televised. The Cold War and the dawn of the nuclear age had increased the importance of choosing a vice president capable of safeguarding the nation's security. Americans tuned in to the vice-presidential debates to judge for themselves whether these men and women were up to the task.

Institutional influences on the evolution of the office have included the Twelfth Amendment, which mandated that the president and the vice president be elected separately, and the Twenty-Fifth Amendment, which settled the issue of presidential succession. Prior to the Twelfth Amendment, whichever candidate for the presidency received the most votes won that office, and the person with the second-highest number became vice president. This created a situation whereby two people with potentially diametrically opposed political views might serve at the top of the same administration. When this practice was changed in 1804, it enabled presidents and vice presidents from the same political party to serve together—increasing the chances that they might establish a working partnership.

In 1967, the Twenty-Fifth Amendment helped clarify under what conditions a transfer of presidential power would be necessary and how exactly it would be conducted. President Eisenhower's heart attack and President Kennedy's assassination had elevated the urgency of resolving these questions. By tightening the institutional links between the office of the president and that of the vice president, the amendment helped raise the importance of the vice presidency. Both presidential candidates and the American public recognized that more needed to be done to ensure that vice presidents were capable and equipped to serve in the event of a constitutional crisis. Presidents began treating their vice presidents more like deputies as they included them in important meetings and briefings, increasing the opportunities for mutual consultation and collaboration.

Before President Andrew Jackson's day, vice-presidential candidates were chosen by party leaders. Starting with Jackson, as presidents began choosing their own vice presidents, personal considerations came into play. The chemistry between men and the extent to which they shared goals affected not only who was chosen but also how much influence he enjoyed. Carter was the first president to conduct thorough, long-term personal interviews of vice-presidential candidates. He eventually chose Walter Mondale because he appreciated his personality, ability and experience. Carter's highly active role in the selection of his deputy soon became standard practice among presidential candidates.

Mondale was involved in every major issue in the administration, including the Camp David Accords, and even functioned as the president's chief intergovernmental and political adviser. At their weekly private lunches, Mondale would help Carter interpret events in Washington, and together they would analyze the president's agenda from a political perspective. Mondale's contribution was vital because the president preferred not to discuss politics with his cabinet and because many of the advisers the president had brought with him from his home state of Georgia were unschooled in the ways of Washington.

Though other vice presidents have served in high-profile roles (Richard Nixon was a member of Eisenhower's National Security Council, Spiro Agnew oversaw intergovernmental affairs for President Nixon, and Nelson Rockefeller ran President Ford's Domestic Policy Council), none of them were members of the president's inner circle. Mondale was the first vice president in the modern era to enjoy that distinction.

Vice Presidents Al Gore, Dick Cheney and Joe Biden all owe Mondale a debt for formalizing this unique partnership with the president, but Cheney raised the relationship to another level. Before Cheney, the vice presidency was sometimes an active and high-profile role, but its potential as the potent extension of the president's power and leadership had yet to be fully explored.

After Cheney, Bush would establish close relationships with others on his staff. None of those men and women, however, ever exercised the sweeping authority that Cheney possessed at the height of his power. Some have speculated that Cheney's influence was a result of his superior skill as a bureaucratic warrior,

which enabled him to marginalize those around him. Bureaucratic skill certainly played a role. Only a handful of people working for Bush possessed Cheney's experience and understanding of Congress and the executive branch. But the source of Cheney's most potent authority as Bush's right hand was his role as vice president. Few would challenge the notion that Cheney was the most powerful American vice president ever to serve in the post. He stands as a testament to what is possible when opportunity, ability and experience meet genuine political might.

Cheney embodied many of the ideal qualities and skills of the presidential right hand while having the added advantage of being vice president. He not only carried the imprimatur of the president, as his chief adviser, but also was clothed in the robes of an office of perceived power. On paper Cheney possessed few authorities, but in reality, if only briefly, he outranked everyone else in the president's orbit.

Cheney's role in the Bush Administration raises an important question about the presidential right hand. Is the vice president the ideal candidate for the role? Is a vice president inherently a better choice than, say, a cabinet officer, a White House counsel or a chief of staff? The answer may depend on who is asking.

For Bush, a president in search of an aide of unquestioned authority, the vice president was the best choice of right hand. As discussed throughout these chapters, other presidents have at various times chosen a cabinet officer, the White House counsel or the chief of staff to fill the role and suit their purposes. When it comes to their number-one adviser or the person with whom they share the most of their executive power, American presidents have a right to choose whomever they want. Obviously, they need someone they can trust. But should public perceptions also impact their decision? For example, some Americans might eye President Trump's choice of right-hand duo, his son-in-law Jared Kushner and his daughter Ivanka Trump, with suspicion, and not just because of their close family relation. Kushner and Ivanka had no government experience, and accountability was clearly not a determining factor in the president's decision to place them in his administration. In light of this, and considering the questionable choices of advisers by other presidents, one wonders whether voter expectations, including expectations about accountability, should play a role in presidents' selection of their right hands.

For most of this book, the relationship between the president and his adviser, and their collective power and influence, has been illustrated and examined from the perspective of serving the president—at the expense of analyzing expectations about right-hand men and women's responsibilities, if any, to the voter. Further, to avoid disrupting the narrative flow of the chapters, there has been little comparison of the evolving changes in the role of the presidential right hand across the arc of its development, and few questions have been raised about its function outside of the context of its utility to the president. But these issues are no less important.

The epilogue will examine aspects of the presidential right hand that are worthy of deeper inquiry and will unpack why one particular type of right-hand man or woman is superior to another—not just in the context of serving the president, but for serving the American voter as well.

RECONSIDERING THE VICE PRESIDENT

PART II

The nation's founding fathers struggled to find consensus on how the presidency should function. Some thought that rather than govern alone, the president should be a member of an executive committee that governed collectively. They also struggled with the role of the vice president in relation to the president. As these two offices evolved and their functions were clarified over successive administrations, they moved progressively toward one another. Sometimes (as in the cases of President Carter and Vice President Mondale, President Clinton and Vice President Gore, President Bush and Vice President Cheney), they worked as a close partnership. The president was still in charge, but the vice president was a powerful, wide-ranging figure, executing the president's will with an authority unchallenged by any other senior official—a true right-hand man.

The nine right-hand men and women profiled in this book represent the progress of the right-hand role from the Washington Administration to the modern day. The chronicles of their relationships with the presidents they served show their strengths and weaknesses as model advisers, alter egos and confidants. Looking back on their stories, we can compare and contrast the five types of right hand they represent—(1) cabinet secretary, (2) senior adviser, (3) chief of staff (or chief of staff analogue), (4) family member and (5) vice president—to determine which is, in general, best suited to serve the president.

Right-hand men and women have often been chosen by presidents for personal reasons. Perhaps a president believed he could work better with one particular adviser than any other, or maybe a certain adviser brought an especially valuable quality or skill to the table. Overall, the profiles of administrations in action in this book have shown the comparative advantages of the vice president as an effective right hand to the president.

Consider the vice president in comparison to a cabinet secretary. While the vice presidency is obviously broader in scope, being a cabinet officer certainly has its advantages. Like the vice president, many cabinet secretaries are constitutional officers and automatically possess recognized authority, which can help energize a reluctant bureaucrat. And, as Commerce Secretary Harry Hopkins (see the introduction) did for FDR, they can effectively cut through government red tape. But, of course, the advantages of appointing a cabinet officer as right-hand man or woman must be weighed against its disadvantages—for example, cabinet rivalries are always a possibility. Recall how the close friendship between President Lincoln and his secretary of state spurred jealousy within the cabinet and how Lincoln had to go out of his way to ease the conflict that he himself had helped create (chapter two).

Aware of such hazards, President Washington strove, sometimes unsuccessfully, to communicate to Secretary of State Jefferson that he and Treasury Secretary Hamilton were on equal ground in his eyes. Like Lincoln, George Washington was a good judge of character, and, while he encouraged vigorous debate within his cabinet, he recognized that showing favoritism threatened the cohesion and effectiveness of his team (see chapter one).

Lincoln and Washington served in the days when the vice president, for reasons discussed above, was rarely welcomed as a member of the president's inner circle. Andrew Jackson was the first president to include his deputy among his closest advisers, but it would be a century before another president would follow his example. President Carter became the first in the modern era to involve his vice president deeply in the work of his administration, strongly influencing the relationships that subsequent presidents shared with their deputies. The important roles played by Vice Presidents Mondale, Gore, Cheney and Biden show that Carter helped establish the vice president as almost as potent an executive as the president himself.

Though the option of a Cheney-like figure (see chapter nine) was unavailable to Washington and Lincoln, they would have benefited from the use of such a politically seasoned and powerful personal adviser. And Cheney's actions are illustrative of how a vice president can be a solution to the problem of cabinet rivalries.

Organizing the American response to 9/11 required the coordination of multiple federal agencies. The heads of the Department of Justice, the Department of Defense, the State Department, the CIA and the NSC could each have asserted a legitimate claim to leadership, but Bush gave Cheney the premier role in the effort. In pursuit of his mission, Cheney had to reach into the portfolio of numerous cabinet officials on multiple occasions. Yet he faced little resistance, because the department heads understood that Cheney was acting on behalf of the president and that, as vice president, he did not owe them the courtesy of seeking their approval. The fact that Cheney and Bush shared a special relationship that was not restrained by portfolio or defined area of expertise only enhanced Cheney's influence within the cabinet. The vice president's broad scope gave him the freedom to address, at a high level and under the same umbrella, issues that stretched across numerous agencies. By assigning Cheney broad oversight of these issues, Bush avoided the inter-agency conflicts that would have undoubtedly arisen.

For similar reasons, the use of the vice president as right hand also has an advantage compared to the use of other senior White House actors, including the assistant to the president, the White House counsel and the chief of staff. Since these are not constitutional roles, these figures must derive their influence predominantly from their relationship with the president. Under such circumstances, they are at risk of having their actions challenged or dismissed by those outside of the executive mansion. Consider the conflict between Clark Clifford and State Secretary Marshall over the recognition of Israel (chapter five). After that, Marshall never spoke to Clifford again, and anyone at the State Department who chose to work with Clifford risked his or her relationship with Marshall. Given these toxic conditions, it would be understandable if a State Department official refused to help Clifford without first seeking the approval of his or her superiors.

The vice president also has huge advantages where opening doors is a major priority. Unlike other government offices, the office of vice president enjoys a level of sweeping access across the executive branch that rivals that of the president. Cheney understood this all too well and routinely reached out directly to lesser officials deep within the bowels of agencies when he needed an answer to a complicated question or a duty quickly performed. Given the friction between them, imagine Thomas Jefferson hearing from one of his subordinates that Alexander Hamilton was ordering around State Department employees the way Cheney had a habit of doing. It would not have been welcome news.

When it comes to raw power, the vice president has advantages over even the president's family members. Over the centuries, presidents' relations have been a popular source of aides of unquestioned loyalty. But this scenario raises its own catalog of dangers.

Recall when President Clinton was sued over the secrecy of the task force on health-care reform (chapter eight). One of the issues the court case turned on was whether Hillary was a government employee. The distinction is important because of federal laws that govern the paid employment of family members of the president. Had the court decided that Hillary was indeed a federal employee, the president would have been open to the accusation that he knowingly committed a crime by employing a member of his family.

A similar debate arose when Jared Kushner and Ivanka Trump were appointed to high-level advisory posts in the Trump White House. Some among the public and in the media expressed concern that the Trump children might use their positions to enrich themselves. Others questioned their qualifications to serve in positions of such high influence in the administration. And, of course, questions regarding nepotism arose. The federal anti-nepotism laws do not exactly forbid family members of the president from serving in the administration, but they do make it illegal for them to receive compensation. So, Trump's lawyers decided that the best solution was for Jared and Ivanka to serve without pay. Though this approach may be legal, there are many good reasons why subsequent presidents may not want to follow Trump's example and consider, instead, the ready-made role of vice president.

Unpaid family members of the president serving in the White House have potentially less influence than regular senior White House employees. Being outside of the official chain of command, their actions on the president's behalf are potentially open to legal challenge and can possibly be deemed voidable on the grounds that these people are not "genuine" representatives of the government. To see how this scenario might play out, consider the blow-up between President

Wilson and Colonel House over the promises House made to delegates during Wilson's brief absence from the Paris Peace Conference (chapter three).

Colonel House was not a member of Wilson's family, like Ivanka and Jared were to Trump, but as a "quasi-official" of the US government he functioned similarly to them. Though he frequently spoke and acted on the president's behalf, his official status hovered in a gray area that was difficult to define. This became a source of problems because, while House was Wilson's chief aide at the peace conference, his unclear governmental standing rendered the promises he made on Wilson's behalf non-binding. For example, in Wilson's absence, House attempted to resolve minor disagreements among the delegates in preparation for the president's return. Any of the decisions he made on Wilson's behalf were subject to challenge because House was not an actual government official.

When access, influence and legitimacy are considered, the advantages of a president using his or her vice president as right hand are clear. The president's power is extended by an assistant who is above the petty squabbles that can fracture a cabinet; the gravitas of the vice president's office will open doors that might open reluctantly for other senior officials; and, unlike a family member of the president, the vice president does not have to face challenges to his or her authority or issues arising from nepotism. The choice of the vice president in the vital right-hand role has advantages for the American voter as well.

Unlike House (chapter three), Howe (chapter four) or Clifford (chapter five), for example—presidential assistants who exercised enormous influence and yet were mysteries to an inquiring public—the vice president is already a relatively well-known figure by the time he or she steps into the office. But consider how little was known about Colonel House when he acted on behalf of the US in Paris. As he made promises for President Wilson and conducted secret negotiations with foreign heads of state, Americans did not have the benefit of understanding his history, nor were they afforded the opportunity to question his qualifications. In Wilson's day, the public was more willing to trust the president's judgment about such matters, but since the Watergate scandal exposed the illegal activities of officials in the Nixon Administration, Americans have been more skeptical of the activities of these shadowy figures. In other words, they are less open to giving the president the benefit of the doubt when it comes to his or her associates.

Recall the uproar that greeted President Trump's appointment of White House strategist Steve Bannon to the National Security Council. Almost as soon as the news of his appointment was made public, Americans began to openly issue challenges about his competency and qualifications. That uproar, and the backlash against the Trump children in their high-level roles, shows the increasing scrutiny to which Americans subject presidential advisers. When citizens perceive that there are options like a knowledgeable, constitutionally authorized vice president, the public demands for the chief executive's closest advisers to have comparable qualifications have merit.

Today, unlike in Wilson's day, Americans expect the people advising the president to be clearly qualified to do so. This may signal an important opportunity for any members of the public hoping to influence the vital selection of right-hand men and women. Given that almost every president has employed a right hand at some point, and given the extraordinary influence these unique individuals possess, shouldn't American voters have a say—or at least the right to have their basic expectations met—regarding who is selected in this critical post?

Some academics may question the utility of the role of right hand to the president or the legitimacy of those who serve in the post. But, as a historical institution, it seems that the role is here to stay. So, considering that Americans have direct influence over who is elected vice president and indirect influence—by way of their representatives in Congress—over who is appointed to head federal agencies, why shouldn't they have a say in who becomes the president's right-hand man or woman? Could the answer to this question be as simple as paying closer attention to who presidential candidates select as running mates?

The rising public esteem in recent years for the office of the vice president has had important consequences for the evolution of the role of president's right hand. Even as Americans have been persistently critical of the ghostlike figures working in the White House, it appears that they have grown more comfortable with the vice president in a position of White House leadership. As a consequence of the convergence of these two vital dynamics—greater scrutiny of presidential advisers and the growing relevance of the vice president—the American public is presented with an opportunity to influence, perhaps for the first time in history, who the president selects as his or her right hand.

The media will continue to ferret out and identify those individuals who are exercising the president's power by proxy behind the scenes, and the American public will undoubtedly continue to object when these figures fall short of their expectations. This is as it should be. Given that reality, and considering the expanding role of the office and the frequency with which vice presidents have been utilized as right hands in recent years, in order to ensure effective and accountable government, Americans should insist that candidates for vice president be legitimately qualified to lead and that they have a genuine working relationship with the presidential candidate. No more left-field selections like former Alaska governor Sarah Palin, who had no Washington expertise and no prior relationship with 2008 presidential candidate Senator John McCain. It is hard to believe, given her questionable qualifications, that President McCain would have selected Vice President Palin to be his most trusted adviser.

If a vice-presidential candidate is extraordinarily capable and gets on well with his or her running mate, chances are that, once the two are in office, the president will draw the vice president into his or her inner circle—which increases the chances of being selected as right hand. That is a win-win scenario for the president and the public. The president will have the benefit of a powerful assistant with gravitas, constitutional relevance and ability, and the American public will have someone who they know has been properly vetted and who, as an elected official, is directly accountable to them.

Given the secret power of presidents' right hands, it is no surprise that Americans are interested in the identities of these people. Of course, those among the public who hope to influence the selection of right-hand men and women must accept the fact that it is ultimately up to the president to choose his or her closest adviser. But engaged Americans should also recognize that by bringing to bear the special influence they possess as voters, they can help guide that decision.

ACKNOWLEDGMENTS

Writing a book is impossible without the help of a community of supporters. Thank you to MAC for your advice, encouragement, ideas and rock-steady support. There were times along the way when I had doubts. Thank you for believing in me.

Thank you to Will DeRooy for helping me find the words.

Thank you to Karen Robb for providing the inspiration for the book. You prove that rock stars aren't always the people on the stage.

Every author needs readers, and I want to thank Camilla McKinney, Rick Gilmore, Elizabeth Hoffman Schmeltz, Richard and Milton Anderson, Tony Jennings and Kelley O'Neill, Becky Levin, Kimberly Overbeek, Diana Meredith and Scott Russell for your patience and advice. I know the rough cuts were just that—rough. I appreciate your time.

And thank you to the staff of the Library of Congress—if not for your sheer strength—for your advice, for your recommendations and for responding to my many stupid questions with generosity and patience.

NOTES

AUTHOR'S NOTE

1. Alexander L. George and Juliette L. George, *Woodrow Wilson and Colonel House: A Personality Study* (New York: Dover, 1964).

2. Edmund Wilson, "Woodrow Wilson at Princeton," in *The Shores of Light: A Literary Chronicle of the Twenties and Thirties* (New York: Farrar, Straus and Young, 1952), p. 322.

3. George and George, *Woodrow Wilson and Colonel House*, p. 318.

INTRODUCTION

1. Churchill's representative Brendan Bracken was joined by a colleague who is reported to have described Hopkins as "so ill and frail that a puff of wind would blow him away" (Michael Fullilove, *Rendezvous with Destiny* [New York: Penguin, 2013], p. 202).

In a letter to his brother Lewis dated September 8, 1939, Hopkins tried to describe the severity of his condition:

> I am not absorbing proteins and fats in any adequate manner. My protein count or whatever you call it, is one-third normal. This is in spite of a very well-regulated diet. In other words, nothing that I can take by mouth seems to make any difference so they are pushing a variety of things intravenously and intra-muscularly, including some material which they are using experimentally here. My eyesight is going back on me, and I have lost about thirty pounds from my top weight a year ago.

2. What became known as the Trail of Tears did not occur during the Jackson Administration, though President Jackson deserves credit for the tragedy. The removal of Native Americans from their ancestral lands east of the Mississippi was initiated by

authority of the Indian Removal Act of 1830. The forced relocation of the Cherokee, Chickasaw, Choctaw and Creek tribes was begun during the Jackson Administration, but the Trail of Tears occurred under the direction of Jackson's successor, President Martin Van Buren, in 1838 and 1839. In his entire eight years as president, the Indian Removal Act was the only law passed at President Jackson's personal behest. John Eaton helped engineer its passage and worked aggressively with President Jackson to encourage the impacted tribes to accept the terms of the law. When, in 1838, Cherokees refused to comply with President Van Buren's order to relocate, Van Buren sent in the military to move them by force.

3. This list is by no means exhaustive. Not all of the presidents' right hands have fit neatly into one of these five categories. Valerie Jarrett, for example, was officially the director of the White House Office of Public Engagement, and Colonel Edward House had no official White House title at all while working for President Wilson. What these five categories represent are frequent models of the presidential right hand over the years. Examining the profiles of the men and women since the Washington Administration who have served in the role will reveal that most of them fit into one of these categories.

4. Another reason for the nickname, besides the fact that he looked the part, was Cheney's penchant for working in the shadows. He notoriously preferred not to put anything down on paper and to conduct business on the telephone or in person whenever possible so as not to leave a trail.

CHAPTER ONE: GEORGE WASHINGTON & ALEXANDER HAMILTON

1. George Washington, letter to Catherine Macaulay Graham, January 9, 1790.

2. Hamilton recognized that he had a talent for organization and management that was appealing to men in leadership, but he preferred his role as captain of artillery. After coming to the attention of Generals Alexander McDougall, Nathaniel Greene, Lord Stirling, and Washington for his role in a battle that led to the capture of a thousand Hessian troops, he was approached by at least two of the generals about serving as their aide-de-camp. He refused each time, out of a belief that the job required a level of "personal dependence" that he found unappealing. On January 20, 1777, George Washington wrote Hamilton a personal letter requesting his service on his staff. Days later, Hamilton published his acceptance in the *Pennsylvania Evening Post.* Hamilton's official appointment and accompanying double promotion to the rank of lieutenant colonel were announced on March 1.

3. Washington's irascibility was particularly apparent when he was in the presence of servants or subordinates. Observers describe him as being two people—the

public Washington who was calm and composed, and the stern, abusive, and violent Washington that emerged in his private dealings with his slaves. Paul Longmore, on page 181 of his book *The Invention of George Washington* (Berkeley: University of California Press, 1988), quotes the wife of the British ambassador, who said of Washington that he "acquired a uniform command over his passions on public occasions, but in private and particularly with servants, its violence sometimes broke out." Biographer Ron Chernow, on page 114 of his book *Washington: A Life* (New York: Penguin, 2010), describes in chilling detail the level of "attentiveness" to Washington's moods that his slaves displayed at Mount Vernon. They watched Washington closely as they went about their work, attentive to his slightest movements, as if even a silent glance in their direction carried a veiled threat.

4. Clinton and Hamilton started out as friends. During the American Revolution, they established a regular correspondence, but, after the war, their political ambitions conflicted. Eventually, Hamilton would count Clinton, along with Jefferson and Burr, as one of his greatest political rivals.

Their roads began to diverge after Clinton defeated Hamilton's father-in-law for the office of governor of New York. Increasingly, as Clinton's political power grew, Hamilton began to resent Clinton's favoring of New York over the country as a whole. Although Hamilton initially regarded Clinton as "a man of integrity," he ended up describing him as "circumspect and guarded" and accusing him of rarely acting "without premeditation or design" (Ron Chernow, *Alexander Hamilton* [New York: Penguin Press, 2005], pp. 220–21).

5. There was always a sense of the theater about Washington. Whether it was in his dress or manner, before a crowd he always seemed to be an actor on a stage. He disliked public speaking, perhaps because it carried the risk of doing damage to his carefully cultivated image and he labored over the physical impression he made the way an actor might in preparation for a scene. It is no surprise that he was a huge fan of the theater. It was not uncommon for him to attend performances five nights a week. He would see plays, puppet shows, musicals, waxworks, almost anything. His letters are filled with theatrical references, and the theater informed even how he interacted with the people around him. The story of him trying to convince his officers to remain in the army during the Revolution by making them feel sorry for him is well known. They found it difficult to criticize the "old man" when he needed glasses to read his prepared remarks. Washington knew that wearing glasses would communicate to his men how the war had aged him and that their pity for him would convince them to stay.

6. Of course, Mary Ball had the assistance of slaves to help ease her burden. George himself, even as a young boy, owned ten slaves. (They had been willed to him upon the death of his father, but George would not take full possession of them until he came of age.)

7. Washington believed that outward appearance was the best indication of a man's inner qualities. Throughout his life, he took great pains to ensure that he and those representing him adhered to exacting sartorial standards. His own close attention to the details of his dress can be gathered from a 152-word letter written to his tailor describing a coat he wanted made. Ron Chernow included in his biography of Washington a few lines from the letter:

> a lapel breast, the lapel to contain on each side six button holes and to be about 5 or 6 inches wide, all the way equal, and to turn as the breast of the coat does: to have it made very long-waisted and in length to come down to or below the bent of the knee, the waist from the armpit to the fold to be exactly as long or longer than from thence to the bottom, not to have more than one fold in the skirt etc. (Ron Chernow, *Washington: A Life* [New York: Penguin, 2010], p. 21.)

8. *The American Experience*, season 5, episode 6, "George Washington: The Man Who Wouldn't Be King," directed by David Sutherland, written by William Martin and David Sutherland, aired November 18, 1992, on WGBH/PBS, Boston.

9. To accuse John Adams of being slow to let go of a grudge or of having a mean streak would be a gross understatement. If he disliked a person, as he grew to dislike Hamilton, his criticism could be scathing and personal. He insulted Hamilton virulently, in ways that seem embarrassingly beneath the stature of a man of Adams's reputation. Referring to Hamilton's youth in the Caribbean, Adams described him to friends as the "creole bastard" or "the Scottish Creolian of Nevis" (Richard Brookhiser, *Alexander Hamilton: American* [New York: Touchstone, 1999]). Adams also seemed obsessed with Hamilton's love life, often accusing him of infidelity in the most lewd ways, such as when he said that Hamilton had "a superabundance of secretions which he could not find whores enough to draw off" (James Thomas Flexner, *The Young Hamilton: A Biography* [New York: Fordham University Press, 1997], p. 62). Adams even accused Hamilton of being a habitual drug user. He once told a friend that Hamilton "never wrote or spoke at the bar or elsewhere in public without a bit of opium in his mouth" (John Adams correspondence, *Statesman and Friend: Correspondence of John Adams and Benjamin Waterhouse, 1784–1822* [New York: Little, Brown, 1927]).

10. Alexander Hamilton, letter to Edward Stevens, November 11, 1769.

11. Thomas Jefferson's assessment of Washington's decision-making style, made years after the Revolution, reveals how little Washington had changed in his later years. Jefferson describes the president as an assiduous and careful planner, but also someone who readjusted only with great difficulty if his plans were disrupted. Jefferson believed Washington to be smart but lacking a nimble cast of mind, which prevented him from

being spontaneous and creative. It was as if Washington had spent so much of his life training himself to control his emotions that he had lost the ability to react naturally to his surroundings. Thomas Jefferson, *Writings*, ed. Merrill D. Peterson (New York: Library of America, 1984), p. 1318.

12. For the better part of a year, Hamilton was being blackmailed by his mistress Maria Reynolds and her husband, James. They had lured Hamilton into the sexual relationship and then demanded regular payments from him. Hamilton's enemies got hold of their letters and shared them with the press while accusing Hamilton of using US Treasury funds for speculation purposes. Apparently valuing his public reputation more than his privacy, Hamilton published a pamphlet in 1796 admitting to the affair in great detail and even including details from the Reynolds's letters.

13. Chernow, *Washington*, pp. 581–82.

14. Jay was suggested because he had negotiated with the British at the Paris talks in 1783. He had served as secretary of foreign affairs under the US confederation government between 1783 and 1790 and as minister to Spain for the Continental Congress in 1779.

15. See Forrest McDonald, *Alexander Hamilton: A Biography* (New York: W. W. Norton, 1982), pp. 285–305.

16. A good description of the strengths and weaknesses of the treaty can be found on pages 71 through 103 of Todd Estes, *The Jay Treaty Debate: Public Opinion and the Evolution of Early American Political Culture* (Amherst: University of Massachusetts Press, 2008).

17. In his letter of July 29, 1795, to Alexander Hamilton, George Washington wrote: "To judge of this work from the first number, which I have seen, I augur well of the performance; & shall expect to see the subject handled in a clear, distinct and satisfactory manner" (Founders Online, July 29, 1795, https://founders.archives. gov/documents/Hamilton/01-18-02-0318 [accessed September 20, 2017]).

18. For a fuller account of Hamilton's media campaign and an understanding of how extraordinary the accomplishment was, see Estes, *Jay Treaty Debate*, pp. 83–85, and Ron Chernow, *Alexander Hamilton* (New York: Penguin, 2005), pp. 493–97.

19. John Alexander Carroll and Mary Wells Ashworth, *First in Peace*, vol. 7 of *George Washington*, ed. Douglas Southall Freeman (New York: Scribner's, 1957), p. 273n45.

CHAPTER TWO: ABRAHAM LINCOLN & WILLIAM SEWARD

1. Eulogy given by Abraham Lincoln at the funeral of former president Zachary Taylor, July 25, 1850.

2. Richard B. Harwell, ed., *The Union Reader: As the North Saw the War* (New York: Longmans, Green, 1958), pp. 326–30.

3. *The American Experience*, season 13, episode 8, "Abraham Lincoln and Mary Lincoln: A House Divided," directed by David Grubin, written by David Grubin and Geoffrey C. Ward, aired February 20, 2001, on WGBH/PBS, Boston.

4. The relationship between Abraham and Mary changed when they reached the White House. Before then, if Abraham was at work and Mary fell into "one of her moods," he would come home to personally and lovingly console her. But once he became president, he no longer had the time, or perhaps the interest, to take care of her in the same way. Her moods grew worse, and, as a consequence, the marriage suffered. Before they entered the White House, Abraham and Mary had shared a close political partnership. In Illinois, he had looked to her for strategy advice. She was politically active, was well informed and had good political instincts. But in Washington, the politics and the people were new, and Mary became less central to Lincoln's planning.

Seward's wife, Frances, disliked politics and politicians. As Seward built his career, Frances preferred to stay behind to raise their children. She hated the idea of Seward serving in the cabinet, because of the social demands it placed on her. Frances's lack of interest in politics became a main reason she and Seward spent so much time apart. The separation strained the marriage and, according to some historians, was the impetus for Frances to start a semi-romantic relationship with one of Seward's friends.

5. Frederick Seward, *Reminiscences of a War-Time Statesman and Diplomat* (New York: Putnam, 1916), p. 253.

6. Lincoln and Seward discussed their strategy at least twice. First, after deciding to send Seward to meet with Stephens, Lincoln wrote a short list of instructions describing how Seward should conduct himself and what he should say. James Conroy, *Our One Common Country: Abraham Lincoln and the Hampton Roads Peace Conference of 1865* (Guildford, CT: Lyons, 2014), p. 131. During the actual meeting, Lincoln and Seward entered the room together after holding back for a few minutes to permit Stephens and his party to get settled. During this period, Lincoln and Seward discussed again what they would say.

7. William Shakespeare, *Othello*, act II, scene 3, line 243.

8. For a well-paced and more detailed depiction of the nominee selection proceedings, see Doris Kearns Goodwin, *Team of Rivals: The Political Genius of Abraham Lincoln* (New York: Simon and Schuster, 2005), pp. 237–56.

9. Journal entry of John Austin, May 18, 1860.

10. Ibid.

11. Ibid.

12. Seward rarely voiced his disappointment about losing the nomination to Lincoln. One of the few documented instances occurred during an exchange between Seward and a member of Congress in which Seward said: "Disappointment! You speak to me of disappointment. To me, who was justly entitled to the Republican nomination for the presidency, and who had to stand aside and see it given to a little Illinois lawyer! You speak to me of disappointment!" Glyndon Van Deusen, *William Henry Seward* (New York: Oxford University Press, 1967), p. 336.

13. Seward was not only one of the best-traveled men in America, but also one of the best-traveled members of the Republican Party, having served for many years on the powerful Senate Foreign Relations Committee.

14. A copy of the memo and Lincoln's unsent response can be found in John M. Taylor, *William Henry Seward: Lincoln's Right Hand* (New York: HarperCollins, 1991), pp. 308–310.

15. Lincoln's Uncle Mordecai and at least one of the cousins of Lincoln's father, Thomas, an uncle, and an aunt were also stricken with depression. Other Lincoln family members struggled with insanity. The many sources on this subject include Michael Burlingame, *Abraham Lincoln: A Life*, vol. 1 (Baltimore: Johns Hopkins University Press, 2008), p. 6.

16. Lincoln suffered at least two nervous breakdowns in his life. Each time he is reputed to have contemplated suicide. These periods are well covered by many historians; however, one volume specifically dedicated to Lincoln's bouts with depression and his thoughts of suicide is noteworthy: Joshua Wolf Shenk, *Lincoln's Melancholy: How Depression Challenged a President and Fueled His Greatness* (Boston: Houghton Mifflin, 2005), pp. 19–23.

17. Doris Kearns Goodwin, as featured on Lillian Cunningham, "His Hand and His Pen," *Presidential*, produced by the *Washington Post*, podcast, April 24, 2016.

18. Lincoln's mother died from milk poisoning in 1818, when Lincoln was still a boy. His older sister, Sarah, took over caring for him. She helped him grieve, and she raised him as if he was her own child, even teaching him to read. Sadly, she died when Lincoln was a teenager as a result of complications associated with the birth of her first child. By his own admission, he was devastated by her death. In adult life, Lincoln also lost his four-year-old son Edward in 1850 and his twelve-year-old boy "Willie" in 1862.

19. Mary Lincoln did not like Seward, whom she referred to as the "abolitionist sneak" for his immutable views on the subject. She chafed at reports that Seward was the puppet master in the White House; one time, she even threatened to personally show the secretary of state which of them had the most influence with Lincoln. Her dislike for Seward extended to the rest of his family. She once refused to meet with

Seward's wife during a rare social call at the White House. When the Seward women sent up a message with the footman that they would like to meet with Mrs. Lincoln, she sent down word that she was not receiving visitors that day.

20. There are a number of sources for this quote. Here, the source is David Herbert Donald, *We Are Lincoln Men: Abraham Lincoln and His Friends* (New York: Simon & Schuster, 2003), p. 171.

21. He went on to say, "The Emancipation Proclamation was uttered in the first gun fired at Sumter and we have been the last to hear it. As it is, we show our sympathy with slavery by emancipating slaves where we cannot reach them and holding them in bondage where we can set them free." For further commentary on Seward's views, see Allen C. Guelzo, *Lincoln's Emancipation Proclamation: The End of Slavery in America* (New York: Simon & Schuster, 2006), p. 222.

22. Border states included Maryland, Delaware, Kentucky and Missouri.

23. President Lincoln made this comment to artist Francis Bicknell Carpenter. Francis Bicknell Carpenter, *Six Months at the White House with Abraham Lincoln: A Story of a Picture* (New York: Hurd and Houghton, 1866), p. 22. The proclamation was officially issued on September 22, 1862. Lincoln, taking Seward's advice, waited until the Union Army achieved a battlefield victory—in this case, the Battle of Antietam.

24. That Lincoln would assign Seward oversight of such an unusual project for a secretary of state indicates the nature of their special partnership. Right hands are often asked to perform special duties for the presidents they serve. Lincoln could have asked his attorney general to oversee the project, but instead he went to Seward. Perhaps he did so because he understood that the maneuvers necessary to enable such a controversial piece of legislation might entail conduct beneath the dignity of a president and, because he would need to be close to whoever oversaw the project, he wanted that person to be someone he could trust completely.

25. The Amendment passed the US Senate on April 8, 1864, and the US House of Representatives on January 31, 1865.

26. Since notes were not taken at this meeting, most of what is known is drawn from official accounts submitted to Congress afterward by Lincoln and Seward. Their reports are deliberately incomplete. The account recorded here is based largely on the writings of Stephens, Campbell, and Hunter. Historian James Conroy assembled the recollections of each of the participants and combined them with newspaper reports to create a very readable description of the meeting. That work is the basis of this section. James Conroy, *Our One Common Country: Abraham Lincoln and the Hampton Roads Peace Conference of 1865* (Guildford, CT: Lyons, 2014), pp. 172–99.

27. When it was signed, the proclamation covered only those states in active rebellion—which did not include Missouri, Kentucky, Maryland and Delaware. Tennessee, and some parts of Virginia and Louisiana, were also excluded from coverage.

CHAPTER THREE: WOODROW WILSON & EDWARD HOUSE

1. Charles Seymour, a former Sterling Professor of History at Yale, recorded this quote in his biography of Colonel House in 1926. The date and person to whom Wilson supposedly addressed this comment are not identified. Charles Seymour, *The Intimate Papers of Colonel House: Arranged as a Narrative* (Boston: Houghton Mifflin, 1926).

2. House never served in the military. The honorific of "colonel" was bestowed upon him as a courtesy similar to that enjoyed by Muhammad Ali, George H. W. Bush and Whoopi Goldberg, who were also "colonels."

3. Had House decided to run for office, it would not have been difficult. There were many in Texas politics who would have supported his candidacy and, given his reputation, challengers would have been few. For an insightful description and analysis of House's reasons for not running, see Charles Neu, *Colonel House: A Biography of Woodrow Wilson's Silent Partner* (New York: Oxford University Press, 2015), taking special note of pp. 37–38.

4. This is recorded by Edwin A. Weinstein based on a memorandum of an interview with Cary T. Grayson on February 18–19, 1926, and included in the public papers of Woodrow Wilson as cited in Weinstein's book, *Woodrow Wilson: A Medical and Psychological Biography* (Princeton, NJ: Princeton University Press, 1981), p. 15.

5. Ibid.

6. Alexander L. and Juliette L. George, *Woodrow Wilson and Colonel House: A Personality Study* (New York: Dover Publications, 1964), pp. 6–7.

7. Weinstein's theory is that Wilson had a type of dyslexia that was different from that caused by brain damage, lack of social stimulation, low intelligence, or emotional trauma. Weinstein, *Woodrow Wilson*, pp. 16–19.

8. According to Weinstein, the strongest proof of Wilson's childhood dyslexia emerged in 1896, when, after he suffered his first stroke, Wilson displayed the "mixed cerebral dominance and bilateral representation for language, associated with childhood dyslexia" (*Woodrow Wilson*, p. 18).

9. Alexander George was the Graham Stuart Professor of International Relations and professor of political science at Stanford University. He was also a head of the social science department at the RAND Corporation. His wife, Juliette George, was a senior scholar of international studies at Stanford. They collaborated on the book *Woodrow Wilson and Colonel House: A Personality Study* (New York: Dover Publications, 1964).

10. George and George, *Woodrow Wilson and Colonel House*, pp. 6–7.

11. Weinstein, *Woodrow Wilson*, pp. 10–13.

12. A. Scott Berg, *Wilson* (New York: G. P. Putnam's Sons, 2013), p. 37.

13. Louis Koenig, *The Invisible Presidency* (New York: Rinehart, 1960), p. 197.

14. Neu, *Colonel House*, pp. 57–58.

15. Weinstein, *Woodrow Wilson*, p. 266.

16. Seymour, *The Intimate Papers of Colonel House*, p. 93.

17. Wilson wanted to prevent banking crises such as the one that had occurred during the Cleveland Administration and which necessitated J. P. Morgan to single-handedly bail out the US economy. In 1895, a banking panic caused a run on gold. The Treasury Department was required to hold $100 million in gold reserve at all times, but so many Americans had traded their bank-account balances for gold that US gold reserves dropped to below $50 million. J. P. Morgan offered to lend the US government $60 million in gold in return for US bonds. President Cleveland demurred. Then, Morgan informed the president that he knew, on good authority, that a large US company was planning to redeem $10 million in gold bonds on the following day, and he knew that the New York treasury held only $9 million in gold. If the bonds were redeemed, as Morgan fully expected, the New York treasury would be insolvent and an already deep banking crisis would worsen. Morgan knew his information was true because a member of his board of directors sat on the board of the company in question.

18. Woodrow Wilson, letter to Joseph Daniels. Baker, *Woodrow Wilson*, p. 13.

19. Koenig, *The Invisible Presidency*, pp. 215–17.

20. Ibid.

21. Ibid.

22. Comment by British diplomat Sir William Wiseman conveyed by Colonel House to Woodrow Wilson on April 4, 1917, and August 4, 1917, and contained in the House papers.

23. August Heckscher, *Woodrow Wilson* (New York: Charles Scribner's Sons, 1991), p. 334.

24. Ibid., p. 335.

25. Comment by Woodrow Wilson to Colonel House. Journal entry by House on November 6, 1914.

26. Edith Galt, a widow, had been in a loveless marriage and was at first unsettled by Wilson's passionate pursuit. Wilson might have proposed earlier, but Colonel House urged him to wait a year. For a description of Wilson and Edith's whirlwind courtship, see Weinstein, *Woodrow Wilson*, pp. 279–97.

27. Phyllis Lee Levin, *Edith and Woodrow: The Wilson White House* (New York: Scribner, 2001), p. 105.

28. Ibid., p. 294.

29. Koenig suggests that House uncharacteristically chose to "throw his weight around" as a way to speed the conference proceedings along. Koenig, *The Invisible Presidency*, p. 246.

30. George and George, *Woodrow Wilson and Colonel House*, p. 197.

31. Ibid., p. 261.

32. Neu, *Colonel House*.

33. George and George, *Woodrow Wilson and Colonel House*, pp. 240–67.

CHAPTER FOUR: FRANKLIN ROOSEVELT & LOUIS HOWE

1. James Roosevelt, *My Parents: A Differing View* (New York: Playboy, 1976), p. 75.

2. The relationship between the two remained strained throughout their married lives together. They were a family, but Howe and Grace did not go out of their way to be together in the way that two spouses in a loving relationship might. Even when they ran out of excuses to separate, they preferred to live apart. In 1927, Grace inherited enough money to live in comfort for the rest of her life. This wealth should have made it easier for Howe and Grace to live together, but their living situation did not change.

3. Grace Howe, letter to Louis Howe, September 28, 1901, personal papers of Louis Howe.

4. The original letter can be found among Louis Howe's personal papers for years 1905–1911 held at the FDR Library. An excerpt follows, but the entire letter can be found in Julie M. Fenster, *FDR's Shadow: Louis Howe, the Force That Shaped Franklin and Eleanor Roosevelt* (New York: Palgrave Macmillan, 2009), p. 86.

Dearest Wife of Mine,

It is now 2:30 AM and I am forced to go to bed for lack of anyone to sit up and keep me company. I must first dear write you a line, for I want to put something down on paper that you can have and keep and perhaps some time when what I say may make things easier, read. It is only this, dear.

You read my thoughts and my actions wrong, dear.

I trust you trust you trust you—Ever since that night dear when—for the sake of the little son that is gone and the little girl that is here we agreed to drop Willie out of our lives, I have felt that was over. Little girl I didn't want to see you go away because I was afraid—just what I was afraid of I will tell you sometime but believe me, dear, that was not it. If I acted cross it was not that, it was because, when I realized all I had tried so hard to do to compensate for so much I had asked you to give up had been—like everything I had tried to do—a failure. That, if the doctors warnings came true—you would have no other recollection of our last winter than that I had taken you away from all that you cared for and given you in its place—"the worst winter you had ever had in your life."

... Forgive me dear for the misery and sorrow I have caused you for the failure I have made of everything, for I can never forgive myself.

I love you I love you I love you

Your Husband

5. Joseph Lash, *Eleanor and Franklin* (New York: W. W. Norton, 1971), p. 199.
6. Eleanor Roosevelt, *This I Remember* (New York: Harper & Brothers, 1949), p. 30.
7. Eleanor Roosevelt *Autobiography* (New York: HarperCollins, 1961), pp. 108–11.
8. Roosevelt, *My Parents*, p. 85.
9. David McCullough, *Truman* (New York: Simon & Schuster, 1992), p. 327.
10. Roosevelt, *My Parents*, p. 92.
11. Elliott Roosevelt and James Brough, *An Untold Story: The Roosevelts of Hyde Park* (New York: Putnam Adult, 1973). Also see H. W. Brands, *Traitor to His Class: The Privileged Life and Radical Presidency of Franklin Delano Roosevelt* (New York: Doubleday, 2008), p. 194.
12. Fenster, *FDR's Shadow*, p. 205.
13. Alfred Smith, *Up to Now; an Autobiography* (New York: Viking, 1929), p. 288.
14. Roosevelt, *My Parents*, p. 93.
15. James Roosevelt gave Howe the lion's share of the credit for getting FDR back "on his feet" politically. He wrote in his memoirs about his parents: "When father was stricken and later when it became clear that he had a long, hard road to any sort of recovery, I am convinced he would have dropped from public life completely had it not been for Louis Howe. Father was too busy with his fight for his life to think of his political future. It's easy now to look back and see that just up the road was the governorship and then the presidency. It was all but impossible then. He had a modest background, and unsuccessful vice presidential candidates generally fade fast into obscurity. It was Louis who decided that the exposure of the campaign, even one they were bound to lose, would be beneficial" (Roosevelt, *My Parents*, p. 76).
16. Patrick Anderson, *The President's Men; White House Assistants of Franklin D. Roosevelt, Harry S. Truman, Dwight D. Eisenhower, John F. Kennedy, and Lyndon B. Johnson* (Garden City, NY: Doubleday, 1968), p. 10.

CHAPTER FIVE: HARRY TRUMAN & CLARK CLIFFORD

1. Harry S. Truman, letter to his sister, November 14, 1947.
2. The need for policy synthesizers grew out of a change in leadership as a result

of the increasing size of the government and of government programs. In Clifford's case, the function was associated with the responsibilities of the White House counsel. Later, the responsibilities would be folded into the functions of the chief of staff.

3. David McCullough, *Truman* (New York: Simon & Schuster, 1992), p. 614.

4. Clifford also played an important leadership role in Truman's political campaign affairs—something Marshall would have been fully aware of.

5. Journalist Bill Moyers included Clifford among the influential politicos he interviewed for his 1980s television show *A Second Look*. Viewers got a sense of the theatrical quality of Clifford's communication style: Clifford used all the elements of communication, from inflection to body language, to add authority to his comments. Even at his advanced age (Clifford was eighty-three at the time) his gifts were apparent. See *A Second Look*, directed by Bill Moyers, "Former Presidential Advisor: Clark Clifford," aired May 28, 1989, on PBS, available online at http://billmoyers.com/content/clark-clifford/ (accessed September 20, 2017).

6. David McCullough, *Truman*, p. 616.

7. Clark Clifford, *Counsel to the President: A Memoir* (New York: Random House, 1991), p. 12.

8. Ibid., p. 13.

9. Ibid., p. 12.

10. Ibid.

11. Merle Miller, *Plain Speaking: An Oral Biography of Harry S. Truman* (New York: Berkley Press, 1974), p. 32.

12. McCullough, *Truman*, p. 47.

13. At the very moment that Truman's press announcement publicized US recognition of Israel, the UN was about to consider a resolution to put the city of Jerusalem under trusteeship. Truman's release was simple: "This Government has been informed that a Jewish state has been proclaimed in Palestine, and recognition has been requested by the provisional government thereof. The United States recognizes the provisional government as the de facto authority of the new State of Israel." See Robert J. Donovan, *Conflict and Crisis: The Presidency of Harry S. Truman 1945–1948* (New York: W. W. Norton, 1977), pp. 384–85.

14. Taking the job would drive Clifford deeply into debt. His solution for making his financial ends meet would be frowned upon today and might even violate ethics. According to Clark Clifford biographer John Acacia, Alfred Lansing, a wealthy St. Louis businessman, subsidized Clifford's White House salary throughout his service to Truman. In total, Clifford received $35,000 from Lansing—almost $350,000 in today's dollars. Clifford also received personal loans from DC lobbyist George Allen totaling $20,000, or $200,000 in today's dollars. See John Acacia, *Clark Clifford: The Wise Man of Washington* (Lexington: University Press of Kentucky, 2009), p. 162.

15. It is clear from the interviews of Steelman and others conducted for the Oral Histories Project by the Truman Presidential Library in the 1960s that Clifford and Steelman were not friends and that their rivalry was real. Steelman's own interviews suggest an intent to correct the record about the Clifford legend. Transcripts of the interviews are available and searchable by name at https://www.trumanlibrary.org/oralhist/oral_his.htm.

16. Maintaining control over the national security elements of the government had been particularly frustrating for Truman's predecessor, FDR.

17. Acacia, *Clark Clifford*, pp. 57–58.

18. Although for years Clifford claimed the credit for the report, which was so well done that it significantly influenced how the US government as a whole viewed the Soviets, it is now widely accepted that George Elsey wrote it with little aid from Clifford. Truman asked Clifford to prepare for him a report to explain the rising influence of the Soviets, and Clifford assigned the task to Elsey. When Elsey had completed a comprehensive study of US-Soviet relations, he handed it to Clifford, who made only cosmetic changes before presenting it to Truman. Clifford took immediate credit for the work, first in a note to Truman and later in a succession of interviews across decades. He acknowledged Elsey as a contributor but took full credit for its organization and writing. Elsey remained quiet about his true role for years, in probable deference to Clifford's growing power. But by the late 1990s, Elsey began to claim the credit he deserved.

CHAPTER SIX: DWIGHT EISENHOWER & SHERMAN ADAMS

1. Patrick Anderson, *The President's Men; White House Assistants of Franklin D. Roosevelt, Harry S. Truman, Dwight D. Eisenhower, John F. Kennedy, and Lyndon B. Johnson* (Garden City, NY: Doubleday, 1968), p. 35.

2. The job of chief of staff has become a sobriquet for the right hand to the president, but it did not start out that way. John Steelman, who was unofficially the first White House chief of staff, might be confused today with the secretary of the cabinet—a sort of traffic cop regulating the flow of paper between the White House and the various agencies. Eisenhower's conceptualization of the role was the first example of the sweeping administrator we think of today. Adams and Eisenhower reimagined the Steelman role as a right-hand man to the president—not just an administrator, but an all-encompassing figure with oversight of everything within the president's reach. The role would see later changes that would ultimately weaken the position, but the all-powerful "right hand" connotation would endure for decades.

3. Dr. Snyder was one of the president's closest friends. He started working for the Eisenhower family in the 1940s when Dwight asked him to look after Mamie, who suffered from the effects of valvular heart disease. When Eisenhower was elected president in 1953, he brought Snyder with him to the White House. Critics had major reservations about Snyder in the role of presidential physician. They thought at seventy-three he was too old for the job and that his lack of experience and out-of-date training disqualified him for the post.

4. Charles Lasby, *Eisenhower's Heart Attack: How Ike Beat Heart Disease and Held onto the Presidency* (Lawrence: University of Kansas Press, 1997).

5. Lasby devotes the introduction of his book to the story of how he discovered the cover-up about Eisenhower's illness. As he tells it, he was researching a book idea about how men under extraordinary stress—like presidents—can suffer a serious heart attack and yet survive to continue in their stressful jobs. His research took him to the papers of Dr. Howard Snyder at the University of Wyoming and to Eisenhower's medical files. It was while reviewing Snyder's notes on the heart attack that he discovered Snyder's "shocking misdiagnosis." Ibid., pp. 1–5.

6. Stephen Kinzer, *The Brothers: John Foster Dulles, Allen Dulles, and Their Secret World War* (New York: Henry Holt and Company, 2013), p. 15.

7. Ibid., p. 124.

8. See William Manchester, *The Last Lion: Winston Spencer Churchill: Visions of Glory, 1874–1932* (New York: Bantam Books Trade Paperback Edition, 1983), p. 34.

9. *The Brothers* by Stephen Kinzer helps explain the far-reaching impact of Eisenhower's covert actions in Iran, Vietnam, Guatemala, and Indonesia.

10. In addition to an overall negative impression of politicians, Eisenhower harbored concerns about Nixon's general lack of experience and what he often referred to as Nixon's intellectual immaturity.

11. In essence, the press release laid out how the federal government would function without its chief executive at the helm. In just three short paragraphs, Dulles covered all the issues that might pose difficulties for him in Eisenhower's absence.

First, we see Dulles's assurance to the public that the cabinet is of sound mind and good intentions: "After full discussion of pending matters, it was concluded that there are no obstacles to the orderly and uninterrupted conduct of the foreign and domestic affairs of the nation during the period of rest ordered by the President's physicians."

Then Dulles secures Adams's removal from Washington: "Governor Sherman Adams, the Assistant to the President, will leave for Denver today and will be available there, in consultation with the President's physicians, whenever it may become appropriate to present any matters to the President."

Finally, Dulles ensures that no other cabinet officials will interfere with his work, while also securing their cooperation if he needs their help: "The Policies and programs of the administration as determined and approved by the President are well established along definite lines and are well known. Coordination of the activities of the several departments of the government within the framework of these policies will be continued by full cooperation among the responsible officers of these departments so that the functions of the government will be carried forward in an effective manner during the absence of the President."

12.   According to his memoirs, Adams recognized the fact that Dulles was the obvious originator of the release and that its true intent was to "vigilantly protect his position as the maker of foreign policy." Sherman Adams, *Firsthand Report: The Story of the Eisenhower Administration* (New York: Harper, 1961), pp. 185–87.

13.   Stephen Ambrose, *Eisenhower: Soldier and President* (New York: Simon & Schuster, 1990).

CHAPTER SEVEN: RONALD REAGAN & "THE TROIKA"

1.   President Ronald Reagan at the Gridiron Dinner, Washington, DC, March 28, 1987.

2.   Lou Cannon, *President Reagan: His Rise to Power* (New York: Public Affairs, 1991), pp. 158–59.

3.   Bob Schieffer and Gary Paul Gates, *The Acting President* (New York: E. P. Dutton Books, 1989), pp. 90–91. Also see Jimmy Carter, *Keeping Faith: Memoirs of a President* (New York: Bantam Books, 1982).

4.   Colin Powell, *My American Journey: An Autobiography*, with Joseph E. Persico (New York: Random House, 1995), pp. 395–96.

5.   Stephen Knott and Jeffrey Chidester, *At Reagan's Side: Insiders' Recollections from Sacramento to the White House* (New York: Rowman & Littlefield, 2009), p. 136.

6.   Nancy Reagan, *My Turn: The Memoirs of Nancy Reagan* (New York: Random House, 1989), p. 106.

7.   Knott and Chidester, *At Reagan's Side*, p. 136.

8.   Schieffer and Gates, *The Acting President*, pp. 78–79.

9.   The actual memo with Baker and Meese's handwritten notes can be found in Schieffer and Gates, *The Acting President*, p. 83.

10.   *James Baker: The Man Who Made Washington Work*, directed and written by Eric Strange, aired March 24, 2015, on PBS.

11.   Laurence Barrett, *Gambling with History: Ronald Reagan in the White House* (Garden City, NY: Doubleday, 1983), p. 230.

12.   Fred I. Greenstein, *The Presidential Difference: Leadership Style from FDR to Clinton* (New York: Free Press, 2000), p. 120.

13. Smith would write a series of important articles starting in 1981 for the *New York Times* describing the leadership of the White House during Reagan's tenure. The lengthy articles would eventually form the backbone of his book *The Power Game: How Washington Works* (New York: Ballantine, 1998).

CHAPTER EIGHT: BILL CLINTON & HILLARY RODHAM CLINTON

1. Gail Sheehy, "What Hillary Wants," *Vanity Fair*, May 1992, http://www.vanityfair.com/news/1992/05/hillary-clinton-first-lady-presidency.html (accessed July 22, 2017).

2. William Henry Chafe, *Bill and Hillary: The Politics of the Personal* (New York: Farrar, Straus, and Giroux, 2012), pp. 225–28.

3. "Our key hypothesis about the power seeker is that he pursues power as a means of compensation against deprivation. Power is expected to overcome low estimates of the self, by changing either the traits of the self or the environment in which it functions" (Howard D. Lasswell, *Power and Personality* [New York: W. W. Norton, 1948], p. 39).

4. Of course, Lasswell's theory might also be applied, to some degree, to the political partnerships of people who are not married to each other, like Wilson and House or Roosevelt and Howe. But one must make allowances for the fact that such relationships do not include the assumption of "equality" that often accompanies a marital relationship. Political partnerships based on marriage, like the Clintons', often involve additional pressures that partnerships such as the Wilson/House arrangement do not encounter. Therefore, while Lasswell's observations might apply to the Wilson/House partnership, they may not apply in the same way.

5. Carl Bernstein, *A Woman in Charge: The Life of Hillary Rodham Clinton* (New York: Alfred A. Knopf, 2007), p. 63.

6. Ibid., p. 84.

7. Ibid., p. 140.

8. Ibid., p. 12.

9. Ibid., p. 14.

10. Ibid.

11. Roger Morris, *Partners in Power: The Clintons and Their America* (New York: Henry Holt, 1996), p. 115.

12. Bernstein, *A Woman in Charge*, p. 15.

13. Ibid., p. 23.

14. Ibid., p. 26.

15. Ibid., p. 12.

16. Unnamed author, "The Class of '69," *Life*, June 20, 1969, vol. 66, no. 24. Incidentally, Hillary's future partner on the president's health-care reform taskforce, Ira Magaziner, was profiled in the same article.

17. Biographer David Maraniss paints an unflattering portrait of Virginia Clinton in his book on Bill Clinton: "Virginia Clinton layered her face with makeup, dyed her hair black with a bold white racing stripe, painted thick, sweeping eyebrows high above their original position, smoked two packs of Pall Mall cigarettes a day, bathed in a sunken tub, drank liquor, was an irrepressible flirt, and enjoyed the underbelly of her resort town, with its racetrack and gaming parlors and nightclubs" (David Maraniss, *First in His Class: A Biography of Bill Clinton* [New York: Simon & Schuster, 1995], p. 13).

18. Ibid., p. 32.

19. Ibid., p. 38.

20. Ibid., p. 313.

21. Chafe, *Bill and Hillary*, p. 91.

22. Ibid.

23. Amy Chozick, "The Road Trip That Changed Hillary Clinton's Life," *New York Times*, October 28, 2016, https://www.nytimes.com/2016/10/29/us/politics/hillary-clinton-road-trip.html (accessed November 5, 2017).

24. Ibid.

25. *American Experience*, season 24, episode 3, "Clinton," directed by Barak Goodman, aired February 20, 2012, on WGBH/PBS, Boston.

26. Bernstein, *A Woman in Charge*, p. 167.

27. Almost every American president in the twentieth century has been involved with health-care reform in some way. Theodore Roosevelt was the first to publicly advocate for reform. He included the idea as a part of his party platform when he ran against President Taft and Governor Woodrow Wilson in the 1912 general election. FDR pursued health-care reform for years, first taking up the issue when he began work on his Social Security plan and later by convening a national health-care conference to recommend legislation. President Truman's reform efforts were thwarted by Southern Democrats, who thought reform might lead to desegregation, and Eisenhower tried to create a federal fund to supplement the resources of private insurers with the goal of broadening the number of groups they insured.

Presidents Kennedy and Johnson added to their list of legislative priorities the goal of insuring the elderly and the poor. Kennedy's efforts failed; Johnson's did not. Presidents Nixon and Carter proposed their own comprehensive health-insurance plans. Both men ran out of time: Carter lost reelection, and Nixon resigned early in his second term. Even the great Ronald Reagan can be said to have carried the ball a few yards when he proposed that states pay more for the care of the elderly and the poor. When he passed the ball to his successor, President George H. W. Bush, he dropped it. It did not matter—Bill Clinton came to Washington determined enough for the both of them.

It is no surprise that Bill and Hillary would devote so much of those first years to the pursuit of such a noble mission. They came of age in the time when John F. Kennedy was asking every American to make sacrifices for the public good.

In the 1960s and '70s, Bill and Hillary did not just dress and act like hippies, they thought like hippies too. Of the pair, Hillary possessed the stronger social compass. While Bill was traveling and thinking about what he would do once he finally ran for office, Hillary was working on women's and children's rights. Bill cared about social matters, of course, but it was Hillary who was a committed devotee. By steering Bill's energies toward issues of social import, Hillary lent a moral aspect to what might have otherwise been read as naked ambition on Bill's part. In Little Rock, the pair settled upon the goal of improving the educational infrastructure of the state. In Washington, they chose health care.

28. On March 10, 1993, US District Judge Royce Lamberth ruled that Hillary was not a government employee, and, for this reason, ruled that the meetings of the task force she chaired must be held in public whenever it convened meetings for the purpose of gathering information. Staff-level working groups were permitted to continue meeting in private, but other meetings, it was ruled, must be public.

29. Chafe, *Bill and Hillary*, p. 214.

30. Bernstein, *A Woman in Charge*, p. 276.

31. Ibid., p. 309.

32. Carl Sferrazza Anthony, *First Ladies: The Saga of the Presidents' Wives and Their Power*, vol. 2 (1961–1990) (New York: HarperCollins, 1993), p. 276.

CHAPTER NINE: GEORGE W. BUSH & DICK CHENEY

1. Bush officially announced his selection of Cheney for vice president at the Frank Erwin Center, University of Texas at Austin, July 25, 2000.

2. Bush is related to fifteen American presidents and can trace his bloodlines back to the *Mayflower*.

3. James Mann, *George W. Bush* (New York: Henry Holt, 2015), p. 7.

4. Stephen F. Hayes, *Cheney: The Untold Story of America's Most Powerful and Controversial Vice President* (New York: HarperCollins, 2007), p. 19.

5. Ibid., pp. 24–25.

6. Ibid., p. 67.

7. Jake Bernstein and Lou Dubose, *Vice: Dick Cheney and the Hijacking of the American Presidency* (New York: Random House, 2006), pp. 136–42.

8. Hayes, *Cheney*, p. 281.

9. Bob Woodward, *State of Denial*, vol. 3, *Bush at War* (New York: Simon & Schuster, 2006), p. 420.

10. Powell was concerned about Bush's desire to fight the war without the help of allies if necessary. Bush was not convinced that he needed the support of the United Nations or Congress. Powell was concerned about the long-term consequences of ignoring these important institutions. In the case of the UN, Powell thought that fighting a war without international support would undermine the purpose and value of the UN and establish a dangerous precedent that, in the event of a future crisis, the US would have difficulty walking back from.

11. Peter Baker, *Days of Fire: Bush and Cheney in the White House* (New York: Doubleday, 2013), p. 5.

12. *Frontline*, season 25, episode 10, "Cheney's Law," directed by Michael Kirk, aired October 16, 2007, on WGBH/PBS, Boston.

13. Ibid.; former vice president Dan Quayle paid Cheney a visit in the early days of George Jr.'s first term, to help acquaint the new vice president with the ceremonial duties of his office. Their exchange was described by *Washington Post* reporter Barton Gellman in the *Frontline* documentary "Cheney's Law":

> Dan Quayle went to see Dick Cheney, who he'd known for a long time, right around Inauguration Day in Bush's first term. He sort of went in, one vice president to another, to let him know how things were going to be. And he said, "You know, Dick, you're going to be doing a lot of traveling, going to a lot of funerals, lot of fundraisers. You're going to be doing the things that presidents don't want to do, and that your president doesn't want to do." And Cheney just looked at him with that little half-grin and raised his eyebrow and said, "I have a different understanding with the president." He didn't elaborate too much, and he doesn't tend to elaborate very often, but they talked a bit more about it. What Quayle told the *Washington Post* is that Cheney was going to be, in effect, a super-chief of staff.

14. Ibid.

15. Baker, *Days of Fire*, p. 10.

16. By the time he and Bush started working together, Cheney had developed strong views about presidential power. Under President Ford, he had watched as Congress slowly stripped, one by one, the executive office of the powers it had had under Nixon. To move his policy agenda, Ford had needed to become one of the most prolific users of executive orders in White House history. Cheney carried his belief in a strong executive with him when he was elected to Congress. As he moved up the congressional ladder, he became a strong supporter of President Reagan's national

security agenda—including aiding the Contras. At the time, he met with Reagan's staff to discuss strategies for circumventing Democratic opposition to Reagan's actions.

Cheney also acted against efforts in Congress to cut Reagan's presidential powers by working to prevent the passage of a law that would have forced Reagan to notify Congress within forty-eight hours of any covert action.

When Cheney reentered the administration under George H. W. Bush as secretary of defense, as the war in Kuwait was building, he counseled the president to pursue action without congressional or international coalition support if necessary, saying that in times of war, the president had almost unlimited powers. (In an interview with PBS in 1996, Cheney confessed to having made this recommendation.) Similarly, after the terrorist attacks of September 11, 2001, Cheney emphasized to President George W. Bush his belief that the president had no choice but to use all available means to pursue the enemy, and the president agreed.

17. Another argument used often centered on the concept of the "Unitary Executive." This theory, first raised by such leading figures as Alexander Hamilton during the original constitutional debates, argues that the founders chose to establish a single president atop the executive branch (as opposed to a two- or three-party executive council—which was also under consideration), so that he would have the power to act with dispatch and in secret, using executive-branch officers to execute his will in times of crisis.

18. According to the *Frontline* documentary "Cheney's Law," when Bush was considering what to do about captured enemy combatants and asked for Cheney's help, the vice president handled the situation in characteristic fashion. Ron Suskind commented on the situation: "[With the decision to try enemy combatants in military tribunals], here you've got this thing that Lincoln pulls his hair out over, Roosevelt frets over in terms of the spies. And it happens at lunch, Cheney and Bush. Cheney kind of lays it out and Bush says, 'Sounds good to me.' That's it. There wasn't a lot of deliberation. . . . Cheney pretty much framed it all for him and then at lunch he said, 'Here are the options.' Bush says, 'Check Box A,' and off we go."

Bush also preferred certainty from his advisers. His decision-making style depended on achieving a level of certainty about an issue so that he felt confident in the decisions once they were made. His advisers picked up on this and crafted their presentations in order to convey certainty. Thus, high-ranking officials would, uncharacteristically, use phrases like "slam dunk" to characterize their assessment of an issue for the president.

In lesser matters, this management approach might be a fitting way to cut through the tall grass of complex issues, but the matters Cheney was dealing with were more than merely complex; they had a constitutional sweep and dealt with life and death. Reducing such matters to simple "yes" and "no" decision points bordered on executive irresponsibility. *Frontline*, "Cheney's Law."

19. Baker, *Days of Fire*, pp. 5–7.

INDEX